David

Thank you for presenting
at our 2003 Conference

I hope there is something
in this book that will
help you build ONCO-TCS
into a global biobrand!
(or maybe just a way
profitable #800mm product)

Cheers,
Michael

*f*P

BUILDING GLOBAL
BIOBRANDS

Taking Biotechnology to Market

Françoise Simon

Philip Kotler

Foreword by Kevin Sharer, Chairman and CEO, Amgen

Free Press

New York   London   Toronto   Sydney   Singapore

*f*P

FREE PRESS
A Division of Simon & Schuster, Inc.
1230 Avenue of the Americas
New York, NY 10020

For information regarding special discounts for bulk purchases,
please contact Simon & Schuster Special Sales:
1-800-456-6798 or business@simonandschuster.com

Designed by Publications Development Company of Texas

Manufactured in the United States of America

10 9 8 7 6 5 4 3 2 1

Library of Congress Cataloging-in-Publication Data

Simon, Françoise.
     Building global biobrands : taking biotechnology to market / Françoise Simon
and Philip Kotler.
          p.   cm.
     Includes index.
     1. Biotechnology industries. 2. Biotechnology—Marketing. 3. Pharmaceutical
biotechnology industry. I. Kotler, Philip. II. Title.
     HD9999.B442S56   2003
     660.6′068′8—dc21

                                                                                    2003040810

ISBN 0-7432-2244-X

To Yvonne David and in memory of Louis Simon, my parents, who made it possible.

FRANÇOISE SIMON

To my mother Betty Kotler and in memory of my father, Maurice Kotler.

PHILIP KOTLER

ACKNOWLEDGMENTS

This book is based on a field study of biopharma strategy, including executive interviews and company case studies. We also benefited from many management seminars and consulting engagements that gave us the opportunity to further test our models and concepts.

Many industry experts and executives contributed to this book. At the risk of overlooking several, we first note the experts and analysts who generously shared their insights and studies: Steve Burrill of Burrill and Company, Roger Longman of the Windhover Group, Scott Morrison of Ernst & Young, Anthony Butler of Lehman Brothers, Neal Hansen and Elizabeth Overend-Freeman of Datamonitor, Tim Daley and Shilpa Sawhney of Decision Resources, Ana Maria Zaugg at IMS Health, Karl Engel of Med Ad News, Karen Bernstein at BioCentury, Carl Feldbaum and Sharon Cohen at BIO, Shannon Herzfeld and Peg Willingham at PhRMA, as well as Humphrey Taylor of Harris Interactive.

Within the biotechnology sector, special thanks go to many executives who contributed their time and insightful comments: At Amgen, Kevin Sharer, George Morrow, Craig Brooks, and Dr. Michael Savin; at Biogen, Jim Mullen, Hans-Peter Hasler, John Palmer, and Ted Llana; Dr. Samuel Broder at Celera, Dr. William Haseltine at Human Genome Sciences, Dr. Lothar Krinke at Endogeny, and Kenneth Conway, former CEO of Millennium Predictive Medicine.

We would also like to extend our appreciation to the pharmaceutical executives who generously gave their time and advice and enriched our own store of knowledge: At Novartis, Thomas Ebeling, David Epstein, Andrew Kay, Deborah Dunsire, Kurt Graves, Martin Cross, Rolf Schumacher, Paula Boultbee, Marion Morton, and Matthew Timms; at Pfizer, Peter Brandt, Patrick Kelly, Dr. Olivier Brandicourt, Ngozi Edozien, Neil Levine, and Julie Rubinstein; at Wyeth, Bernard Poussot, Cavan Redmond, Leanne Wagner, Jeff Peris, Tim Fidler, and David McGettigan; at Glaxo, Dr. Allen Roses; and at Merck, Dr. Bennett Shapiro, Linda Distlerath, Dr. Sidney Mazel, and Jennifer Taubert. The biopharma industry now includes information technology companies that are shaping the bioinformatics field; in this sector, we would like to thank Dr. Caroline Kovac, Mike Svinte, and Dr. Ajay Royyuru of IBM Life Sciences for sharing their insights and analyses.

We had outstanding help on the manuscript; we benefited from the expertise of our production team, and we also extend special thanks to Joy Sarsale for her dedication and expert technical assistance. Finally, at the Free Press, we owe a special debt of gratitude to a world-class editor and friend, Bob Wallace, who helped us shape the material into its final form and who offered constant encouragement, insight, and guidance.

FOREWORD

A mgen joins others in welcoming this excellent new book, *Building Global Biobrands*. As the biotechnology sector reaches maturity, we are witnessing the emergence of global biopharma companies, among which Amgen is playing a leading role. Our success comes from one simple fact—we are committed to being a science-based, patient-driven company.

We are a relatively young company. Why do we (and our shareholders) think we have a shot at attaining our aspiration? Why shouldn't we expect "regression to the mean" given our early successes? We think the answer lies in attaining a certain critical mass, something we think of as becoming a "world-scale biopharma" company.

What characterizes a world-scale biopharma company? It starts with reaching sufficient breadth and depth in several core disciplines to take something from a discovery at the biologist's bench to a product useful to the patient and reimbursed by the payors. Let me describe several of the themes that have been essential to our becoming a world-scale biopharma:

- *Scientific expertise in the "New Biology":* A biopharma needs to go beyond its initial platform or product area to develop competencies in several platforms like proteomics or genomics to be able to appreciate subsequent innovations.
- *Technical depth in "enabling technology":* The ability to scale-up and efficiently produce proteins, antibodies, and other materials at industrial scale and clinical quality is essential.
- *Focused infrastructure:* The human resources, finance, legal, and other G&A functions must be adequate to staff, fund, and preserve the patent estate of the enterprise.
- *Customer-focused commercialization:* Marketing, sales, and development must cultivate a customer intimacy that helps turn scientific advances into true patient benefits.
- *Geographic reach:* A world scale biopharma has sufficient presence to market or distribute its product in any market that makes sense. World presence also means the ability to access talent and innovations from throughout the world.

In short, a world-scale biopharma company is focused on commercializing the newest discoveries in molecular biology and has sufficient expertise and resources to succeed.

While our aspiration is straightforward and clear, we realize we must draw on a broad and complex repertoire of talents and skills to attain it. Simon and Kotler's book, *Building Global Biobrands,* provides a comprehensive overview of the breadth of strategies that firms in our industry employ. There is no magic bullet or guaranteed formula for success in our field. As the authors point out, success comes from a melding of best business practices with leading edge science and a bit of good fortune.

KEVIN SHARER
Chairman and CEO
Amgen, Inc.

CONTENTS

PREFACE

With revolutionary biotechnological breakthroughs occurring in every sector, from medicine and defense to food and cosmetics, the twenty-first century is rapidly taking shape as the Biotech Century. The commercial impact of biotechnologies is already estimated to account for a third of world gross domestic product. Healthcare alone is the largest sector worldwide, ranging from 12 percent to 14 percent of gross domestic product in key markets. In the United States, the size of affected industries ranges from $400 billion for chemicals to $800 billion for the food sector and more than $1 trillion for biomaterials. Powerful macro forces will drive expansion—chief among them the need to feed, heal, clothe, and shelter some 9 billion people worldwide by 2050.

Along with the enormous global opportunities presented by this revolution, businesses are faced with an array of unprecedented challenges in building and sustaining brands in this fast-moving market. In the midst of unprecedented turbulence, companies from megapharmaceuticals to biotech startups must fundamentally rethink their structures, business models, and global strategies. Our book is the first to address the business of biotechnology at three levels: innovation, marketing models, and global strategies. Addressing the value chain from discovery to market, we aim to show managers how companies can innovate with bionetworks, win customers with biobrands, and create sustainable advantage worldwide.

Although we focus on the biopharma sector as the innovation and marketing bellwether of the new ecosystem, our findings are relevant to all industries impacted by biotechnology, from consumer goods to industrial products.

BOOK APPROACH

Part One defines the new biosector. Chapter 1 describes how bioscience drives innovation in healthcare, computing, food, materials, energy, and defense.

Chapter 2 then analyzes the interface of three transforming forces at work in the biosector: information technology, consumerism, and systems biology. At the same time as Web-enabled consumers demand personalized medicine, postgenomic research and infotech are coevolving to create new fields such as bioinformatics. As our industry cases demonstrate, the biotech leaders of the coming decades may be IBM, Hitachi, and Siemens—as well as Amgen and Pfizer.

Chapter 3 assesses the bionetworks being formed across industries and pinpoints the winning structures, from equity links to virtual webs.

Part Two focuses on the power of biobrands, from Epogen to Viagra and from ethanol to molecular-targeted therapies. With the right strategy, this power extends over time and space: Bayer aspirin is 105 years old and still the category leader, thanks to sustained innovation. Viagra reached more than 40 countries in one year and antiarthritic Celebrex passed one billion U.S. dollars in global sales in the same time frame—a better reach and return than that of most consumer goods.

Chapters 4 and 5 focus on the key challenge of building global biobrands, which is further complicated by the rise of personalized medicine. As new therapies target specific genotypes, a new brand paradigm is emerging as an alternative to the mass market approach. Firms are now redefining disease and rethinking their segmentation and branding models. We focus on several success stories for both branding models and derive strategic lessons for large and small companies.

Chapter 6 focuses on sustaining biobrands. Innovative strategies at the portfolio, franchise, and brand levels can maximize biobrands during their patent life.

Chapter 7 then shows how biomarketers can, in effect, manage beyond the lifecycle and renew brands by transferring equity to successor molecules or changing their legal status.

Part Three addresses the global challenge of access, price, and communications issues. Chapter 8 reviews the economics of new technologies and outlines how companies can balance profitability and social responsibility, given global regulation dynamics.

Chapter 9 develops a portfolio of global and national biopricing strategies and suggests how companies can build consumer-focused brand value.

Chapter 10 examines the structure of e-health and its impact on integration of online and offline strategies through the value chain.

RESEARCH METHODOLOGY

Our strategic approach arose from a global analysis of public and private research, as well as an extensive series of more than 300 interviews conducted over a three-year period with corporate, R&D, and marketing executives from companies ranging from start-ups to multinationals; these interviews, reflecting the global scope of bioscience, were conducted in the Americas, Europe, and Asia.

PART ONE

NAVIGATING THE GLOBAL BIOSECTOR

THE NEW BIO
MARKETSPACE

The dominant science of the twenty-first century will be biology.

Freeman Dyson[1]

New York, April 2020
At 8 A.M. on a sunny spring day, the Fuller household is in full morning rush mode. John is about to head off for his law office, his wife Cynthia for her pre-workday jog, and eight-year-old Marion for school. At the breakfast table of their Westchester home, Marion has just received her latest inoculation. Shots are a thing of the past; she just ate a banana. Using his wristwatch transmitter, John does his monthly checkup by sending his internist the data collected in his t-shirt's biosensors and in a capsule he swallowed. His health is fine, thanks to diet and exercise, but also to new drugs customized to his genotype. Always on the go, he tended to forget his pills, but he now has a microchip implant that works as a slow-release micropharmacy. In the bathroom, Cynthia is admiring her new makeup, which has just cleared a case of rosacea. She is back on her regular morning jog

schedule, since the knee she injured skiing last winter has been partly reengineered. Meanwhile, John completes a bank transfer and decides to sell a stock that, in his view, has just peaked; thanks to iris scans and other biometric screens, online security is no longer an issue.

Outside, the air is crisp, and the Hudson River looks amazingly clean—biofuels and waste-eating bacteria have worked wonders on the challenging New York ecology in the past decades. Overhead, planes bound for Canada and the West Coast are carrying their passengers with an added degree of safety—their wings and fuselage are now made of biomaterials sensing and self-repairing any stresses or impending cracks, and their avionics include neural networks that can rapidly react to critical events such as hydraulic failures. Two things, however, have not improved; legroom is scarce and airports are still clogged to the gills.

Utopia? Biotech's detractors think so and paint a grim counterpart of Frankenfoods, mutant crops run amok, and the specter of eugenics creating a gene-enhanced "super class."[2] This doomsday vision is unlikely to occur due to regulation, and resisting biotechnology progress amounts to battling the inevitable. Every innovation in our 2020 scenario is already in development or at the pilot market stage:

- Research on edible vaccines has yielded plants that produce hepatitis B surface antigen for oral immunization. A single banana chip would inoculate a child for one-fifteenth of the price of an injection and would not require the "cold chain" that is problematic in many developing economies.
- The distinction between food, cosmetics, and medicine is fading; Unilever is marketing medical foods such as a cholesterol-reducing margarine. Cosmetics such as Johnson & Johnson's Retinol have medical claims. Shiseido funds biopharma research and was first to develop a non-allergenic variety of rice. A strain of "golden rice" yielding provitamin A has been engineered and can open pathways for the production of other vitamins and plants.[3]
- Vivometrics received clearance by the Food and Drug Administration (FDA) for its Life Shirt System that monitors more than 30 vital signs. Its initial focus is on three markets: clinical trials for drugs and devices, home sleep diagnostics, and cardiopulmonary medical research.[4]

- Applied Digital Solutions developed a tracking device using mobile telephone chips in a wristwatch-sized locator and plans a medical version to relay data ranging from pulse rate to blood chemistry. Siemens and Agilent also created prototype medical monitors, and Medtronic's Chronicle links its pacemakers to physicians via the Internet.
- Samsung's vision of a home diagnostic tool is its "Family Doctor," a swallowed capsule that examines internal organs and relays data to a physician.[5]
- MicroCHIPS, an MIT-affiliated startup, plans to launch within five years a chip implant with 400 wells holding drug dosages and a microprocessor releasing them at different intervals. By 2010, a second generation may interact with embedded sensors, allowing the body's own signals to trigger drug release.
- Regenerative medicine ranges from Organogenesis' Apligraf (first engineered skin, FDA-approved for leg ulcers) to the clinical testing of a bioartificial liver. Another tissue engineering company, Gentis, combines scaffolds, molecules, and dermal cells to build new cartilage (a global market of $1 to $3 billion).[6]
- A "carbohydrate economy" is emerging with biofuels, plant-based polymers, and high-efficiency enzymes. Ethanol production is led by Archer Daniels Midland, and Cargill Dow received approval for polylactic acid, a biopolymer that is the first new fiber class since the 1950s.
- Environmental biotech accounts for more than $1 billion in a $17 billion U.S. market. This includes companies such as Regenesis, which markets products to help degrade groundwater contaminants.[7]

For biotechnology to fulfill its potential, companies need to focus on three bases of competition: innovation, branding, and global reach. Innovation is shifting from pharmacos to biotechs, while branding largely remains the forte of Big Pharma. An emerging scenario links a few megamarketers such as Pfizer to a web of biotech satellites. These networks include equity investments as well as virtual links. In addition to their marketing muscle, pharmacos also contribute global reach, which biotechs need to recover their research costs. This chapter covers biotechnology's cross-industry scope, timeline, and global reach; and Chapter 2 discusses transforming trends in the industry. The following chapters focus on bionetworking and biobranding. (See Figure 1.1.)

FIGURE 1.1   Bio Business Model

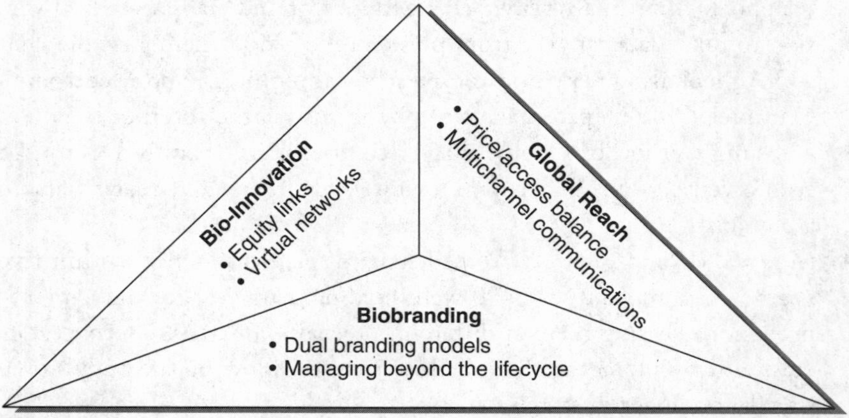

Source: Françoise Simon/SDC Group, 2002.

ECONOMIC IMPACT OF BIOTECHNOLOGY

Broadly defined, the biosector is already estimated to account for more than a third of world gross domestic product (GDP). In the United States alone, the size of affected industries ranges from $400 billion for chemicals to $800 billion for the food sector and more than $1 trillion for biomaterials.[8] Powerful macro forces will drive further expansion—chief among them the need to feed, clothe, and shelter some 9 billion people worldwide by 2050.

Biotechnology will extend well beyond healthcare, which is already the largest industry sector in the world, reaching 12 percent of GDP in Germany and 14 percent in the United States or almost twice the spending on information technology. Population aging will entail the spread of chronic diseases and the need for gene therapies; by 2030, the number of Americans over 65 will more than double from today's 33 million to 75 million. In a decade, the United States could well spend 17 percent of GDP on healthcare.[9]

Biotech innovation has clear results. In its thirty years of existence, the industry has produced more than 100 drugs and has nearly 400 products in clinical trials. Its value to society is also well established.

ECONOMIC RETURN OF BIOSCIENCE

The economic value of investment in bioscience research was recently calculated by Kevin Murphy and Robert Topel. Using a value per life of $5 million to determine the impact of the six years' increase in average life expectancy from 1970 to 1990 alone, they arrived at an average annual worth of $2.4 trillion to Americans. Accounting for the fact that much of the life expectancy increase resulted from non-medical factors (higher incomes, better diet, less smoking, etc.), if even 10 percent of the increased longevity were attributable to medical research, it would still amount to $240 billion a year. Given that medical research was $36 billion in 1995 in the United States, this represents a massive return on investment. More specifically, reducing the death rate from either heart disease or cancer by 20 percent (a possible outcome of postgenomic research) would be worth around $10 trillion to Americans—more than a year's GDP.*

* Kevin Murphy and Robert Topel, "Exceptional Returns: The Economic Value of America's Investment in Medical Research," Mary Woodard Lasker Charitable Trust (May 2000); see also "The Health Effect," *The Economist* (June 3, 2000), p. 78.

While innovation is the lifeblood of biotech firms, they face a set of unique challenges because of their medical focus. These range from ethical concerns to regulation and patenting issues. The evolution of bioscience cannot be extrapolated from that of its twentieth-century digital counterpart. Unlike information technology, bioscience is in a time paradox: Postgenomic research accelerates innovation across industries, but legal and ethical concerns have acted throughout biotech's history as "social brakes"—a trend that is intensifying as we confront issues such as stem cell therapy and human cloning.

INNOVATION TIMELINE

A central issue concerns the biotech timeline. It may be as little as 5 to 10 years before some of the components of our 2020 scenario are realized, while others may never come to pass. Biotech progress since DNA was first identified in 1944 as the "transforming factor" in bacteria (or, further back, since Gregor Mendel discovered plant genetics in 1863) shows that, like information technology, it evolved in discrete innovation clusters spurred by specific inflection points. In 1972, Eldridge and Gould proposed the theory of *Punctuated Equilibrium,* suggesting that rapid evolutionary change takes place in relatively short bursts. Biopharma's first inflection point occurred in the nineteenth century, when scientists synthesized compounds from plants and dyes, leading to innovations such as aspirin, introduced in 1897. The second point—and the beginning of bioscience—came in the 1950s with Watson and Crick's discovery of the structure of DNA. The third inflection point was marked by the drafting of the human genome in 2000, which is leading to the emergence of molecular medicine, with therapies targeting specific patient genotypes.[10] (See Figure 1.2.)

Biotechnology, from the start, coevolved with other sciences; Watson and Crick's 1953 discovery of the double-helix structure of the DNA could not have happened without Franklin and Wilkins' development of x-ray crystallography. Later, bioscience merged with computing when Michael Hunkapiller developed in 1986 the first automated gene sequencer at Applied Biosystems, used by Craig Venter at NIH; a second impetus came in 1998 with the ABI sequencer that allowed Venter, then at Celera, to beat the genome sequencing schedule.

Computing and bioscience continue to merge, creating new fields such as bioinformatics. IBM is leading this area with initiatives such as its Blue Gene supercomputer, whose functions will include the study of protein dynamics.

Because it integrates several fields and deals with complex living systems, bioscience faces R&D costs and time frames much larger than those of information technology. Of 5 to 10,000 compounds screened, only one typically makes it to market, pushing the development cost of a new drug to more than $800 million. Timelines are equally daunting: It took 29 years after the discovery of DNA structure to market the first recombinant DNA therapy (Genentech and Lilly's insulin). Similarly, monoclonal antibodies (Mabs) were first developed in 1975, but companies such as Hybritech tried in vain to commercialize them in the 1980s. The first therapeutic Mab would not reach market until 1998, when IDEC's Rituxan was approved for non-Hodgkin's lymphoma. The main obstacle for the early Mabs was their origin in a mouse hybridoma (fusion of an antibody-producing cell

FIGURE 1.2   Innovation Timelines

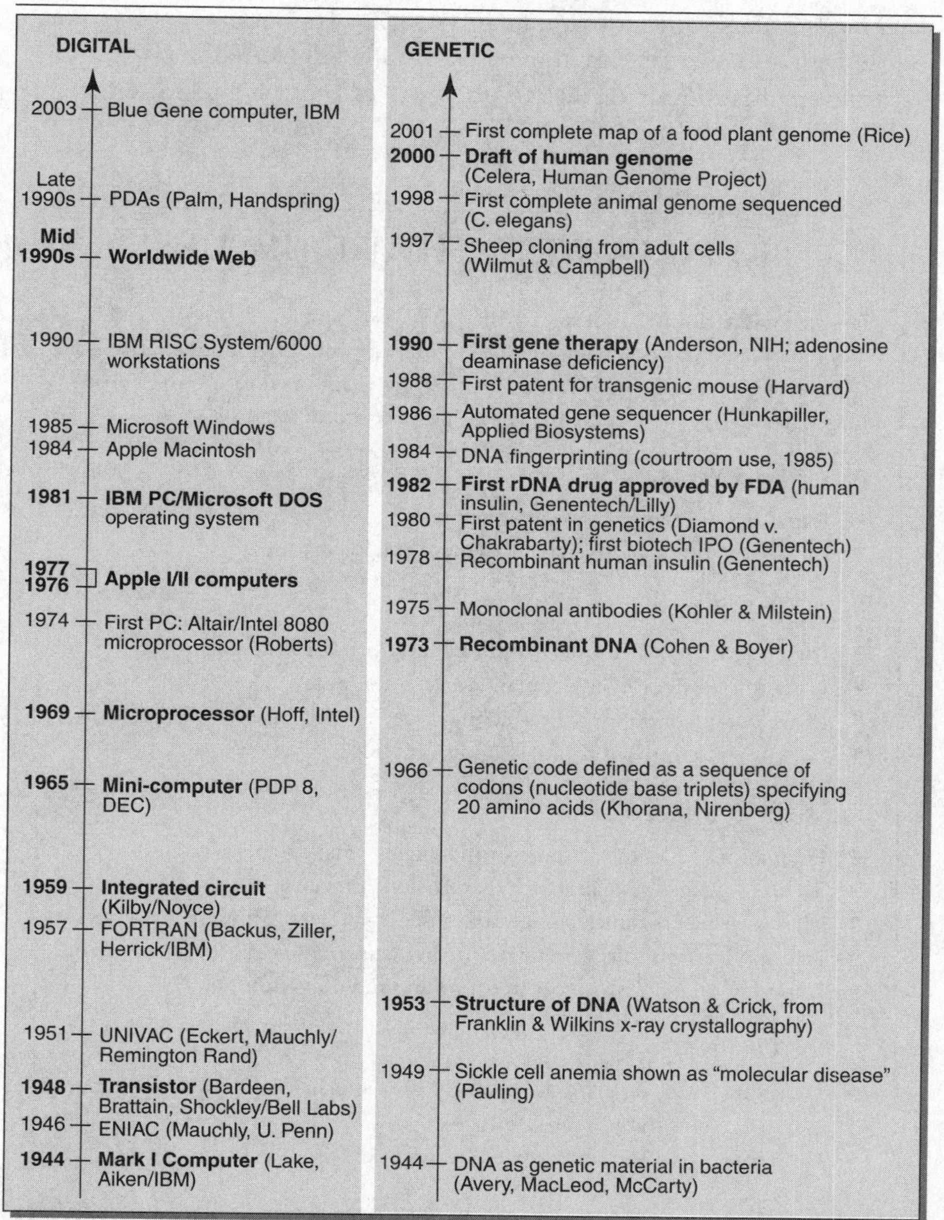

DIGITAL

2003	Blue Gene computer, IBM
Late 1990s	PDAs (Palm, Handspring)
Mid 1990s	**Worldwide Web**
1990	IBM RISC System/6000 workstations
1985	Microsoft Windows
1984	Apple Macintosh
1981	**IBM PC/Microsoft DOS** operating system
1977 1976	**Apple I/II computers**
1974	First PC: Altair/Intel 8080 microprocessor (Roberts)
1969	**Microprocessor** (Hoff, Intel)
1965	**Mini-computer** (PDP 8, DEC)
1959	**Integrated circuit** (Kilby/Noyce)
1957	FORTRAN (Backus, Ziller, Herrick/IBM)
1951	UNIVAC (Eckert, Mauchly/ Remington Rand)
1948	**Transistor** (Bardeen, Brattain, Shockley/Bell Labs)
1946	ENIAC (Mauchly, U. Penn)
1944	**Mark I Computer** (Lake, Aiken/IBM)

GENETIC

2001	First complete map of a food plant genome (Rice)
2000	**Draft of human genome** (Celera, Human Genome Project)
1998	First complete animal genome sequenced (C. elegans)
1997	Sheep cloning from adult cells (Wilmut & Campbell)
1990	**First gene therapy** (Anderson, NIH; adenosine deaminase deficiency)
1988	First patent for transgenic mouse (Harvard)
1986	Automated gene sequencer (Hunkapiller, Applied Biosystems)
1984	DNA fingerprinting (courtroom use, 1985)
1982	**First rDNA drug approved by FDA** (human insulin, Genentech/Lilly)
1980	First patent in genetics (Diamond v. Chakrabarty); first biotech IPO (Genentech)
1978	Recombinant human insulin (Genentech)
1975	Monoclonal antibodies (Kohler & Milstein)
1973	**Recombinant DNA** (Cohen & Boyer)
1966	Genetic code defined as a sequence of codons (nucleotide base triplets) specifying 20 amino acids (Khorana, Nirenberg)
1953	**Structure of DNA** (Watson & Crick, from Franklin & Wilkins x-ray crystallography)
1949	Sickle cell anemia shown as "molecular disease" (Pauling)
1944	DNA as genetic material in bacteria (Avery, MacLeod, McCarty)

Sources: Françoise Simon/SDC Group, IBM, Burrill & Company, 2002.

with a myeloma B cell, leading to an immortal cell line generating the same antibody). These triggered immune system rejections, and success came only with a second generation of partly or fully humanized Mabs.

Given these historical delays, forecasts of biotech innovation vary widely and are likely to be revised often in the coming years.

BIO-INNOVATION: FUTURE TIMELINE

Dr. Francis Collins, director of the U.S. National Institute of Human Genome Research, has made predictions about postgenomic innovation in the next 40 years. A rough consensus emerges from his forecast and that of industry experts such as George Poste and Stephen Burrill:

PHASE I—5 YEARS
- Expansion of molecular diagnostic tests.
- Identification of molecular subtypes of major diseases.

PHASE II—10 YEARS
- Predictive tests for more than 20 genetic conditions.
- Growing number of molecular-targeted therapies.
- Pharmacogenomic markers tracking patients' responses to drugs.
- New imaging probes to assess body functions.

PHASE III—15 TO 20 YEARS
- Populations to be tested to determine genotypes; databases to be created.
- Tailored drugs for diabetes, hypertension, cancer, and other illnesses.
- Mass-market therapies to be subdivided to reflect different genotypes.
- Full applications of regenerative medicine (somatic cells for autografts).
- Gene replacement therapy (in utero and in adult life).

PHASE IV—30 YEARS
- Genes involved in aging to be fully characterized and clinicals under way to extend the human life span.
- Comprehensive genomics-based healthcare.*

* Francis Collins, cited in Charles Craig, "Bio Tries to Keep Political, Business Climate Positive for U.S. Biotech," *Biotechnology Investors' Forum—Europe* (2001), p. 6; Burrill & Company, *Biotech 2001* (2001), p. 44.

IMPACT OF INVESTMENT COMMUNITY

Timeline issues were exacerbated by an investor mindset that often expected short-term returns from a science whose progress should be measured in decades, not quarters. While the industry has attracted more than $200 billion in investment to date, it has also suffered from extreme stock volatility. Major slumps occurred in 1984, 1988, 1994, 1997, and 2001 following boom periods. After the 1982 approval of Genentech/Lilly's Humulin, the boom years of 1982 to 1983 saw nine initial public offerings (IPOs), including those of Amgen, Biogen, and Chiron. Another wave of seven IPOs occurred in 1986 alone, including OSI, Xoma, and Genzyme, but these dropped to zero after the 1987 stock crash. Similarly, the 1991 to 1992 boom collapsed by 1993 with the failure of the sepsis drugs and the Clinton plan for healthcare reform. In March 2000, at the peak of the tech bubble and shortly before the announcement of the draft of the human genome, a presidential declaration implying that genetic information should not be patented sent biotech shares into free fall. Gyrations continued in late 2001, as terrorism was followed by the birth of the biodefense sector.

SOCIAL BARRIERS

Throughout its history, bioscience has also been affected by "social brakes" such as ethical fears and patent controversies. Early on, the development of recombinant DNA in the 1970s prompted a self-imposed moratorium by molecular biologists on gene-splicing research. Since then, most significant discoveries have triggered assorted warnings and limitations. The United States first led the world in stem cell research, when embryonic stem cells were first isolated at the University of Wisconsin in 1998. After a 2001 presidential decision limited U.S. federal funding to cell lines already in existence, the National Institutes of Health (NIH) announced that 48 of the 64 eligible cell lines were in non-U.S. labs. A shift of talent and funding may occur as a result, because Britain, Scandinavia, and the Netherlands have more liberal regulation; most importantly, the U.S. restriction, which affects a huge NIH yearly biomedical budget of almost $20 billion, may further delay the development of stem cell therapy for Parkinson's disease, stroke, or diabetes—already estimated to be at least a decade away.[11] Similarly, the November 2001 announcement by Advanced Cell Technologies (ACT) that it had cloned the first human embryo met with harsh criticism from the public and some legislators. Xenotransplantation was another thorny issue; European parliamentarians called for a moratorium on it because of concerns about animal-to-human viral transmission.[12]

Another potent brake on bioscience research is the controversy surrounding patenting issues. Following the landmark 1980 *Diamond v. Chakrabarty* case, the U.S. Supreme Court approved the principle of patenting genetically engineered life forms (awarded to Exxon for oil-eating microorganisms). The U.S. Patent & Trademark Office (PTO) awarded more than 10,000 patents in the past decade to companies including Incyte, Genentech, and Novartis, but also to academia and the government. New guidelines require medical utility, that is, a "specific, substantial and credible use" for a DNA sequence. A dispute between ACT, Infigen, and Geron (who bought Roslin Bio-Med in 1999) led to a PTO investigation of their patents on cloning technologies. Resolution of this dispute may take up to

TABLE 1.1   Bioscience Benefits and Risks

Industry	Technology	Benefit	Barrier/Risk
Human Diagnostics	Genetic screening (DNA chips).	Prevention, targeted treatment.	Insurance/employment discrimination.
Human Therapy	Somatic gene therapy.	Greater efficacy and tolerability.	Viral vector risk in drug delivery.
	Germline gene therapy.	Eradication of disease trait.	Parental eugenics.
Computing	Bioinformatics.	Global genetic databases.	Patenting, privacy.
	Biometrics.	Travel, e-commerce.	Privacy.
	Biomimetic computers.	Proteomics research.	Cost, complexity.
Agbio	Molecular farming.	Drugs, medical foods.	No predictive ecology.
	Transgenic animals.	Organ replacement.	Viral transmission.
Materials	Nanotechnology.	"Smart" materials (self-assembly, memory).	Development cost, complexity.
Energy	Biofuels.	Reduced pollution, renewable resources.	Development/ production cost.
Environment	Bioremediation.	Efficacy.	No predictive ecology.

Source: Françoise Simon/SDC Group, 2002.

two years; in the meantime, this episode may drive some investment away from companies in the cloning field.[13]

Ethical and legal barriers are compounded by privacy issues—specifically, consumer concerns about insurance and employment discrimination based on genetic testing. (See Table 1.1.)

Biotech firms can draw several lessons from their innovation history:

- Macrotrends are conflictual—positive demographics are countered by pricing and access issues; companies need to stress bioscience's economic value to society.
- Bioinnovation cannot be extrapolated from the digital sector. The biosector is increasingly profitable and productive, but this is partly offset by persistent "social brakes."
- The industry as a whole and individual firms need to be more proactive in addressing ethical and legal concerns.
- Companies should also strive to manage investor expectations to attenuate the boom/bust cycles that have affected the biosector for the past three decades.

GLOBAL REACH OF BIOTECHNOLOGY

BIOTECH/PHARMA FUSION

Biotechnology has now reached a stage where its top-tier firms are full-fledged biopharmaceuticals. Amgen's $16 billion acquisition of Immunex reached Big Pharma scale and was to give it a combined market capitalization of nearly $62 billion by yearend 2002, higher than that of AstraZeneca. Big Pharma global sales still dwarf biotech sales, but the new sector is increasingly profitable and has higher valuations and growth prospects.

Biotech's market cap peaked in early 2000 at nearly $500 billion. By yearend 2002, despite a sharp continuing decline in the technology sector, the top 10 biotechs still accounted for nearly $125 billion in market value—roughly equivalent to Merck's market capitalization. (See Table 1.2.)

Despite the gloom in public markets, the biosector raised $12 billion in 2001 (down from more than $32 billion in 2000), still double the levels

TABLE 1.2   Top Biotechnology Firms

Company	Revenue, 2002 ($M)	Net Income (Loss), 2002 ($M)	R&D Spend, 2002 ($M)
Amgen	5,523	(1,392)	1,117
Genentech	2,719	64	623
Serono	1,547	321	358
Chiron	1,276	181	326
Biogen	1,148	199	368
Genzyme	1,080	179	230
Medimmune	848	(1,098)	144
Invitrogen	649	48	34
Gilead	467	72	135
Celltech*	436	(80)	131
IDEC	404	148	94
Millennium	353	(590)	511
Genencor	350	(1.5)	70
Qiagen	299	23	28
Affymetrix	290	(1.6)	70

* Celltech—2001 data.
Sources: Company reports (unaudited consolidated statements of income, January/February 2003); "Corporate Scoreboard," *BusinessWeek,* February 24, 2003, p. 74.

raised in the late 1990s, and investment rose again in 2002. Annual biotech growth is projected at 15 to 20 percent in the next three to five years, accelerating to 30 percent by the end of the decade.[14]

The biotech/pharma symbiosis is easily summed up: Pharma needs biotech's innovation, and biotech needs pharma's scale. To maintain its sales at the double-digit annual growth rate expected by investors, major pharmacos need to launch an average of four new molecular entities (NMEs) per year, assuming annual sales of $350 million for each. From 1995 to 2000, there was less than one NME launch per year per company, with only 10 percent reaching annual sales of more than $350 million despite multibillion dollar R&D expenditures for major pharmacos.[15] (See Table 1.3.)

In the coming decades, product portfolios will also come closer together. While Big Pharma sales are still dominated by primary-care blockbusters such as Pfizer's Lipitor (atorvastatin) for cholesterol reduction and Viagra (sildenafil) for erectile dysfunction, pipelines are filling up with biologics (nearly 400 are in late-stage clinical trials). Some of the top biologics are marketed by Big Pharma, such as Lilly's recombinant insulin line and Schering-Plough's interferon-alpha franchise. Conversely, Big

TABLE 1.3 Top Pharmaceutical Firms

Company	Ethical Sales, 2002 ($M)	Total Sales, 2002 ($M)	Net Income (Loss), 2002 ($M)	R&D Spend, 2002 ($M)
Pfizer	29,843	32,373	9,126	5,176
GlaxoSmithKline	26,993	31,818	6,941	4,098
Merck	21,446	51,790	7,150	2,677
AstraZeneca	17,343	17,841	2,836	3,069
Johnson & Johnson	17,151	36,298	6,651	3,957
Aventis	15,153	19,500	1,977	2,974
Novartis	13,550	20,911	4,718	2,799
Bristol-Myers Squibb★	12,380 (E)	NA	NA	NA
Pharmacia	12,037	13,993	597	2,329
Wyeth	11,733	14,584	4,447	2,080
Roche	11,529	19,301	(2,614)	2,764
Eli Lilly	10,384	11,078	2,763	2,149
Schering-Plough	8,745	10,180	2,089	1,425
Abbott	7,250	17,685	2,794	1,562
Sanofi-Synthelabo	6,535 (E)	7,042	1,662	1,152

★ BMS to restate financial data.
Sources: Company reports (unaudited consolidated statements of income, January/February 2003); "Corporate Scoreboard," *Business Week*, February 24, 2003, p. 74.

Biotech is adding primary care to its traditional niche products, some of which are blockbusters in their own right, such as Amgen's $2 billion erythropoietin Epogen for anemia; in arthritis, the new compounds are biologics, from Immunex's Enbrel (etanercept) to Centocor's Remicade (infliximab) and the new Kineret (anakinra) from Amgen.

The biotech/pharma synergy now includes a focus on biomanufacturing, which is facing a major capacity crunch; shortages cost Immunex and Wyeth more than $200 million for Enbrel in 2001, and Wyeth invested in two new plants in the United States and Ireland. Fewer than a dozen biopharma firms have the development, manufacturing, quality, and clinical expertise to commercialize biologics. Major companies plan to invest more than $8 billion in biomanufacturing in the next five years, to obtain a total industry capacity of more than 1 million liters.

GLOBAL SPREAD OF BIOTECHNOLOGY

In 2000, thanks in part to a massive capital influx, the biosector became truly borderless, with a wave of cross-border deals, global financing, and dual listings in the United States and Europe. By 2001, there were nearly 5,000 biotech firms worldwide (of which more than 600 were publicly traded) generating $35 billion in revenue and spending $16 billion on R&D. Spurred by public and private investment, European biotechs multiplied to nearly 1,900 firms (versus almost 1,500 in the United States), but remained less mature, generating 22 percent of the world total (against 73 percent in the United States). Asia was still a small fraction of the world sector, but showed high growth in biohubs such as Singapore. (See Table 1.4.)

Europe's Biotech Strategy

While national initiatives have kick-started markets such as Germany, Europe-wide policy is still at the "all talk, little action" level. The German government triggered fast growth in the past decade with aggressive investment. By 2001, the public budget reached €435 million, which was crucial in attracting a similar level of private investment. Germany spent more than four times as much as France, and the market reflected it. Germany now accounts for about one-fifth of European biotechs, with a national market cap over five times that of French companies. The region is led by the United Kingdom, whose biosector accounts for more than half of the total European market value.

France is the second largest pharma market, accounting for almost 20 percent of the European market; it has a strong medical research base, but

TABLE 1.4   Global Scope of Biotechnology

	Global	United States	Europe	Canada	Asia/Pacific
Public Company Data					
Revenues ($m)	34,874	25,219	7,533	1,021	1,001
R&D expense ($m)	16,427	11,532	4,244	474	175
Net income/loss ($m)	(5,933)	(4,799)	(608)	(507)	(19)
Number of employees	188,703	141,000	34,180	7,005	6,518
Number of Companies					
Public companies	622	342	104	85	91
Private companies	3,662	1,115	1,775	331	441
Total companies	4,284	1,457	1,879	416	532

Source: Ernst & Young, *Beyond Borders—The Global Biotechnology Report 2002*, p. 10. (Data for financials largely represent data from October 1, 2000, through September 30, 2001; numbers may appear inconsistent due to rounding.)

its biosector lags because of underinvestment and a culture gap between academia and industry. There are signs of change: A 1999 law allowed public researchers to take equity stakes in their own ventures and offered a tax credit on R&D costs for startups. The Institut Pasteur has taken equity stakes in Hybrigenics and several spinoffs, and the University of Lille also has equity in Genfit.[16]

At the regional level, the European Commission published in January 2002 an action plan to deliver effective policies, attract human and financial resources, and address global challenges. The corporate world was underwhelmed. Novartis announced that it was moving its global research hub to the Boston area, and European biotechs continued their transatlantic investments with two goals: Move downstream toward drug discovery but also gain a foothold in the North American market. Germany's Lion Bioscience bought Trega and NetGenics in the United States for $53 million to strengthen its drug discovery tools and combine its genomics expertise with informatics. Another German firm, MediGene, bought NeuroVir in the United States for $46 million. In 2001, Britain's Shire made a much larger acquisition with Canadian company BioChem for $4 billion. DeCode Genetics of Iceland purchased MediChem in the United States to move from population genetics to drug development.[17]

Big Biotech is now mature enough to develop its own global marketing capabilities. In 2002, Amgen paid nearly $140 million to acquire from Roche the assets and operations related to Neupogen (filgrastim) in the European Union (EU), Switzerland, and Norway. Neupogen, targeting infection in patients on chemotherapy, reached sales of $1.3 billion in 2001. The much smaller U.S. biotech Cephalon bought French pharmaceutical firm Lafon, the licensee for its lead product (modafinil) to recover the 20 percent royalties it had been paying Lafon, but also to gain European production and sales capacity. The deal was notable for its size ($450 million in cash, or five times sales) and for the trend-setting potential of a biotech buying a pharmaco.[18]

Asian Biotech: Priority Sector

While Japan and the rest of Asia share region-specific policy goals and cultural perspectives, their biotech sectors are at very different levels of development. The Japanese pharmaceutical market, second worldwide, is valued at about $60 billion and accounts for more than 15 percent of global

R&D spend. It will grow in parallel with its population of 130 million, which, by 2015, will have the largest proportion of over-65-year-olds in the world.

Japan has four distinct types of biotech players—pharmacos, brewers and food makers with fermentation expertise, electronics firms, and local biotechs:

- Japanese pharmacos are actively acquiring technology via alliances such as those of Takeda/Affymetrix, Eisai/Incyte, and Taisho/Vertex/Neurocrine/IDEC.
- Brewers pioneered biotech investments with Kirin's early funding of Amgen; Takara (leader in distilled spirits) produces biochips for gene testing, and Kyowa Hakko (largest maker of fermented chemicals) also supplies reagents for DNA research.
- Like IBM, major electronics firms have set up internal life sciences groups and entered into alliances with local pharmacos and brewers; Hitachi collaborates with Takara and Yamanouchi, as well as with U.S. biotechs.
- Japanese biotechs multiplied in the late 1990s and include bioinformatics players Pharmadesign and Intec Web, tissue engineering firm J-Tec, drug delivery company NanoCarrier, and genomic firm GenCom; the government has boosted funds for biotech and nanotech research, aiming for a national biosector of at least 1,000 companies by 2010.[19]

Beyond Japan, the Asia/Pacific region shows a wide variance, from the first-world development level of Singapore to the embryonic biosector in China.

Asia's two giants, China and India, present very different pictures in biotechnology. China's biosector is embryonic but high-potential, whereas India has major pharmacos—but these are facing a sharp transition from generic manufacturing to drug discovery. The Chinese pharmaceutical market is valued at only $4 billion but expected to grow annually at a 15 percent rate. While a large part of the market consists of traditional medicines, the government encourages foreign investment and technology transfer for high-tech therapies. The market's potential is shown in the fact that the population of 1.3 billion spends only $7 per capita on healthcare, compared with $200 per capita in the United States; even assuming only about 300 million people in the market for Western medicines, the upside is significant.

SINGAPORE: AN ASIAN BIOMEDICAL HUB

Singapore got on the biotech map through a combination of aggressive public funding, foreign investment, and local talent. The output of the bio-medical industry reached $4 billion in 2000 and is expected to grow to $7 billion by 2005. More than 20 companies operate there, from Merck to Affymetrix and local players S*BIO (partnering with Chiron in drug discovery), ES Cell (stem cell research), and KooPrime (bioinformatics).

The Economic Development Board (EDB), which wants Singapore to be a world-class biohub attracting 15 top biopharma companies by 2010, has aggressively supported its ambitions with a $600 million fund and top research centers such as the Institute of Molecular and Cell Biology, set up as early as 1987, and the Genome Institute. The EDB gave Lilly support to initiate in 2001 its Center for Systems Biology, which will spend $140 million over five years to study whole biological systems. Thanks to Singapore's educated workforce and political stability, private funding is readily available. More than $6 billion in venture capital funds is managed in Singapore. The government also actively encourages new ventures. The EDB and the Agency for Science, Technology & Research are to coinvest more than $1 billion to cover all phases of biomedical research, from the incubation stage to commercialization. A recent initiative aims to make Singapore a "regulatory haven" for stem cell research, thanks to liberal legislation allowing cloned embryos to be kept up to 14 days. Local research planned by Australia's ESI will focus on diabetes and Parkinson's disease.*

---

* "Biotech Hotbed," *Pharmaceutical Executive* (August 2001), p. 24; Ernst & Young, *Beyond Borders* (2002), p. 140; Burrill & Company, *Biotech 2002* (2002), p. 237; P. Chan, "Send in the Clones," *The Economist* (August 24, 2002), pp. 58–59.

China's revenues from the biosector passed the $2 billion mark in 2000, and the country counts more than 50 biotech firms; the largest, Sinogen, has captured more than 60 percent of China's market of 20 million hepatitis sufferers with its recombinant interferon product. The government has designated biotech as a priority sector and backs areas such as the biochip industry, led by Beijing-based Capital Biochip. Serious barriers remain, ranging from weak intellectual property to suboptimal quality standards. These issues may improve in the wake of China's admission to the World Trade Organization (WTO).[20]

While India has a major pharma industry led by multinationals such as Ranbaxy, Dr. Reddy, and Wockhardt, its biotech market is undeveloped, accounting for about $1.5 billion by 2005. It includes human health as well as agricultural and industrial products (genetically modified seeds, enzymes, and organic acids).

A major historical barrier has been India's lack of intellectual property protection. It will not begin to recognize patents until 2005, in accordance with the WTO. The government unveiled its "Biotechnology—A Vision" Report in 2001, calling for a sustainable Indian biotech industry within 10 years; major goals include strengthening the bioinformatics network and conducting a field assessment of large-scale production of transgenic seeds by 2005.

India has several competitive advantages: a low cost innovation and manufacturing base (operational costs are one-seventh to one-tenth of those in developed markets), a research infrastructure (universities, biotech parks, and the National Institute of Biologicals, with a project outlay of $40 million), and an educated workforce.

India's major challenge will be the transition of its pharmacos from generics to original research. This will be helped by investments and cross-border alliances. Wockhardt plans to invest more than $40 million in biotech over two years, and Shantha Biotechnics partnered with Pfizer to commercialize the first indigenous hepatitis B vaccine and to expand markets for its other products.[21]

In summary, the global environment yields several lessons for bio-pharma companies:

- In Europe, government support varies and EU-wide policy is still lacking; the most favorable markets are the United Kingdom and Germany.
- The EU biosector is growing fast but is still immature; consolidation will continue.
- U.S. biotechs are globalizing and investing in EU firms to gain a local production and sales infrastructure.
- Japanese biotech players are diverse, and potential partners can range from brewers to electronics firms.
- Asia/Pacific varies widely; Singapore, Taiwan, and Korea are biomedical hubs that offer attractive investment conditions; the China and India markets are embryonic, legally risky, and best approached with alliances.

CROSS-INDUSTRY SCOPE OF BIOTECHNOLOGY

In parallel with biotechnology's global reach, it has a unique multisector impact. In the same way that computing, media, and telecoms evolved around a binary language, innovation in a much broader array of industries now shares a common genetic code.

This is occurring at two levels: market and technology. Companies previously operating in one market, such as food processing, are branching out with hybrid products such as medical foods. At the same time, companies with a technology platform developed in one industry are leveraging it across sectors—as Japanese brewers did with their fermentation techniques and as chemical manufacturers are doing with combinatorial chemistry and high-throughput screening.

Biopharma is emerging as the innovation driver for sectors ranging from energy to cosmetics, but these have fundamentally different roles in the new biotech ecosystem. *Coinnovators* are academia and the government; *enablers* include computing, telecoms, and media, forming new fields such as bioinformatics and telemedicine. *Hybrids* are emerging as boundaries blur between medicine, food, and cosmetics. *Counterparts* to the biopharma sector range from energy to agrotechnology, which share research areas such as biofuels and molecular farming. (See Figure 1.3.)

This multisector web of research synergies should not be confused with *industry convergence*. The "life sciences" concept was embraced in the late 1990s by firms such as Aventis and Pharmacia, envisioning that drugs, nutrition, and agbio would be housed under the same corporate umbrella. This quickly unraveled under internal and external pressures. European opposition to genetically modified organisms (GMOs) combined with low commodity prices to erode the profitability of agritech operations. In addition to vastly different margins, agbio and human health had different markets, regulators, and distribution channels. As a result, Novartis, Pharmacia, and AstraZeneca all spun off their agritech units, and Aventis followed suit. However, research synergies remain significant across sectors.

The need for scale in postgenomic R&D is acute, given its risks and costs. Many new technologies have a multisector impact: Transgenic plants yield human therapies as well as medical foods and cosmeceuticals. Instead of supporting vertically integrated conglomerates, bioscience is emerging as a matrix of research, supply chain, and marketing relationships, which link

FIGURE 1.3   Bioscience—Innovation Driver

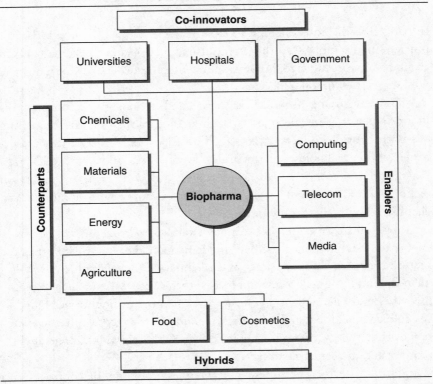

Source: Françoise Simon/SDC Group, 2002.

previously unrelated industries—and spur new ones, from bioinformatics to the biodefense field.

Before the September 2001 terrorist attacks in the United States, biopharma companies had disengaged from vaccines and anti-infectives. Vaccines were not a repeat business like drugs for chronic diseases, prices were low because governments were often the buyers, and liability was significant until legislation passed in 1986 alleviated it somewhat. Vaccine producers had dwindled to four (Merck, Wyeth, Aventis Pasteur, and Glaxo-SmithKline). Similarly, anti-infective drugs had been neglected in favor of oncology or cardiovascular therapies, but the rise of antibiotic-resistant bacterial strains had partly rejuvenated the area—the global infectious disease market was worth more than $37 billion, and vaccines and antivirals had

BIODEFENSE: A CHALLENGING NEW SECTOR

The need to defend against terrorism created a new market for biopharma. A 2002 bill authorized $4.6 billion to fund initiatives against germ warfare, including the expansion of medical stockpiles and grants to accelerate development of vaccines and diagnostics. Customers ranged from the Department of Defense (DOD) to the Defense Advanced Research Projects Agency (DARPA), the Department of Energy (DOE), and the Centers for Disease Control (CDC).

Small biotechs and vaccine companies took the lead. More than 20 biotechs worked in biodefense, including Britain's Acambis, which had won a $343 million contract in 2000 from the CDC to produce smallpox vaccine. Others included:

- Abgenix (transgenic mouse technology to generate monoclonal antibodies against smallpox, Ebola, and Marburg viruses, supported by DARPA grants).
- Bruker Daltonics ($10 million DOD contract for spectrometers for chemical defense—already used in Tokyo subways).
- Cepheid (DOD contract for hand-held detection devices).
- Maxygen (molecular breeding to develop superantigens for use in vaccines; funded by $24 million in DARPA grants).[a]

The new market carried significant risks, in addition to the liability relating to vaccines:

- Overdependence on government contracts could prevent small companies from targeting commercial markets.
- Governments could limit the open publication of pathogen genomes and other scientific data.
- Biodefense technologies could be stolen and used to create new weapons.
- An association with bioweapons could have a chilling effect on the biosector and add public fears to the existing concerns about GMOs, cloning, and stem cells.

The industry asked legislators for greater relief from liability, quick FDA reviews of new vaccines, and long-term financial commitment by the government. However, biodefense remained largely uncharted territory for biotechs.[b]

---

[a] Burrill & Company, *Biotech 2002* (2002), pp. 19–21.
[b] Andrew Pollack, "A Bright Shining Industry," *New York Times* (October 21, 2001), sec. 3, pp. 10–11.

double-digit growth. September 2001 radically changed the dynamics of this market.[22]

BIOMATERIALS: FROM POLYMERS TO NANOMEDICINE

The merging of biotechnology and materials science will have an unparalleled scope of applications and impact an enormous market of more than $1 trillion. Biomaterials are made in nature or by biotransformation and include drugs, enzymes, industrial chemicals, and crop protection/production compounds. In medicine alone, biomaterial products range from $200 vascular grafts to the $50,000 Left Ventricle Assist Device. Major players include Johnson & Johnson, Guidant, and Medtronic.

Further afield, biomaterials are revolutionizing energy, mining, and environmental cleanup. The biofuels initiative announced by the U.S. government in 2000 aims to generate biofuels equivalent to 348 million barrels of oil a year and to lower greenhouse gas emissions by 100 million tons (equivalent to the amount from 70 million cars).

Major corporate initiatives are underway. DuPont intends to generate 25 percent of 2010 revenues from biomaterials. By then, the second generation of its high-performance polymer, Sorona, will be produced directly from cellulosic biomass. It also leads in biosilks and is researching with Cornell University ways to engineer spiders to produce nonsticky web silk—a polymer 5 to 10 times stronger than steel. Applications range from artificial ligaments to parachute strings. Similarly, Cargill and Dow Chemical have formed a joint venture, Cargill Dow Polymers, and are investing more than $300 million to manufacture plastics from corn.[23]

In engineering, the central innovation will come from nanotechnology, producing composites tailored at the molecular or atomic level. Smart materials will emulate biological systems and use adaptive learning to self-repair. End products will range from automotive panels "remembering" their shape after dents, to lightweight airplane composites that sense and self-repair impending stress cracks.

The "killer application" is expected to be a DNA-type process to create integrated circuits. Traditional silicon technology may reach its limits in 2010 to 2015, when circuit lines may shrink to 0.01 micron and be vulnerable to quantum physics effects. To address this, DARPA intends to fund molecular electronics, in which molecules are designed to have electrical as well as chemical properties. The National Science Foundation estimates that nanotech as a whole will be a $1 trillion market by 2015.

Another high-potential area is nanomedicine, in which materials combine with drugs to create novel delivery systems. Startup C-Sixty was founded in Toronto to develop a fullerene-based therapy for AIDS. Because buckyballs (or buckminster fullerenes, carbon molecules discovered in 1985) can be shaped to fit into cell surface receptors, they can be coated with drugs that disrupt the cell's reproductive cycle; these are in development in oncology, AIDS, and other areas.[24]

BIOHYBRIDS: COSMECEUTICALS AND MEDICAL FOODS

For decades, the boundaries between cosmetics and drugs have been blurring, with incentives in both sectors: For cosmetics manufacturers, pharmaceutical margins are highly attractive; for drugmakers, new delivery systems (from creams to transdermal patches) are well-suited to some therapeutic areas. Johnson & Johnson's Ortho division pioneered this convergence with tretinoin, initially indicated for acne. The drug was later rebranded as Renova as an antiwrinkle agent.[25]

The market is growing, especially in Germany, France, and Japan. To reduce its dependence on cosmetics and move into preventive health, Shiseido made massive biopharma investments and developed a portfolio of dermatology products. Beyond this area, it gained approval seven years ago to market a chemically treated form of rice as a medicine for children who are allergic to rice—an unfortunate affliction in Japan. This made Japan the first country to approve a medical use for food.[26]

Nutraceuticals, which include supplements, organic foods, and medical foods, reached global sales of $140 billion by 2000. Growth rates peaked around 10 percent in the late 1990s and are projected to continue at the 6 percent level in the coming years. About 65 percent to 85 percent of U.S. consumers claim to use food to help manage their health, and the Japanese have favored functional foods throughout their history.

The appeal of higher growth rates and margins prompted deals such as PepsiCo's purchase of Gatorade in 2000, Kellogg's acquisition of

Worthington Foods for $307 million, and Kraft's purchase of Boca Burger in 1999/2000.[27] The latter two firms focus on soy products.

For several reasons, the business reality of medical foods has not met expectations. Consumers are fad-sensitive and many products had fuzzy positioning and inadequate scientific support for their medical claims. After investing $50 million on its Intelligent Cuisine frozen line, Campbell discontinued it in 1998. Procter & Gamble's fat substitute Olestra was a disappointment, and the newer cholesterol-reducing phytosterols marketed by Unilever and McNeil have not had a stellar performance. Novartis chose to exit this sector, which may be better suited to consumer goods companies. In 2001, Archer Daniels Midland and Kao formed a joint venture to produce and sell diacylglycerol oil in major markets. It is approved in Japan for the management of serum triglycerides, and ADM Kao will conduct further clinicals in the United States and abroad.[28]

AGBIO: THE NEXT GENERATION

Following the collapse of the "life sciences" concept, spinoffs led to the creation of "pure play" agbio giants. Novartis and AstraZeneca merged and floated their agrochemical businesses under the name of Syngenta in November 2000; Aventis later announced the sale of its Crop-Science operation to Bayer for $6.6 billion, and Pharmacia spun off the agbio part of its Monsanto acquisition. On the other hand, DuPont increased its exposure to agribusiness with its $7.7 billion purchase of Pioneer Hi-Bred in 1999, and BASF bought American Cyanamid the following year. By 2001, after a consolidation wave, the top seven agbio companies had revenues of $23 billion.

While research synergies are clear, the downstream businesses are too different in terms of regulation, economics, customers, and distribution channels to warrant mergers. Collaborative potential is high in several areas, including transgenic animals for drug production, edible vaccines, and nutraceuticals, but its realization depends on a radical rethinking of the consumer strategies of agbio companies.

Historically, agrichemical companies focused on their direct customers, that is, farmers. While nutraceuticals changed this business model by introducing consumers as a critical component of the food chain, agbio companies largely continued to ignore them.

GMOs benefited farmers through *input traits* (better crop productivity) but had no *output traits* (advantage to the end user). This was compounded by external disasters, including British mad cow disease and the dioxin scare in Belgium. More media coverage followed when Aventis' StarLink corn, approved for animal feed but not human consumption, was found in U.S. fast food. The cost to Aventis was more than $1 billion for the recall and compensation to growers. Farmers also questioned Monsanto's bioengineering that prevented its "terminator" seeds from being reproduced, thereby condemning them to eternal dependence on the company. This was an acute issue in emerging markets such as India, where farmers could not afford to pay for the high-priced seeds. Monsanto eventually capitulated in India, but the public relations damage was done. The result was disastrous: Gerber led food processors in rejecting use of bioengineered ingredients, Archer Daniels Midland asked farmers to segregate crops, and the EU imposed a 1998 moratorium on the approval of new genetically engineered seeds.

The only way to turn the debate around is to produce a second generation of GMOs with clear and tangible consumer benefits, such as an increased nutrition value. The new strain of "golden rice," first developed at the Swiss Federal Institute of Technology, contains enough beta-carotene to meet daily Vitamin A requirements and boost iron levels. Vitamin A deficiency affects 400 million people worldwide and can lead to learning disabilities and blindness, and iron deficiency is found in 3.7 billion.[29]

For these reasons, India and other emerging markets including Brazil, China, and South Africa are actively expanding genetically modified (GM) crops. Some 125 million acres of transgenic crops were grown in 2001, and China was reported to have the second largest investment in plant biotechnology after the United States—with spending to quadruple by 2005. Argentina has the second-largest acreage of GM crops after the United States, and India and Brazil are expected to adopt transgenics in the near future.

The biggest challenge remains public opinion in developed countries. An EU report summarizing 81 research projects conducted over 15 years at a cost of $64 million concluded that there were no new risks to human health or the environment—but the EU still passed legislation to mandate the labeling of GM foods, which requires producers to track the products from seeds to grocery stores.[30]

SUMMARY POINTS

✓ Biotechnology has reached an inflection point where it is increasingly profitable and productive, but also vulnerable to negative forces ranging from pricing and access issues to public concerns about privacy.

✓ The biosector's evolution is unique, and the industry must be more proactive in minimizing the "social brakes" that have negatively impacted its progress.

✓ Big Biotech and Big Pharma are now indistinguishable, and an emerging scenario links pharmaceutical megamarketers to a web of satellite biotechs; accordingly, the next chapters deal with the biopharma sector as a single unit.

✓ The top-tier biotechs are developing their own global capabilities and need region-specific strategies in Europe and Asia.

✓ Cross-border deals are linking the United States and Europe, but high-potential, high-risk markets such as China and India are best approached with alliances.

✓ Biotechnology is the innovation driver for many sectors, but these vary widely in their business appeal; while biomaterials and nanomedicine hold high promise, hybrid fields such as medical foods may be better suited to consumer goods players than to biopharma companies.

TRANSFORMING FORCES
IN THE BIOSECTOR

There is a market emerging now around the marriage of information technology with life sciences research and genetics that I personally believe represents the next major revolution—not only in this industry, but for society at large.

Louis Gerstner, former chairman and CEO, IBM[1]

While particle physics and computer science were last century's driving forces, bioscience is this century's core technology, creating new links between industries and prompting new business models. No cross-industry linkage will have a more powerful impact on innovation than the fusion of bioscience and information technology, creating new sectors such as bioinformatics.

Major milestones in bioscience and computing could not have happened without a coevolution of technologies. Biology, particularly at the molecular level, amounts to an information science. As Freeman Dyson remarked, "Hardware processes information; software embodies information. These two components have their exact analogues in the living cell; protein is hardware and nucleic acid is software."[2]

29

The bioinformatics field links software and hardware companies and drug discovery firms. It is driven by twin forces: the proliferation of biological information and the search for new high-growth markets by information technology companies. In an accelerated parallel to Moore's law, biological information is estimated to double every six months. Most importantly, bioinformatics promises to increase R&D efficiency by reducing costs and time to market—although this will take several years. When the markets for high-performance computing, storage, and e-commerce are added to that of data management, the global market for IT products and services in the life sciences may surpass $40 billion by 2004, according to a study commissioned by IBM.[3]

In addition to information technology, two other transforming forces are impacting the biosector: systems biology and consumerism. (See Figure 2.1.)

Systems biology integrates analyses of cellular components and studies how they interact to create biological systems. Beyond genomics research, proteomics investigates the protein products of the genome and how they interact to determine biological functions—this multiplies the structures targeted and the computational capacity required. Beyond the proteome, the metabolic system and the entire human physiology present even higher complexity. Because this requires large-scale computation, it leads to the integration of wet biology and digital biology. The market opportunity in systems biology has attracted companies ranging from IBM and Microsoft to Hitachi, Agilent, and Corning.[4]

FIGURE 2.1 Transforming Forces

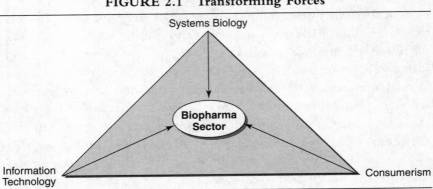

Source: Françoise Simon/SDC Group, 2002.

Both information technology and systems biology are related to a third transforming force, *consumerism*. At the same time as IT takes whole-genome biology to the next level, it helps consumers take a proactive role in healthcare—from information seeking on the Internet to networking, advocacy group building, and interactive communications with manufacturers. While physicians retain their primary influence on medical research, patients can directly impact it—especially in life-threatening areas. In AIDS and oncology, several therapies came to market in record time because of patient activism.

Another reason that consumers deserve attention from biopharma companies is their ambivalence: While they may welcome the advent of personalized medicine, they may also be vocal in expressing concerns about privacy and genetic discrimination—thus influencing legislators and negatively impacting the industry.

This chapter focuses on information technology, consumerism, and systems biology and draws the implications of these transforming forces for biopharma companies.

INFORMATION TECHNOLOGY

Informatics is driving biology, from data mining and molecular modeling to complex cell and organ simulation. However, bioinformatics still lacks the standards and integration needed to extract an optimum value from the databases and technology platforms already developed. It resembles the pre-Windows/Intel computing sector, with its different operating systems and developers.[5]

To develop common protocols for data exchange, more than 40 biotech and IT companies formed the I3C group in 2001 (Interoperable Informatics Infrastructure Consortium). Members range from IBM and Oracle to Affymetrix, Incyte, and the National Cancer Institute.[6]

BIOSCIENCE/COMPUTING INTERFACE

Molecular-based medicine will emerge from the interface of bioscience and computing. On the bioscience side, massive datasets are evolving from the genomic to the proteomic levels. Automation helps develop these datasets and facilitate data mining and pattern discovery. On the IT side, the massively parallel architecture of IBM's Blue Gene supercomputer will be critical to studying protein dynamics. Grid computing is already in use at companies such as Monsanto, and optoelectronics is creating new fields such as biometrics. (See Figure 2.2.)

To address the new market opportunities, many IT companies have formed internal bioscience groups. Sun Microsystems set up a computational biology unit to work with nonprofits, and Agilent Technologies formed a life sciences group to provide DNA chips and bioinformatics tools. In 1999, Agilent entered into a licensing agreement with Rosetta (since acquired by Merck) to manufacture and sell custom DNA arrays. In 2001, Agilent started an alliance with MDS Proteomics to develop new protein analysis products.[7] Japanese companies are also active in this field. Hitachi has built an ambitious web of collaborations. In 2000, it formalized a 10-year, $200 million partnership with Nanogen to develop biochip instrumentation. In 2001, Hitachi concluded a $185 million deal with Myriad, Oracle, and Switzerland's

FIGURE 2.2   Bioscience/Computing Interface

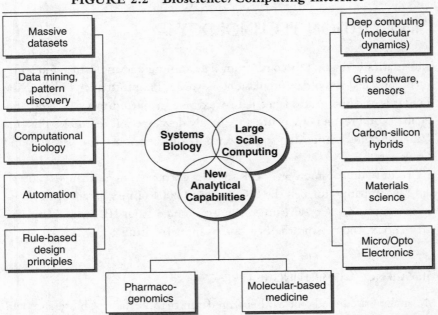

Source: Françoise Simon/SDC Group, 2002; partly adapted from George Poste (cited in *Biotech 2002*, Burrill & Company, p. 22).

Friedli to set up Myriad Proteomics as a 50 percent-owned subsidiary of Myriad, with the objective to develop a database of human protein interactions and pathways, as well as a catalog of purified proteins by 2004.[8]

BIOCHIP PLAYERS: FROM AFFYMETRIX TO HITACHI

The biochip market is expected to reach more than $3 billion by 2004, at a compound annual growth rate of 65 percent. Biochips include microarrays and microfluidics-based chips, but microarrays have been dominant since they were pioneered by Affymetrix in the mid-1990s. Microarrays use nucleotide probes set in a grid of microwells and exposed to DNA samples; the probe's hybridization with a target gene is signaled by a fluorescent enzyme. Chips are crucial to gene expression profiling, that is, determining which genes are active at a given time to make specific proteins. Biochips are also used in genotyping; new therapies depend on the detection of single nucleotide polymorphisms (SNPs), that is, genetic variations among individuals or populations. These can be linked with disease and with phenotypes (observable traits). A map of 1.42 million SNPs was published, coinciding with the partial sequencing of the genome.[9]

Given their hybrid nature, biochips have attracted IT companies who share the field with biotechs such as Nanogen, Orchid, and Sequenom. Motorola formed its Biochip Systems Division in 1998 and expanded it in 2000 with the $280 million acquisition of Clinical Micro Sensors. In this two-year time frame, another $220 million was spent on equity investments in Molecular Staging (amplification technology for DNA arrays), Iconix (chemogenomics database), SurModics (PhotoLink technology), Genometrix (electronic hybridization), and Orchid (microfluidics). On the content side, Motorola was the first biochip producer to license Incyte's datasets. Based on these alliances and academic collaborations, Motorola is positioning itself as a low-cost, high-volume producer of bioarrays.[10]

LARGE-SCALE COMPUTING

Beyond biochips, computing itself is changing to accommodate the flood of bioscience data. *Grid networks* aggregate the power of smaller machines for a fraction of the price of a supercomputer. Incyte uses a 1,000-unit grid for its genomic databases, and Monsanto's subsidiary Cereon Genomics has

BIOCHIPS: A KEY TO PERSONALIZED MEDICINE

In the future, DNA chips may allow personalized medicine, that is, custom therapies based on individual genotypes. Affymetrix pioneered biochips in 1994. Current costs are $1,000 to $2,500, but they will gradually decrease. The molecular diagnostics market now splits into two tiers:

1. *The research market* ($500 million to $2 billion) is dominated by Affymetrix. While pharmacos may spend $100 million or more on bioarrays, this market remains fragmented; it is targeted by Corning and Agilent.
2. *The clinical market* has a much higher potential. Bioarrays used in reference laboratories and, ultimately, in physicians' offices could optimize drug selection and medical outcomes, especially in areas such as oncology.

Both markets face some barriers. The widespread adoption of molecular diagnostics is not expected for another 5 to 10 years. There is a resistance from pharmacos to use genotyping in clinicals: Linking a drug to a genotype or eliminating genotypes linked to adverse reactions could improve outcomes but also reduce the market. Physician training and consumer concerns about privacy and reimbursement may also slow adoption of the technology. Beyond healthcare, biochips are increasingly used in agriculture, defense, energy, and the environment.★

★ Mark Ratner, "Motorola: Paging Diagnostics," *In Vivo,* March 2001, pp. 47–51; Burrill & Company, *Biotech 2002* (2002), p. 32; see also D. Lockhart and E. Winzler, "Genomics, Gene Expression and DNA Arrays," *Nature,* vol. 405 (2000): 827–836; and Hadley King and A. Sinha, "Gene Expression Profile Analysis by DNA Microarrays," *Journal of the American Medical Association* (November 14, 2001): 2280–2283.

boosted its gene analysis productivity by switching to grid computing. Economic benefits are also compelling; whereas a midrange supercomputer can cost $30 million, basic grid software and services start around $25,000. IBM and Hewlett-Packard are incorporating grid software into their product lines.

At the same time as this cost-saving innovation is giving small biotechs significant computational power, the high end of the sector is also evolving, led by IBM and its "one-stop shop" offerings in hardware, software, and consulting services, as well as its web of partnerships.

In 2000, IBM formed a life sciences unit that focuses on data management, electronic enablement of clinical trials, and high-performance computing. IBM's Computational Biology Center focuses on genomic pattern discovery, molecular modeling, and gene-chip data analysis. The Deep

---

BLUE GENE: MODELING PROTEIN DYNAMICS

In December 1999, IBM announced a five-year, $100 million initiative to build a petaflop-scale supercomputer to attack problems such as protein folding. Because typical proteins contain thousands of atoms and forces on each one must be evaluated for each time-step, this requires the calculation of millions of separate forces. Simulating the behavior of a small protein for a millionth of a second took three months on a Cray T3 supercomputer. To address this, Blue Gene will be 100 times faster than IBM's champion, ASCI White, used to simulate nuclear explosions, and it will have more than 2 million times the power of a single PC.

Modeling the folding trajectories of a protein would address questions such as these:

- Why do proteins consistently fold into specific structures?
- Are there one or several folding pathways per protein?
- Are some structures more stable or faster-folding?

Beyond protein dynamics, Blue Gene will test the validity of the "force-field" models (simplified mathematical models of molecules) used in computational biology. The supercomputer will have other applications in climate and materials science. Its massively parallel architecture is also self-healing; each of the chips containing processor cores will be fault-tolerant, so that it will work even if some cores fail: This could apply to e-commerce and other situations where servers must operate around the clock.★

★ Personal communications to Françoise Simon by Dr. Caroline Kovac, Vice President, IBM Life Sciences (April 12, 2001); Mike Svinte, Vice President of Marketing and Ajay Royyuru, Manager of Structural Biology (April 2002); "Big Blue's Big Bet," *The Economist* (December 9, 2000), pp. 32–35.

Computing Institute oversees the development of Blue Gene, a supercomputer with unprecedented power.[11]

Pharmacos have invested in their own systems, they are wary of open standards and information sharing, and they are paying high prices for drugs, not information. In the late 1990s, the first wave of bioinformatics companies such as NetGenics and Pangea mostly underdelivered, in part because they offered piecemeal solutions. The two viable avenues in bioinformatics now appear to be either forward integration toward drug discovery on the Incyte model or a "one-stop shop" approach on the IBM model.[12]

SUSTAINING VERSUS DISRUPTIVE INNOVATIONS

The fusion of IT and bioscience leads to what Clayton Christensen called *sustaining innovations* as well as *disruptive innovations.*[13] Deep computing needs the massive resources of a dominant player such as IBM and will offer applications at the high end of the market, that is, sustaining innovations.

At the same time, disruptive innovations are emerging in several areas, as some companies target the low end of the market in grid computing and biochips. DNA microarrays may move from research labs to point-of-care "labs-on-a-chip" used by physicians to determine patient genotypes, find the molecular basis of diseases, and prescribe targeted therapies.

Disruptive innovations will be helped by consumerism. The trend toward self-care has combined with technological change to create the home diagnostics market. In the same way as diabetics now carry miniature blood glucose monitors, future patients may use home diagnostics for genetic testing—thus bypassing lab reports to insurers.

In the same way, biologics may move closer to consumer products as they migrate from niche areas to primary care and as new delivery systems such as nasal sprays become more available.

The fusion of infotech and bioscience has several implications for biopharma companies:

- The competitive field has vastly broadened and includes new IT entrants; market power in bioinformatics is shifting from startups to major players such as IBM.
- The emerging innovation structure is a web of cross-industry collaborations such as Hitachi, Oracle, and Myriad's joint venture.

- Postgenomic research requires unprecedented computational capacity, which may be derived from both high-end and low-end systems (deep computing and grids).
- The field is evolving through both sustaining and disruptive innovations; consumer trends and technology advances will accelerate disruption and drive diagnostic and therapeutic applications.

CONSUMERISM

Across major world markets, many consumers have become active managers of their own health and have gained a direct influence on healthcare decisions. While the proactive segment first emerged in the United States, the trend has spread to Europe and, to a lesser degree, Japan.

A 2001 survey commissioned by McKinsey of 1,500 consumers in Germany, the United Kingdom, and Italy found that most were confident in their ability to self-medicate (83 percent) and most made health-driven lifestyle choices (67 percent) and were willing to pay out-of-pocket for additional products and services (59 percent).

Across the three countries, 35 percent of respondents were proactive (driven by a need for control or fear of illness). However, only 26 percent asked their doctors for specific treatments—reflecting the fact that direct-to-consumer advertising (DTC) is allowed in the United States but not in Europe for prescription drugs.[14]

A related trend in major markets is a high interest in biotechnology, but also a high variance in actual knowledge. Surveys were sponsored by the European Commission in the 1990s, and similar studies were done in Japan. In 1997, only about half of Europeans were familiar with the term *biotechnology,* and the proportion dropped to one-third in Japan. The following year, a survey commissioned by the National Center for Genome Resources polled more than 1,000 U.S. households. Although 91 percent thought they knew the meaning of *gene,* less than half understood *gene therapy* and only about 50 percent were aware that genetic tests were available. However, there was high acceptance for genetic testing: 93 percent for early diagnosis and 86 percent for identification of predisposed individuals—even in untreatable diseases.[15]

This finding was confirmed by another U.S. survey, in which 79 percent of the respondents said they would take a hypothetical genetic test to predict whether they could develop Alzheimer's disease. They were also willing to pay more than $300 for a fully predictive test; they would use a positive result for socioeconomic purposes (get finances in order and purchase long-term care insurance).[16]

Concurrently the public has expressed concerns about privacy and ethics. While consumerism has grown for many years, the biopharma industry has only recently engaged consumers directly—although its outreach remains largely at the brand or company level and has not included education about new technologies. This has led to a disconnection between producers and end users, and the resulting dissatisfaction is reinforcing consumerism.

DRIVERS: ECONOMICS, DEMOGRAPHICS, AND INFORMATICS

Consumer activism arose from multiple factors. Worldwide cost containment efforts by public and private payers mean a greater economic burden for patients—at a time when the price of new therapies is escalating and the aging of populations raises the prevalence of chronic diseases. Concurrently, the Internet gives consumers access to previously restricted medical information and empowers them to form global advocacy networks. Finally, telemedicine, home diagnostics, and the switch of several drug classes to over-the-counter (OTC) status act as disruptive innovations, allowing consumers to self-medicate or comanage their health.

This confluence of forces has lasting power and will continue to be fed by deep dissatisfaction with health systems that ration care and shift costs to consumers. In a 2001 survey, public satisfaction with national health systems ranged from more than 90 percent in Denmark to less than 60 percent in Germany and the United Kingdom and only 40 percent in the United States. A 2002 telephone survey by Harris Interactive of more than 1,000 American adults found that managed care was ranked at the bottom of industries "doing a good job serving customers"—just above tobacco and below oil companies. While nearly 75 percent of respondents thought well of banks and hospitals, only 59 percent were favorable to pharmaceutical manufacturers, and 33 percent liked managed care.[17] These multiple drivers of consumerism can be summarized as follows:

Driving Forces	Key Components	Consumer Impact
Economics	• Government cost containment • Employer activism • Uninsured populations	• Rising copayments • Cost shifting • Political activism
Demographics	• Population aging • Caregiver segment	• Spread of chronic diseases • Strain on long-term care
Medical Innovation	• Postgenomic advances • Home diagnostics, OTC drugs	• Demand for genetic testing • Self-diagnosis and medication
Informatics	• Global spread of Internet • Online/offline media	• Access to medical information • Global patient advocacy networks

CONSUMER AMBIVALENCE: HIGH-TECH/HIGH-TOUCH MEDICINE

These complex forces have led to paradoxical consumer attitudes: On one hand, patients demand sophisticated healthcare information and therapies. On the other hand, consumers on both sides of the Atlantic have concerns about issues ranging from GM foods to cloning.

These pro- and antitechnology stances drive purchase behavior. At the same time as activist groups demand new cancer or AIDS therapies, consumers are turning to complementary medicines—seeking *high-touch care* as an alternative to *high-tech medicine.*

In two studies led by David Eisenberg, use of at least 1 of 16 alternative therapies, ranging from acupuncture to herbal remedies, rose from 34 percent in 1990 to 42 percent in 1997. Visits to alternative medicine practitioners reached 629 million by 1997 and thereby exceeded visits to U.S. primary care physicians. Total 1997 out-of-pocket expenditures for alternative therapies were conservatively estimated at $27 billion, which was comparable to projected out-of-pocket expenditures for all U.S. physician services that year.[18] In Europe, alternative medicine is even better entrenched, as

FIGURE 2.3   Alternative Therapies

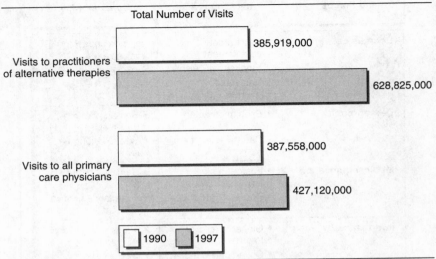

Source: David Eisenberg et al. "Trends in Alternative Medicine Use in the United States, 1990–1997," *Journal of the American Medical Association* (November 11, 1998): 1569–1575.

herbal and homeopathic medicines are regulated alongside allopathic therapies in countries such as France and Germany. (See Figure 2.3.)

The high-tech/high-touch paradox is a double-edged phenomenon for biopharma companies. On the negative side, consumerism, like informatics, creates entirely new sets of competitors, from chiropractors to herbal supplement manufacturers. In Germany, doctors prescribe St. John's Wort for depression 20 times more often than Prozac. On the positive side, this trend is expanding the market for pharmacos, as they broaden their product lines to include nonconventional therapies. In arthritis, Johnson & Johnson now has a complete high-tech/high-touch range, from its biologic Remicade (infliximab) to its dietary supplement Aflexa, a glucosamine derived from shellfish. The dual impact of consumerism can be visualized as shown in the table at the top of page 41.

LEGAL AND ETHICAL CONCERNS

While the high-tech/high-touch trend can be turned to the advantage of biopharma companies, stronger barriers arise from the fact that regulators

Negatives	Positives
• Internet access: increased price transparency.	• Biopharma firms become information partners.
• Complementary medicine: new competitors, lower margins.	• New market for pharmacos, product line expansion.
• Proactive consumers.	• Increase compliance.
• Physician resistance: time and control issues.	• Consumer as physician's partner: possibly better outcomes.

have not caught up with scientists. Genetic tests are already marketed, national genetic databases are being built, stem cell therapy and cloning are in progress—and are facing a patchwork of local regulations that falls far short of protecting consumers' rights.

In a 2002 Harris survey of more than 1,000 U.S. adults, the vast majority (over 80 percent) did not want their employers to know the results of genetic testing, and more than 60 percent also excluded their health insurers. However, in an American Management Association study of large and mid-size U.S. companies, one-third admitted to gathering genetic information about employees, and 7 percent said that they used it for hiring and promotion—despite the fact that this violates the Americans with Disabilities Act. Health insurance is equally problematic: while more than 20 American states prohibit denying insurance due to genetic information, this does not apply to self-funded insurance plans—and 85 percent of larger companies are self-insured.[19]

In the United Kingdom, the government and the Association of British Insurers reached an agreement in 2001 that applied to life and long-term care insurance; companies will be unable to approve or deny claims on the basis of genetic testing—but this applies only to the next five years; a long-term policy still needs to be developed. The World Health Organization (WHO) stated that genetic testing should not be introduced by countries without clear and enforceable legal prohibitions of its use in employment or insurance decisions—but current reality falls far short of this ideal.[20]

Genetic Databases

Other ethical issues relate to genetic databases. A high-visibility public/private partnership is the deCode Genetics national database in Iceland, which triggered a debate on informed consent—in particular, whether to use an "opt-in" process mandating explicit consent before inclusion in the database or an "opt-out" process automatically including data unless individuals object to it. The public was assured that data would not be individually identifiable and that the database would be under the control of the Icelandic government.[21]

Gene Therapy and Cloning

The public does not clearly differentiate the various types of gene therapy, that is, the treatment of disease by altering the genetic makeup of cells.

Somatic cell gene therapy modifies cells with inserted or altered genes, which applies only to an individual lifespan. By contrast, *germ cell gene therapy* alters an egg with the insertion of a foreign gene, and this modification is passed on to future generations. Germ cell therapy raises ethical issues depending on its purpose; interventions to prevent serious disease would not in themselves be suspect, unlike parental desire to enhance normal traits and produce "designer children." For these reasons, research on germ cell therapy and reproductive cloning is banned in most countries.

Legislation varies widely on stem cell therapy. The United Kingdom permits research on embryos up to 14 days of development for therapeutic cloning (but not reproductive cloning). By contrast, the United States has banned federal funding for human embryo research, with the exception of embryonic cell lines obtained with private funds and derived before August 2001.[22]

Given these legal inconsistencies, consumers remain highly conflicted. Outcomes for consumerism yield four different scenarios:

- The positive convergence of consumers and technologies would lead to personalized medicine.
- A positive technological outcome, combined with consumer ambivalence, would lead to a hybrid system where mass-market drugs coexist with targeted therapies.
- A positive consumer outlook offset by technological delays would entail a continuation of the status quo.
- A negative consumer mindset and scientific difficulties would reinforce skepticism about mainstream medicine and support further expansion of alternative therapies. (See Figure 2.4.)

FIGURE 2.4   Consumerism/Technology Scenarios

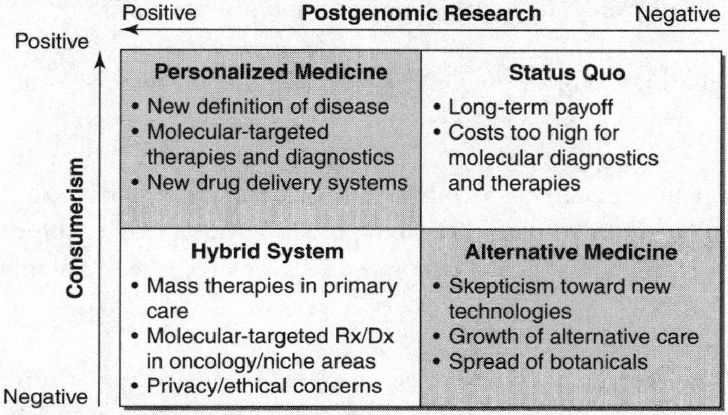

	Positive ← **Postgenomic Research** Negative	
Personalized Medicine	**Status Quo**
• New definition of disease • Molecular-targeted therapies and diagnostics • New drug delivery systems	• Long-term payoff • Costs too high for molecular diagnostics and therapies
Hybrid System	**Alternative Medicine**
• Mass therapies in primary care • Molecular-targeted Rx/Dx in oncology/niche areas • Privacy/ethical concerns	• Skepticism toward new technologies • Growth of alternative care • Spread of botanicals

Source: Françoise Simon/SDC Group, 2002.

STRATEGIC IMPLICATIONS

The evolution of consumerism has strategic implications for all healthcare stakeholders. Internet access, postgenomic technology, and a trend toward self-management of health have led to dysfunctions in patient/physician/payer/manufacturer relationships.

Patients' access to medical information leads to a greater communication need, which conflicts with physicians' time constraints. Online messaging does not help: Surveys find that most physicians use the Internet for research and professional contacts, but fewer than 15 percent use e-mail with patients. The main barriers are liability and reimbursement concerns. California-based Healinx is addressing these in a program with several Silicon Valley self-insured companies; in a plan administered by Aetna, Web visits are structured to meet malpractice insurers' guidelines and provide basic reimbursement.

This presents an opportunity for biopharma companies to capture the common ground between physicians and patients. Manufacturers could develop educational materials for patients at a quasi-professional level to complement the current basic brochures—thus meeting the needs of consumer segments with different knowledge levels.

Relationships also may be expanded between patients and biopharma companies and integrated with their payer and provider outreach. (See Figure 2.5.)

Biopharma companies could become more customer-centric with these steps:

- Redefine the market space from the consumer viewpoint.
- Develop a broader portfolio, from products and services to information.
- Shift from one-way DTC communications to a true dialogue with consumers.

A consumer-driven view of the market considers the entire range of available therapies, from biologics to botanicals. It also entails an integrative portfolio. Merck, for instance, is a scientific leader with several first-in-class products, but it is also a health information provider with the Merck Manual (both offline and online). Finally, consumer insights also need to be integrated into the development process at an early stage because end users and physicians have different expectations.

For instance, antiobesity drugs have generally underperformed, in part because their clinical endpoints (5 percent decrease in body mass index, or four pounds lost per month in the first few months) were not attractive enough for consumers, and their significant side effects did not pass physicians' risk/benefit assessments.[23]

FIGURE 2.5   Rethinking Relationships

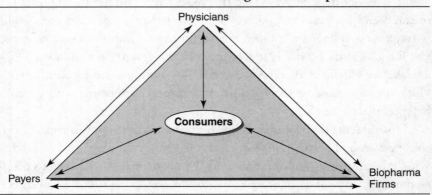

Source: Françoise Simon/SDC Group, 2002.

Biopharma companies, therefore, need to adopt a *push-pull strategy* with equal weight on the "push" to physicians and payers and the "pull" from consumers. Several key lessons emerge from consumer trends in major world markets:

- Consumerism is here to stay; it will be fed in future years by a confluence of economic, demographic, and technological factors.
- Consumers are ambivalent toward biotechnology and want both high-tech and high-touch therapies.
- Regulation lags science, resulting in insufficient protection for consumers; the biosector should continue to work with governments to assure more consistent legislation.
- Companies must rethink their relationships with patients, physicians, and payers and expand their role from pill sellers to healthcare partners.
- Consumer insights should be integrated into the development process at an early stage, so that clinical endpoints reflect expectations from end users as well as prescribers.

SYSTEMS BIOLOGY

Because systems biology studies complex sets of cellular components by integrating all their elements, this poses a new set of challenges. While the starting place was the draft of the human genome, the study of its functional output or proteome will unleash much greater value. The genome cannot always indicate which proteins are expressed, in what form and with what functions—nor can it identify the biological basis of multigenic processes such as disease, stress, and aging. Proteins are vastly more numerous and complex than genes, and they are not a closed set, since they undergo continuous change during their lives. The physiome itself reaches a much higher level of complexity. Proteomics has direct applications in many fields:

- *Diabetes:* Proteomic profiles of insulin signaling pathways to guide therapy.
- *Infectious diseases:* Rapid profiling of antibiotic sensitivity.
- *Oncology:* Profiling of proteomic signal pathways to guide and monitor therapy.

- *Immunology:* Proteomic profiling of T- and B-cell activation to evaluate the immune response to vaccines, illness, or injury.[24]

The ultimate goal of systems biology is preventative medicine, that is,
the development of diagnostics and drugs that block disease at its molecular source. To do this, it must integrate functional and structural genomics,
proteomics, pharmacogenomics (linking drug response to genetic variations), SNP research, and informatics. (See Figure 2.6.)

New Technologies: Time to Full Impact

The key question remains the time frame required for this process to yield
personalized medicine. Projections by Recombinant Capital and Lehman
Brothers are that the proteome might be mapped by 2005 to 2007; biological pathways would follow, but profiling complex diseases on protein
chips would not occur until a decade later.

This long time frame does not help pharmacos, which may face a "productivity cliff" until 2005. One problem is the sharp rise in drug targets
caused by genomic discovery. While current therapies are directed at fewer
than 500 drug targets, genomics may yield 5,000 to 10,000. Trial and error
costs are much higher for new targets, which entail novel chemistry and
toxicology tools.[25]

Pipeline problems are compounded by the fact that the cost of clinical
development has skyrocketed. Regulators impose added scrutiny on first-
in-class therapies, and highly publicized drug recalls resulting from adverse
reactions have made them even more cautious: The average number of patients in a regulatory submission dossier has grown from 1,700 in the early
1980s to more than 4,000 today. A drug development timeline still aver-
ages 15 years, 40 percent of which is spent in clinical trials: Costs (including cost of capital and failures) are estimated at $880 million, and
two-thirds of those are incurred at the clinical stage. (See Figure 2.7.)

Role of New Technologies through the R&D Chain

New technologies have already started to reduce time to market. Their impact on costs is more nuanced; several studies are projecting an initial cost
increase as new investments are made, followed by long-term optimization.

FIGURE 2.6 Systems Biology

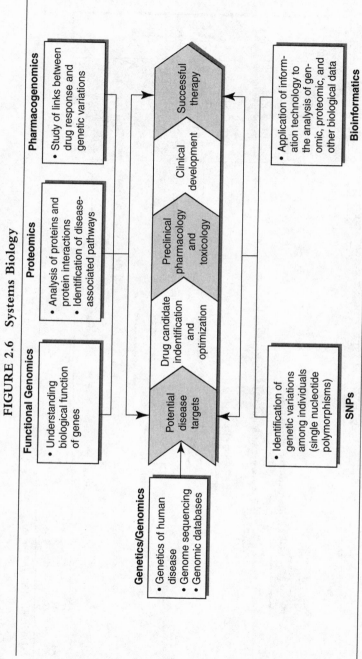

Source: Françoise Simon/SDC Group, 2002; Partly adapted from T. Bumol and A. Watanabe, "Genetic Information, Genomic Technologies and the Future of Drug Discovery," Journal of the American Medical Association (February 7, 2001): 552.

FIGURE 2.7 Biopharma Research Stages

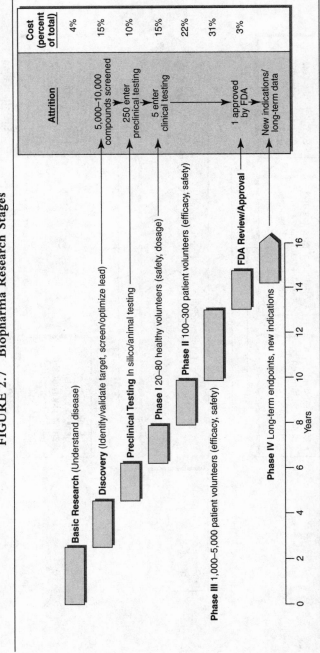

Source: PhRMA, SDC Group, 2002.

48

At Novartis, drug discovery now includes a multiparallel approach with target validation throughout the process; this has reduced the time from target prioritization to early clinical stage from six years to four.[26] Some technologies such as biochips are used through the R&D process, but downstream technologies have a nearer-term impact than upstream ones. E-management of clinical trials can accelerate time to market and reduce costs at the most expensive research stage.

Other technologies industrialize the discovery process: High-speed chemistry and ultra-high-throughput screening greatly reduce the time needed to identify chemical leads. Finally, pharmacogenomics is used throughout the R&D process to identify polymorphisms and link genotypes with drug response—which leads to a new basis of segmentation (patients with genetic mutations, adverse reactants, slow and fast metabolizers). Table 2.1 summarizes these new technologies and their impact.

INVESTMENT COST OF NEW TECHNOLOGIES

Postgenomic research requires the integration of two very different research models, as practiced by first- and second-generation biotech firms. Pioneers such as Amgen and Biogen depended on focused biological insights and small-scale experiments to develop their initial products. A new generation of companies, such as Millennium, Human Genome Sciences, and Cura-Gen, is relying instead on large-scale genomic and proteomic analysis and massively parallel assays.

As these models merge, investment costs are escalating because large-scale platforms are expensive to build. Capital requirements are 5 to 10 times greater for the new model than for the classical one. Both are required because large-scale computation facilitates but does not replace biological experimentation. Animal models, protein chemistry, and molecular biology are all essential to drug development.[27]

Lehman Brothers and McKinsey estimate that a fully integrated postgenomic capacity requires a threshold investment of $70 to $130 million. For an average large-cap pharmaco with a $2 billion R&D budget (including 20 percent, or $400 million for research), this is affordable—and most have already acquired it. On the biotech side, Millennium spent more than $100 million to build an integrated technology platform. Many biotechs are building this capacity through mergers or alliances. For

TABLE 2.1　Gene to Drug: Impact of New Technologies

	Technologies	Output	Time to Full Impact*	Competitive Advantage
Basic Research	Gene databases.	Databases and biochips identify genes coding for potential targets (receptors, enzymes).	S	Low
	mRNA and protein profiling via biochips.		S–M	Low
	Structural proteomics.		M–L	Low
	Model organisms.		S–M	Medium
	Bioinformatics.		M–L	High
Discovery	Functional genomics/ proteomics.	Validate target.	M–L	Medium-high
	Structural proteomics.		M–L	Medium
	Closed-loop chemistry.	High-speed chemistry and high-throughput screening identify leads against target.	S	Low
	Pharmacogenomics (SNP scoring).		M–L	Medium-high
	Cheminformatics.		M–L	High
Preclinical Stage	Animal models of disease.	Leads confirmed in animal models; clinical candidates identified.	S–M	Medium
	In vitro modeling.		S	Medium
Clinicals	E-trial management.	Clinical safety and efficacy in patient groups.	S	High
	Genotyping.	Polymorphisms (SNPs) linked to drug response.	M–L	High
	Clinical informatics.		M–L	High

*Time to full impact—S: Short term (0–2 years), M: Mid term (3–5 years), L: Long term (>6 years).
Source: Françoise Simon/SDC Group, 2002; partly adapted from *The Fruits of Genomics, II* (January 30, 2001), Lehman Brothers, pp. 7, 39, 56.

pharmacos, mergers are less beneficial since scaling up a postgenomic investment does not yield a significant return. Investment costs break down as follows:

- Informatics: $20 to $40 million.
- Target validation: $20 to $40 million (including database subscriptions).
- Lead optimization: $10 to $20 million.
- Genomics/proteomics applications in clinical trials: $20 to $30 million.[28]

IMPLICATIONS FOR BUSINESS MODELS

Postgenomic technologies will act as a disruptive force on biopharma business models, branding strategies, and portfolios. In particular,

IMPACT OF POSTGENOMIC RESEARCH ON PRODUCTIVITY

A consensus has emerged that postgenomic research will initially increase not only R&D costs, but also the average cost per new molecular entity (NME). However, beyond a five-year time frame, new technologies are expected to have a substantial positive impact. The Lehman Brothers/McKinsey estimate—assuming a moderate improvement in technology—is as follows for an average pharmaco:[a]

	2000	*2005*	*2010*
Total annual R&D budget ($B)	$1.6	$2.6	$2.7
Number of NMEs	2	2	4.4
Annual R&D budget per NME ($B)	$0.8	$1.3	$0.6

Similarly, a Boston Consulting Group (BCG) estimate was that postgenomic technologies could save on average $300 million and two years per drug (out of the $880 million and 15 years now required). This would be partly offset by the initial costs of addressing a greater number of molecular targets; after three to five years, costs could return to average.

BCG also broke down cost and time savings at each research stage:

- Target discovery (databases, biochips): $140 million, one year of time to market.
- Screening and optimization (in-silico chemistry, high-throughput screening): $130 million and 0.8 year of time to market.
- Preclinical/clinical testing (animal models, pharmacogenomics): $20 million and 0.3 year.[b]

---

[a] *The Fruits of Genomics*, II (Lehman Brothers, January 30, 2001), p. 26.
[b] P. Tollman, P. Guy, J. Altshuler, A. Flanagan, and M. A. Steiner, *A Revolution in R&D: The Impact of Genomics* (Boston Consulting Group, June 2001), pp. 3–4, 7, 11.

pharmacogenomics has been called the "Pandora's box" of the industry because it transforms both products and markets. Traditionally, pharmacos have developed drugs designed to the disease, not the patient, and marketed them as if they were effective in 100 percent of the population, even though only 70 percent might respond. With pharmacogenomics, the "one-size fits all" drug concept changes into customized medicine: the right drug, at the right dose, for the right patient. This may fragment and shrink the market but also increase market share. While blockbuster drugs effectively treat 30 percent to 40 percent of a mass market, targeted therapies capture an 80 percent share of a global niche. In the future, some blockbusters may also subdivide into molecular subtypes. This would replace the mass model with a dual one, which entails different economics, distribution channels, pricing, and communications.

While blockbusters may persist in primary care, targeted therapies will prevail in areas such as oncology, where less than half of patients respond to current drugs. This may not happen until the end of the decade, because of several factors:

- Costs are projected to drop by 2005, but they are still too high (at least $1 to identify one SNP in one patient—while he or she may have tens of thousands of SNPs).
- Regulators still lack the infrastructure needed for pharmacogenomics evaluation.
- Pharmacos fear that genotyping will shrink their markets and taint some drug candidates if it leads to excluding patients with adverse reactions.
- Physicians need training for molecular diagnostics and therapies.
- Consumers need legal protection from insurance and employer discrimination before they accept routine genetic testing.[29]

This will delay the wide use of pharmacogenomics, but biopharma firms are now banking clinical samples, which can be genotyped at a later date. The market itself may drive faster adoption, as physicians and patient advocacy groups demand better treatment, and as payers recognize the cost effectiveness of targeted therapies. As regulators become able to evaluate pharmacogenomics, they may even require its use—thus mandating a genotype-based microsegmentation of the market. These factors are summarized in Table 2.2.

Pharmacogenomics will also transform products and portfolios. Because targeted therapies require genetic testing, the concept of a product will expand to include both diagnostics and therapeutics. The molecular diagnostics market is now only about $1 billion (versus $30 to $40 billion for traditional chemistry/pathology diagnostics), but it is growing at a

TABLE 2.2   Pharmacogenomics—Drivers and Barriers

	Drivers	*Barriers*
Regulators	• FDA: Drug approval more likely if PGx data support NDA in case of adverse effects in some populations.	• Lack of FDA infrastructure for PGx evaluation. • Restricted labeling limits the market and may "taint" a drug.
Payers	• Cost effectiveness of earlier, more efficacious and safer therapies.	• High member turnover → no long-term incentivization to improve patient health. • Consumer privacy issues.
Physicians	• Reduce/eliminate adverse reactions. • Increase patient compliance in chronic diseases.	• Education needed to prescribe Rx/Dx combination. • Primary care physicians less likely to prescribe Rx/Dx than specialists.
Consumers	• Demand personalized medicine. • Better drug efficacy, safety.	• Privacy concerns. • Need for genetic counseling.
Biopharma Companies	• Reduce time to market and size/cost of Phase III trials. • Income recovery via Phase IV drug rescue.	• High cost of genotyping; need for Dx. • PGx erodes blockbuster business model. • Difficult to remarket a withdrawn drug.

Source: Françoise Simon/SDC Group, 2002.

30 percent to 50 percent annual rate (against 2 percent to 10 percent for classical technologies).[30]

Finally, portfolios may shift as new technologies become fully developed. While they are now organized by therapeutic areas such as cardiology, they may partly shift their focus to the biological mechanisms that cause diseases. This is already the case for many biotechs. Starting from a chemistry platform (in-silico modeling), Vertex has focused its discovery on target classes that respond best to in-silico technologies—especially kinases. This has yielded an $800 million–plus alliance with Novartis.[31] As new technologies mature, biopharma firms may shift their portfolios from saturated areas such as cardiology and develop expertise in areas such as cancer and its biological mechanisms, which will benefit most from postgenomic research.

SUMMARY POINTS

The biopharma industry is facing three transforming forces—the twin technologies of informatics and postgenomic research, and the grass-roots trend of consumerism. Success depends on integrating these key changes into company strategies:

✓ Innovation is driven by a web of cross-industry collaborations, which expands the range of available partners for biotechs; the competitive field has vastly broadened to include sectors such as IT and food.

✓ Informatics leads to both sustaining and disruptive innovations, as it offers high-end and low-end solutions to biopharma firms.

✓ Consumerism combines with technology to accelerate disruption; biopharmas need to evolve from drug sellers to health partners.

✓ Consumer ambivalence about biotechnology needs to be addressed through legal protection concerning genetic testing.

✓ The high-touch/high-tech paradox expands the competition, but also offers an opportunity to broaden product lines with nonconventional medicines.

✓ Consumer insights must be integrated into the development process at an early stage, so that clinical endpoints reflect end user as well as prescriber expectations.

✓ Postgenomic technologies may increase R&D costs in the next three to five years but reduce costs and time to market in the long term.

✓ New technologies disrupt the blockbuster model and create an alternative paradigm (targeted therapy with a dominant share of a global niche).

✓ Postgenomic research is impacting company portfolios. These may partly shift from saturated therapeutic areas to high-growth fields or biological mechanisms of action.

While bioscience impacts many fields, the biopharma industry can be seen as the bellwether for these sectors. The next chapters, therefore, focus on biopharma because it drives innovation across sectors. Chapter 3 focuses on the industry restructuring (mergers, acquisitions, and alliances) partly prompted by technological change; the following chapters then analyze the new branding strategies that leverage postgenomic innovation.

INNOVATING WITH BIONETWORKS

The future of the biotechnology industry depends crucially on its relationship with the pharmaceutical sector.

William Haseltine, chairman and CEO, Human Genome Sciences[1]

The biosector's search for new drugs has yielded important biologics, but it has not reduced research risk or improved pharmaceutical productivity. In 2002, 35 of the 78 new products (including extensions) approved by the FDA came from biotechnology, and seven biologics generated more than $1 billion. The largest, Epogen/Procrit, an anemia drug comarketed by Amgen and Johnson & Johnson (J&J), was in the top tier of all therapeutics. In addition, hundreds of biotech therapies were in late-stage trials.[2]

PHARMACEUTICAL INNOVATION GAP

While biotech output surged, pharmaceutical productivity declined. A decade ago, an annual R&D spend of $15 billion produced 50 new chemical entities (NCEs); the industry now spends more than $35 billion to

55

produce 30 new compounds. Postgenomic research has not helped. In a 1997 Accenture survey, pharmaceutical R&D chiefs predicted that it would make their research 50 percent faster and 300 percent more productive. When queried again in 2001, they showed no such progress.[3] Pharmacos are under a triple pressure to generate new products:

- Greater R&D risk and long payoff for postgenomic technologies.
- Increased pricing pressure worldwide.
- Patent expirations on drugs worth $100 billion in this decade.

Scale is another issue. The top 10 firms now all have annual sales above $10 billion. The double-digit earnings growth expected by investors requires, at a minimum, $1 billion in new sales each year. This means that pharmacos must generate at least three new products annually, but they average only one or two. As a result, research spending is shifting to external sourcing—from 5 or 10 percent of total 10 years ago to about 30 percent at many firms currently. This is reflected in actual output: Many blockbusters are in-licensed. This includes Pfizer's Lipitor (Warner-Lambert), GlaxoSmithKline's Epivir (BioChem), and J&J's Procrit (Amgen).[4]

The quest for products explains megamergers such as that of Pfizer and Pharmacia, driven by megadrug Celebrex (celecoxib) as well as complementary portfolios and access to new categories such as oncology. Without the deal, Pfizer's earnings growth would have dropped by 2006 or 2007 with patent expiries on big brands, including its antidepressant Zoloft (sertraline) and cardiovascular Norvasc (amlodipine). The same pressure drove Big Biotech's largest deal, Amgen's $16 billion acquisition of Immunex; its antiarthritic Enbrel (etanercept) would support Amgen's 20 percent planned earnings growth, and its inflammation and cancer pipeline would help Amgen diversify its portfolio. Intrabiotech consolidation reached an all-time high in 2001, including three deals above $1 billion.[5]

In addition to market factors, the very nature of bioscience dictates that it continue to evolve in a network structure because it is multidisciplinary. It is also multi-institutional, as it depends on universities and government agencies for basic research, teaching hospitals for clinical trials, and venture capitalists for financing.[6] Moreover, systems biology requires a consortium approach: The Human Proteome Organization, formed in 2001, includes Celera, Roche, Harvard Medical School, the Scripps Research Institute, and the Universities of Utrecht and Tokyo. The scale of postgenomic research

FIGURE 3.1 Biopharma Restructuring

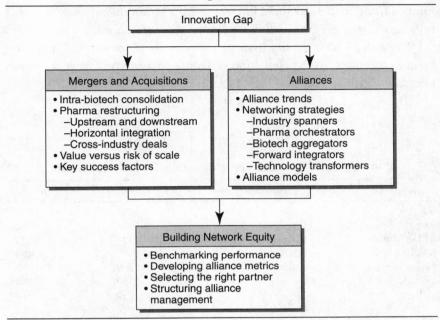

Source: Françoise Simon/SDC Group, 2002.

and the need to sustain earnings growth will continue to drive both mergers and alliances. Accordingly, this chapter focuses first on mergers and acquisitions (M&As), then analyzes alliances, and derives from both the key elements of a networking strategy. (See Figure 3.1.)

BIOSECTOR RESTRUCTURING: MERGERS AND ACQUISITIONS

Megamergers have not changed the industry's concentration. While the top six auto makers hold three-quarters of their world market, the top six pharmacos still account for only about one-third of world sales.[7]

INTRABIOTECH CONSOLIDATION

While restructuring was driven by Big Pharma in the 1990s, biotechs later took the lead—helped by higher valuations and cash left from pre-2001 financing. According to Recombinant Capital, intrabiotech deals jumped from 26 in 1999 to 52 in 2001, with a total value of more than $23 billion, surpassing that of nonbiotech pharma transactions.[8]

These deals have greatly increased their scale. A new trend may have begun with Cephalon's acquisition of Lafon—for the first time, a biotech bought a pharma company. (See Table 3.1.)

TABLE 3.1   Intrabiotech Consolidation—Major Deals

Acquirer	Company Acquired	Date	Price ($M)
Chiron	Cetus	1991	650
Amgen	Synergen	1994	262
Millennium	Chemgenics	1997	103
Medimmune	U.S. BioScience	1999	492
Millennium	Leukosite	1999	635
Gilead	NeXstar	1999	550
Celltech	Medeva	1999	914
	Chiroscience		535
Corixa	Coulter	2000	900
Invitrogen	Life Technologies	2000	1,500
	Dexter		400
Chiron	PathoGenesis	2000	730
Amgen	Kinetix	2000	170
Evotec	Oxford Asymmetry	2000	475
HGS	Principia	2000	120
Celgene	Signal	2000	200
Cephalon	Anesta	2000	444
Celera	Paracel	2000	283
	Axys	2001	174
Genzyme	GelTex	2001	1,000
	Novazyme		138
Sequenom	Gemini Genomics	2001	235
Vertex	Aurora	2001	592
Pharmacopeia	Eos	2001	197
Millennium	Cor	2001	2,000
Medimmune	Aviron	2001	1,500
Amgen	Immunex	2001	16,000
Cephalon	Groupe Lafon	2001	450
Berna Biotech	Rhein Biotech	2002	257
Serono	Genset	2002	106

Source: Company reports; Françoise Simon/SDC Group, 2003.

Big Biotech: Sustaining Shareholder Value

Like Big Pharma, Big Biotech needs to sustain earnings growth. The Amgen/Immunex deal gave the company a combined market capitalization higher than that of AstraZeneca.[9] This deal was key in several ways:

- Revenue growth was slowing on the first-generation products, Epogen (epoetin alfa) and Neupogen (filgrastim), and successor brands were still new to the market.
- The portfolio would be strengthened by Enbrel; combined with Amgen's Kineret (anakinra), it would add a third franchise in inflammation.
- The continued Immunex-Wyeth alliance would strengthen marketing and sales.

SECOND-TIER BIOTECHS: PRODUCT AND MARKET ACCESS

Because investors now value products more than technologies, the second generation of biotechs is moving downstream. This is shown by Millennium's string of acquisitions—from Leukosite ($635 million in 1999) to Cor ($2 billion in 2001). Cor provided commercial infrastructure and cardiovascular expertise—which Millennium needed to realize its goal of being a top-10 firm by 2010.[10]

Other deals combined product and market access. This was the case for Cephalon's acquisition of Lafon for a steep $450 million (or five times sales, all in cash). Cephalon gained a foothold in Europe, doubled its sales force, added production, and eliminated the 20 percent royalties it had paid Lafon since 1993 for Provigil (modafinil), a drug treating narcolepsy-related sleepiness.

European biotechs followed a similar pattern. When Berna acquired Rhein in 2002, it moved closer to its goal of becoming the number one pure-play vaccine company by 2005; Rhein is the world's third-largest producer of hepatitis B vaccines.[11]

Technology Players: Integrating for Drug Discovery

Technology firms are also using acquisitions to move toward drug discovery. The most radical platform-to-product transformer is Celera. Founded as a genomic database firm by Craig Venter, who wanted it to be the

"Bloomberg of biotechnology," the company is now using its $1 billion in cash to become a biopharmaceutical—realizing that a mere subscription business would not bring the return expected by investors. To this end, Celera purchased Paracel and Axys, the latter contributing chemistry capabilities.[12] A similar objective drove Vertex's 2001 purchase of Aurora and its screening and cell biology capabilities.

Market access is driving transatlantic mergers. In 2002, Iceland's De-Code Genetics gained a U.S. foothold as well as proteomics and chemistry capabilities with its purchase of MediChem. That same year, Germany's Lion bioscience acquired U.S.-based NetGenics.[13]

PHARMACEUTICAL CONSOLIDATION

While the Pfizer-Pharmacia transaction might trigger other mergers, it is not expected to lead to massive consolidation. Limiting factors are lower valuations and investors' dim view of megamergers. With its strong market cap and high price/earnings (P/E) ratio, Amgen could afford a large acquisition better than larger pharmacos. Mergers also have a poor track record and some acquisitions were criticized; Bristol Myers Squibb's (BMS) 2001 purchase of DuPont Pharmaceuticals brought drugs for depression, cancer, inflammation, and obesity, but investors doubted that these justified the $7.8 billion price.

Other acquisitions were more focused; in 2001, J&J's Alza purchase contributed drug delivery systems, and Roche's acquisition of a 51 percent interest in Chugai strengthened its presence in Japan.[14] Pharmaceutical restructuring followed four different models with varying degrees of success. (See Figure 3.2.)

Vertical integration included both upstream and downstream expansion, that is, the purchase of biotech innovation or distribution channels. Horizontal integration occurred within Big Pharma, but it also drove cross-industry deals.

Upstream Expansion: Buying Innovation

Vertical moves into biotechnology yielded uneven results for Big Pharma.

The Roche/Genentech acquisition, phased from 1990 to 1999 and followed by a partial spinoff of Genentech, worked well because of its relative

FIGURE 3.2 Pharma Restructuring

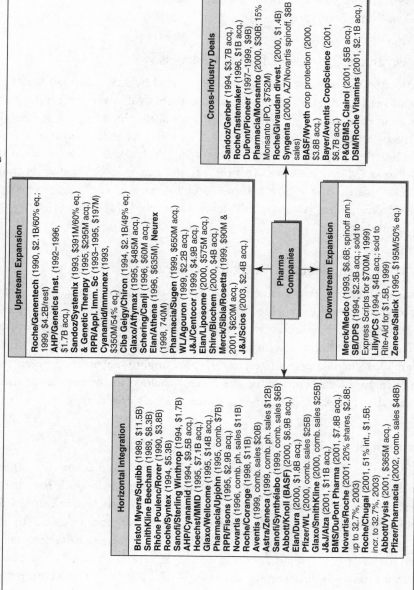

Upstream Expansion

Roche/Genentech (1990, $2.1B/60% eq.; 1999, $4.2B/rest)
AHP/Genetics Inst. (1992–1996, $1.7B acq.)
Sandoz/Systemix (1993, $391M/60% eq. & Genetic Therapy (1995, $295M acq.)
RPR/Appl. Imm. Sc (1993–1995, $197M)
Cyanamid/Immunex (1993, $350M/54% eq.)
Ciba Geigy/Chiron (1994, $2.1B/49% eq.)
Glaxo/Affymax (1995, $485M acq.)
Schering/Canji (1996, $60M acq.)
Elan/Athena (1996, $635M); **Neurex** (1998, 740M)
Pharmacia/Sugen (1999, $650M acq.)
WL/Agouron (1999, $2.2B acq.)
J&J/Centocor (1999, $4.9B acq.)
Elan/Liposome (2000, $575M acq.)
Shire/Biochem (2000, $4B acq.)
Merck/Sibia/Rosetta (1999, $90M & 2001, $620M acq.)
J&J/Scios (2003, $2.4B acq.)

Cross-Industry Deals

Sandoz/Gerber (1994, $3.7B acq.)
Roche/Tastemaker (1996, $1B acq.)
DuPont/Pioneer (1997–1999, $9B)
Pharmacia/Monsanto (2000, $30B; 15% Monsanto IPO, $752M)
Roche/Givaudan divest. (2000, $1.4B)
Syngenta (2000, AZ/Novartis spinoff, $8B sales)
BASF/Wyeth crop protection (2000, $3.8B acq.)
Bayer/Aventis CropScience (2001, $6.7B acq.)
P&G/BMS, Clairol (2001, $5B acq.)
DSM/Roche Vitamins (2001, $2.1B acq.)

Pharma Companies

Horizontal Integration

Bristol Myers/Squibb (1989, $11.5B)
SmithKline Beecham (1989, $8.3B)
Rhône Poulenc/Rorer (1990, $3.8B)
Roche/Syntex (1994, $5.3B)
Sanofi/Sterling Winthrop (1994, $1.7B)
AHP/Cyanamid (1994, $9.5B acq.)
Hoechst/MMD (1995, $7.1B acq.)
Glaxo/Wellcome (1995, $14B acq.)
Pharmacia/Upjohn (1995, comb. $7B)
RPR/Fisons (1995, $2.9B acq.)
Novartis (1996, comb. ph. sales $11B)
Roche/Corange (1998, $11B)
Aventis (1999, comb. sales $20B)
Astra/Zeneca (1999, comb. ph. sales $12B)
Sanofi/Synthélabo (1999, comb. sales $6B)
Abbott/Knoll (BASF) (2000, $6.9B acq.)
Elan/Dura (2000, $1.8B acq.)
Pfizer/WL (2000, comb. sales $25B)
Glaxo/SmithKline (2000, comb. sales $25B)
J&J/Alza (2001, $11B acq.)
BMS/DuPont Pharma (2001, $7.8B acq.)
Novartis/Roche (2001, 20% shares, $2.8B; up to 32.7%, 2003)
Roche/Chugal (2001, 51% int., $1.5B; incr. to 32.7%, 2003)
Abbott/Vysis (2001, $365M acq.)
Pfizer/Pharmacia (2002, comb. sales $48B)

Downstream Expansion

Merck/Medco (1993, $6.6B; spinoff ann.)
SB/DPS (1994, $2.3B acq.; sold to Express Scripts for $700M, 1999)
Lilly/PCS (1994, $4B acq.; sold to Rite-Aid for $1.5B, 1999)
Zeneca/Salick (1995, $195M/50% eq.)

Source: Françoise Simon/SDC Group, 2003.

61

autonomy and a clear market split, with Roche handling ex-U.S. sales. By contrast, some biotech purchases were rejected; these included Immunex, purchased in 1992 by Cyanamid and resold eight years later, and Affymax, bought in 1992 by Glaxo for $485 million and resold in 2001 for only $50 million.

Downstream Expansion: Buying Channels

Downstream forays were disastrous. Motivated by a desire to get closer to consumers through pharmacy databases, these deals were undermined by different economics and competencies. Two of the three major acquisitions (DPS by SmithKline Beecham and PCS by Lilly) were divested at losses totaling $4 billion. As the first trend-setting deal, the 1993 acquisition of Medco by Merck benefited from its strength in mail-order distribution. While contributing almost half of Merck's revenues, its much lower margins decreased profitability and Merck announced that it planned its partial spinoff.[15]

Horizontal Integration: Megapharma Deals

Pharma mergers have a mixed record. On the positive side, the Pfizer/Warner-Lambert deal yielded $1.4 billion in cost reduction by the end of 2001 and—more importantly—grew Lipitor to nearly $8 billion in worldwide sales by 2002, partly thanks to a huge salesforce.[16] On the downside, many deals had an opposite effect. Roche bought Genentech, Syntex, and Boehringer Mannheim; while the biotech yielded important cancer therapies, the pharma deals did not enhance Roche's productivity.

Cross-Industry Deals: The Life Sciences Fallacy

Led by the "life sciences" concept of agbio, food, and cosmetics joining health care under one corporate umbrella, cross-industry deals have had a near-complete failure rate. While hybrid categories such as nutraceuticals showed promise, they collided with consumers' fears about GMOs. In addition, while there were research benefits in applying genomics across several fields, their economics diverged; R&D costs, channels, and profit margins were too different to yield synergies. This led to divestments. Astra-Zeneca and Novartis spun off their agbio operations as Syngenta in 2000,

Pharmacia did an IPO of Monsanto, Aventis sold its crop science unit to Bayer, and Wyeth sold its crop protection group to BASF.

The consumer sector did not fare better. In 2000, Roche divested its Givaudan division and, two years later, sold its vitamins unit to Dutch specialty chemicals firm DSM. Cosmetics followed the same pattern: BMS sold its Clairol Unit to P&G in 2001.[17]

Is Bigger Better? Value versus Risk of Scale

The value of scale is debated on three counts: innovation, marketing, and global reach. *Research scale* was the focus of a 2002 report that compared the net present value of new products to R&D spend for Big Pharma over the past decade; it found no correlation between budget size and return on investment.[18] Scale does work downstream, as companies can run global clinicals faster and more efficiently. However, mergers often entail high diseconomies of scale because of talent losses and culture clashes. R&D may also become unmanageable. Table 3.2 illustrates these trade-offs.

Marketing scale yields the clearest competitive advantage, but it also has a downside. Blockbusters depend in part on armies of sales reps—and Pfizer/Pharmacia now has a global strike force of 30,000. In the United States, the addition of consumer promotion to medical marketing has inflated adspend to levels beyond the reach of small firms. Scale may also facilitate negotiations with payers.

However, it is not a panacea. Highly visible ad campaigns have fed a consumer backlash about drug prices, and salesforces have grown faster than physician numbers—which may be a sign that the "brute force" blockbuster model will yield diminishing returns in the future.

Geographic scale is needed to recover R&D costs, ensure fast product rollout, and hedge against macroeconomic risk—but some ex-U.S. markets are political minefields, generating negative press coverage about patents and pricing. Companies also need to balance central strategy and local execution, as they address persistent tensions between corporate branding and country management.

Consolidation will continue for both biotechs and pharmacos but for different reasons—while biotechs are acquiring critical mass, Big Pharma deals have been largely defensive; this may explain why they have had doubtful results.

TABLE 3.2   Value versus Risk of Scale

	Value	Risks
R&D Scale	• Allows upfront investment in key new technologies. • Helps attract biotech partners. • Faster global trials, efficient e-trial management. • Integrated platform technology.	• New technologies not scalable. • Partners may fear limited attention and possible buyout. • Mega-R&D may become unmanageable. • Diseconomies of scale (talent loss, culture clashes).
Marketing Scale	• Megasalesforces for blockbuster launches. • Dominant share of voice via large ad budgets. • "One-stop shop" thanks to broad disease portfolio. • Marketing scale is a draw for biotech partners.	• Physician market saturated; targeted therapies need few reps. • Advertising blitz may lead to regulator, consumer backlash. • Category size matters more than overall size. • Megamarketing may need to be split into smaller units.
Global Scale	• Fast rollout in global markets. • Hedge against economic risk. • Higher long-term growth in emerging markets.	• Coordination issues, global versus local conflicts. • More useful for Japanese and European than U.S. firms. • Exposure to patent/pricing issues in emerging markets.

Source: Françoise Simon/SDC Group, 2002.

MERGER AND ACQUISITION PERFORMANCE—A DUBIOUS RECORD

M&As were assessed by three measures: innovation, market share, and economic return. By all three, nonmerged firms have outperformed merged ones across industries.

INNOVATION

A survey of 776 firms over 15 years found that aggressive acquirers spent less on R&D and generated fewer new products than less active firms. Another study tracked the opportunity cost of pharma acquisitions: the all-cash $14 billion purchase of Wellcome by Glaxo in 1995 could have funded

39 new products (based on an average $360 million drug development cost at that time).[a]

MARKET SHARE

Postmerger shares also suffer. A McKinsey study of the top 10 companies in 1989 and 1999 showed that the top tier of 1999 was derived from the mergers of 23 firms, which held 49 percent of the world drug market in 1989. By 1999, these top 10 companies had only a 46 percent share, and their growth was below industry average.[b]

ECONOMIC RETURN

Merger effects on shareholder returns were also found to be negative. An analysis by Financial Times Pharmaceuticals showed that, in the 1994 to 1998 period, shareholder returns of nonmerged companies were roughly double those of merged companies in the sample.[c] Cost savings were more than offset by merger disruptions and loss of key talent. As a percentage of combined company sales, as tracked by Bear Stearns, they averaged 5.6 percent—but these effects were short term, did not help top-line growth, and were limited ex-U.S., where labor laws precluded massive layoffs and plant closures.[d]

---

[a] Michael Hitt, "The Market for Corporate Control and Firm Innovation," *Academy of Management Journal,* vol. 39 (1996), p. 6; Barrie James, "The Pharmaceutical Industry in 2005: A Strategic Reality Check," *Spectrum* (April 17, 1998), p. 5-16.
[b] Rajesh Garg, R. Berggren, and M. Holcomb, "The Value of Scale in Pharma's Future," *In Vivo* (September 2001), pp. 78–83.
[c] Cited in Burrill & Company, *Biotech 2001* (2001), p. 184.
[d] Joseph Riccardo, *Global Pharmaceutical Industry Review and Outlook, 2000–2001* (New York: Bear Stearns, 2001).

KEY SUCCESS FACTORS

Despite the fact that M&A results have been less than stellar, a vast literature deals with ways to improve success rates—starting with partner selection and due diligence.

Because all value creation occurs after the deal, this section focuses on postmerger integration. The key issue at that stage is the balance between strategic interdependence (needed to transfer knowledge and create efficiencies) and autonomy (necessary to retain the acquired firm's scientific assets). This balance varies according to three transaction types:

1. A *preservation deal* is typical of pharma/biotech acquisitions, which must be managed at arm's length to protect the biotech's innovation culture, but which should also ensure technology transfer to the parent company.
2. An *absorption deal* reflects many big pharma transactions where value comes from a full integration of portfolios, functions, and systems; these tend to fail when defined as "mergers of equals" rather than pure acquisitions, due to leadership uncertainties, turf battles, and culture clashes.
3. *Symbiosis deals* are the most challenging because both autonomy and interdependence are needed; this is most often the case in intrabiotech M&As, which must protect each firm's scientific assets while integrating technologies and portfolios.[19] These M&A types are summarized as follows:

Deal Type	Autonomy Need	Inter-Dependence Need	Examples	Strategies
Preservation	High	Low	Roche/ Genentech	• Protect boundaries. • Nurture acquired R&D, transfer learning.
Symbiosis	High	High	Amgen/ Immunex	• Gradually integrate knowledge. • Strategic control, operational autonomy.
Absorption	Low	High	Pfizer/ Warner-Lambert	• Set up single leadership. • Trim redundancies. • Move to best practices.

In all cases, M&A success hinges on three factors: leadership, timing, and strategic fit:

1. *Leadership* is key to reducing resistance from the target firm, which can destroy value through staff losses and reduced knowledge transfer. This is easiest to implement in absorption deals. When Pfizer took over Warner-Lambert, it set up a clear, single leadership and quickly

implemented workforce reduction with generous severance terms—but it also retained some R&D leaders and preserved a key Warner-Lambert asset, its sales force.[20]

2. *Timing* is critical: Many M&As are defensive deals, hastily negotiated when key products are about to lose patent protection. BMS bought DuPont Pharma at a time when its core oncology and cardiology franchises were threatened by patent expiries and product delays. By contrast, Pfizer moved early with its Pharmacia acquisition; its generic threats would not begin until 2006 to 2007, when patents were due to lapse on several drugs. Because Pharmacia's key products were protected for years, Pfizer diminished its generic exposure from 20 percent to about 10 percent of sales.[21]

3. *Strategic fit* includes R&D, product portfolio, marketing, operations, and culture. In all deal types, it is critical to maintain internal research as well as external alliances; Millennium increased its R&D spend at the same time as it was escalating its alliances. Strategic fit also relates to portfolios, as deals should avoid large overlaps leading to value-reducing product divestitures. Operational integration is critical for information systems, which can delay product launches if they are not well-linked.

The last element of strategic fit, culture, is the most problematic, especially in cross-border deals. An example is the 1995 merger of Upjohn and Pharmacia—two years after the latter had combined Swedish and Italian companies. Managerial styles clashed as the Swedish consensus approach collided with the U.S. command-and-control style and the Italian hierarchical culture. A new headquarters in London added a layer of management and conflict, and the Italian operations became known as "Fortress Milan" because of its impenetrable accounting, powerful labor unions, and management resistance. By early 1997, restructuring costs had reached $800 million ($200 million higher than projected), and the CEO had resigned.[22] Preventing culture clashes is easiest in absorption deals, where a single leadership entails a dominant culture, and in preservation mergers, where the two cultures coexist at first and only gradually combine. In symbiosis deals, intrabiotech mergers are likely to be the most successful because they share innovation-driven cultures and do not involve globally dispersed operations.

NETWORKING STRATEGIES

ALLIANCE TRENDS: INTRABIOTECH LINKS, PRICE ESCALATION

Intrabiotech alliances have gained ground for five years; in 2001, there were nearly 550 worldwide versus 480 for biotech/pharma deals. Their scale is also rising, including Abgenix's $150 million antibody partnership with CuraGen and Amgen's $130 million licensing of a Phase III lymphoma treatment from Immunomedics.

Pharma/biotech deals have shifted from technologies to products. Phase III compounds grew from 8 percent of the 2000 deals to 14 percent of those concluded in 2001 and also commanded record prices.[23]

The top deals of 2001 all focused on drugs or diagnostics:

Partners	Value ($M)	Focus
ImClone/BMS	2,008	Codevelop and market Erbitux.
Bayer/Curagen	1,340	Develop small molecules in metabolism.
Celltech/Pharmacia	280	Copromote Celltech's CDP-870.
Isis/Lilly	259	Antisense (metabolism, inflammation).
Millennium/Abbott	250	Develop Rx/Dx in metabolism.
BMS/Exelixis	200	Discover and develop cancer drugs.
Genentech/Roche/OSI	187	Copromote OSI's Tarceva (oncology).
MorphoSys/Schering AG	180	Develop drugs and diagnostics.
Novartis/Immusol	150	Oncology discovery.
Merck KgGaA/Biomira	150	Codevelop cancer vaccines.[24]

FIVE NETWORKING APPROACHES

Biopharma alliances follow four main strategy models, which depend on company size and competencies. The newest entrants are industry spanners shaping the bioinformatics field; these range from IBM to Sun Microsystems. Top-tier pharmacos are becoming network orchestrators as they manage a diversified alliance portfolio. Big Biotech leaders have become aggregators in their own right, with linkages ranging from in-licensing to acquisitions. Second-tier biotechs such as Millennium are moving downstream. These forward integrators have spent years building platforms and are now

TABLE 3.3 Networking Strategies

Strategy Type	Company Leaders	Objectives
Industry Spanners	IBM, Hitachi, Oracle, Motorola	• Leverage computing expertise to shape the bioinformatics field. • Provide supercomputing power (IBM).
Pharma Orchestrators	Merck, Pfizer, GlaxoSmithKline	• Gain scale and products with mergers (Pfizer) or joint ventures (Merck/Schering-Plough). • Acquire technology (Merck/Rosetta). • Manage alliance portfolio through value chain.
Biotech Aggregators	Amgen, Biogen	• Gain scale and products with acquisitions (Amgen/Immunex). • Adopt selective in-licensing (Biogen).
Forward Integrators	Millennium, CuraGen, Vertex	• Shift from technology to drug discovery. • Develop drugmaker skills via large alliances.
Technology Transformers	Celera, Incyte	• Build integrated technology platforms and acquire discovery skills. • Move from tools to drug discovery.

Source: Françoise Simon/SDC Group, 2002.

developing their drugmaking skills through pharma partnerships. Finally, smaller technology specialists are moving from platforms to products. These technology transformers include Celera and Incyte.[25] (See Table 3.3.)

INDUSTRY SPANNERS: GENERAL ELECTRIC AND IBM

The biosector is attracting infotech worldwide, from Oracle to Hitachi and Siemens. General Electric (GE) leads a related field, molecular imaging, which has a significant potential in oncology applications. GE Medical announced in 2001 an alliance with Genometrix and the University of Texas to better detect risk levels in oncology—with prostate cancer as the first target.[26]

Although a relative newcomer, IBM now has a network of technology and marketing alliances as well as a joint venture, and it is active in a consortium. Its life sciences unit has invested more than $200 million to grow four solution areas: knowledge management, high-performance infrastructure, clinical/regulatory, and information-based medicine.[27] Goals are threefold: Build critical mass on IBM platforms, establish links with firms that have technologies to fill gaps in its solutions portfolio, promote industry standards, and expand customer and market base.

Partnerships cover the R&D chain, from biological modeling to the physician's office:

- *High-performance intrastructure* includes academic alliances in North America, Europe, and Asia Pacific and links with firms ranging from Accelrys to Physiome Sciences.
- *Data and knowledge management* includes links with Agilent, Lion bioscience, MDS Proteomics, and Spotfire to help researchers access and integrate disparate data sources.
- *Proteomics hardware and software drives* deals with GeneFormatics, MDS Proteomics, and structural Bioinformatics.
- *Drug discovery optimization* alliances added a European partner (Lion) as well as three-way deals; IBM and Spotfire are to supply an end-to-end discovery platform to Aventis with the aim to cut R&D time.
- *Clinical and regulatory solutions* are developed with partners such as Phase Forward (trial automation) and Documentum (electronic submissions). This is a high-potential market, as the industry spends $20 billion a year on clinicals.
- *Information-based medicine* enables physicians to offer individualized treatment options; IBM's partners in this area include deCode Genetics.
- *Medical management software* is the focus of the Amicore joint venture that IBM, Pfizer, and Microsoft announced in 2001; its Web-based software and services will streamline physicians' practice workflow and will be marketed by Pfizer's and Amicore's salesforce. (See Figure 3.3.)

While IBM collaborates with venture capitalists, it clearly differentiates its equity investment strategy from theirs, as it chooses partners for their fit with IBM's research rather than for their financial potential. Selection hinges on two factors:

1. *Strategic fit* covers technical compatibility, competitive relationships, potential to fill solution gaps, and organization structure and culture.
2. *Market impact* includes position and growth, value of customer base, and potential influence on industry standards.

FIGURE 3.3 IBM Bionetwork

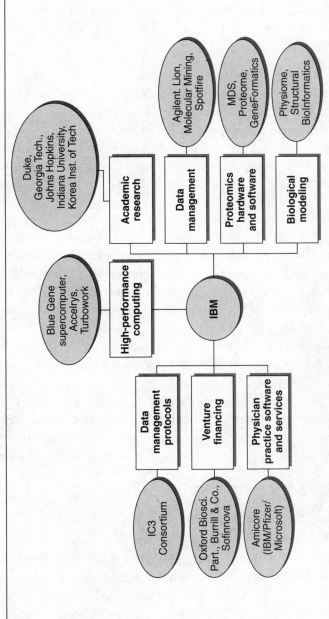

Source: Françoise Simon/SDC Group; IBM Life Sciences, 2002.

PHARMA ORCHESTRATORS: MERCK AND PFIZER

The alliance philosophy of top-tier pharmacos is reflected in these statements from R&D executives: "Power comes from the ability to integrate," but also "we don't want to be held hostage to one biotech company."[28]

Merck: Internal Research Focus

Merck retains a focus on internal research, which totaled nearly $3 billion in 2002 and yielded two top products, the antiarthritic Vioxx and the anti-asthmatic Singulair. However, faced with patent expirations, Merck has stepped up its networking. One-third of current dollar sales come from external research, and several top products were in-licensed, from Cozaar (DuPont) and Pepcid (Yamanouchi) to Fosamax (Gentili) and Noroxin (Kyorin).

Merck's approach is to balance internal expertise and external collaborations; for every partnership, it has a strong internal group. While it disengaged from several alliances, including a copromotion with Wyeth on Fosamax, it negotiated in 2000 a joint venture with Schering-Plough for the codevelopment and copromotion of complementary drugs. It also acquired two biotechs; Sibia brought neuroscience expertise and Rosetta, its array technology, which identifies gene functions by comparing expression patterns.

Merck has a clear vision of what should be researched in-house and what can best be outsourced: The latter includes informatics, genomic/proteomic databases, and delivery systems. Accordingly, Merck's alliance portfolio consists of four main clusters through the R&D chain, including basic research (Celltech, Cubist), platform technologies (Affymetrix, Incyte), clinical development (Isis, Vical), and delivery technologies (Elan/Nanosystems, CytRx).

Pfizer: Master Integrator

Like Merck, Pfizer sees itself as the integrator of a suite of alliances; by 2001, its portfolio included 510 partnerships (up from fewer than 100 in 1995). For Pfizer, scale does matter, and research management is not an oxymoron.

The scope of its network adds to Pfizer's R&D complexity. About 25 percent of discovery phase investment is for external research; after Phase I, about 20 percent of R&D spend is external (including contract research organizations).

What counts is not just the scale of its alliance portfolio, but also how it strategically supports each R&D stage. Gene targets are accessed through the genomics databases of Celera and Incyte. Gene families are identified through bioinformatics and structural genomics. Other alliances provide access to transgenic models, and gene functions are determined by tools such as the Affymetrix microarrays. In a series of 1999 deals, Pfizer optimized its parallel processing in alliances with Aurora (high throughput screening), Evotec (accelerated biochemical screens), ArQule (rapid chemical synthesis) and Neurogen (chemoinformatics). In 2001 to 2002, Pfizer added deals with Tripos, Chembridge, and Pharmaceutical Discovery to create new combinatorial megalibraries. These meant a $650 million commitment to attack "the root causes of the real nemesis in R&D: attrition." They were structured as technology transfers with high value to partners but full ownership of compounds by Pfizer.[29]

Further downstream, copromotions were critical to blockbuster-building. Pfizer comarketed Zyrtec with UCB and Daiichi, Lipitor with Warner-Lambert, and Celebrex with Pharmacia—and all became leading brands in competitive categories.

Pfizer's scale impacts its networking in three ways:

1. The fact that Pfizer is now present in most major therapeutic categories gives it the most exposure to antitrust challenges by the FTC.
2. Licensers of major drug candidates may have fears of being ultimately engulfed, as were Warner-Lambert and Pharmacia.
3. In-licensed drugs may compete for marketing resources with Pfizer's blockbusters, and originators may feel they would get more attention from smaller partners—although contracts may specify terms such as the number of details per year.

These factors may affect Pfizer's alliance equity, built since the mid-1990s thanks to flexible terms and record-high fees (the Warner-Lambert deal had an upfront and milestone value of $195 million and a commitment to fund half of clinical and marketing costs, while collecting only about 45 percent of net sales). Pfizer's deal making has slowed down against that of Glaxo or Lilly.[30]

BIOTECH AGGREGATORS: AMGEN AND BIOGEN

Amgen and Biogen adopted historically distinct strategies but are now both focusing on a selective alliance strategy.

Amgen: Changing Course

The Epogen/Procrit saga may have played a part in Amgen's historical policy of limiting alliances. J&J licensed epoetin alfa from Amgen in 1985 and renamed it Procrit for its share of the U.S. market (nondialysis use). The dialysis-related anemia market in the United States remained Amgen's. Ten years later, Amgen started arbitration proceedings, claiming that J&J breached the agreement by selling Procrit for dialysis use. After protracted litigation, an arbitrator ruled in favor of Amgen in 2002 and awarded $150 million in damages.

Amgen is now accelerating its alliances. Recent in-licensing includes epratuzumab for non–Hodgkin's lymphoma from Immunomedics and an ALS treatment from Regeneron.

Amgen has three key objectives:

1. Portfolio diversification (gain of an inflammation franchise from Immunex).
2. Technology integration (acquisition of Kinetix for its small-molecule and protein kinase expertise; compound-screening alliance with Pharmacopeia).
3. Geographic expansion (continued reliance in Asia on long-standing Kirin partnership, but more direct control in Europe through the $138 million buyback of Neupogen's European rights from Roche).[31]

Biogen: Focused In-Licensing

As it evolved from a research firm to a top-tier biopharmaceutical, Biogen shifted from early out-licensing to its current combination of internal research and selective in-licensing with a focus on key therapeutic areas with high unmet need.

Over 20 years ago, Biogen outlicensed its recombinant alpha interferon to Schering-Plough on a worldwide basis, and sales of Intron A contributed royalties that allowed Biogen to grow its autoimmune franchise and build its research and manufacturing infrastructure.

Over a decade ago, Biogen also licensed to SmithKline (now Glaxo SmithKline) exclusive rights to market hepatitis B vaccines in major markets excluding Japan. In 1990, both entered into a sublicense agreement with Merck, and the Glaxo and Merck deals continue to generate royalties.

While Biogen continues its high level of internal research investment (R&D accounted for 32 percent of 2002 revenues), it is also strengthening its key franchises with in-licensed products and complementing its own discovery with technology alliances.

Recent alliances include a 2001 deal with ICOS to codevelop and co-market small molecule LFA-1 antagonists to treat inflammatory conditions. In this deal, Biogen's strengths in the biology of inflammatory disease and in clinical development will translate to small molecules.

In 2000, an alliance was concluded with Elan to codevelop and comarket Antegren (natalizumab), an alpha 4 integrin inhibitor targeting Crohn's disease and multiple sclerosis. The deal leverages Biogen's strong presence in multiple sclerosis and its state-of-the-art manufacturing capability—particularly its high capacity mammalian cell culture technology that will assure uninterrupted supply worldwide.

A recent partnership with IDEC aims to codevelop three promising oncology therapeutics from Biogen's early-stage development candidates and to speed time to market through this joint work.

Biogen's shift from its early outlicensing to its current combination of internal research and in-licensing deals, plus selective partnering of its early-stage pipeline, may be applicable to many biotechs as they mature from research organizations to full-fledged biopharmaceutical companies.[32]

FORWARD INTEGRATORS: MILLENNIUM AND VERTEX

While Big Biotech and Big Pharma are growing ever closer, the newer wave of genomic firms is also evolving into protopharma entities. The leaders have transformed their deal structures, shifting from licensing agreements to full cost- and profit-sharing partnerships allowing them to develop their drugmaking skills. Recent deals stand out by their scope and value: Millennium/Abbott ($250 million) in metabolism, Millennium/Aventis ($450 million) in inflammation and toxicogenomics, and CuraGen/Bayer (potential $1.5 billion over 15 years) for toxicogenomics. Among these forward integrators, Millennium and Vertex are both leaders.[33]

VERTEX/NOVARTIS: THE KINASE ALLIANCE

Like Millennium, Vertex spent years building its technology platform and, in 2000, leveraged it into a six-year alliance with Novartis, with a total potential value of $800 million. Vertex sold its expertise in the kinase family, an area that Novartis had already validated with the successful launch of its leukemia drug Gleevec, targeting the bcr-abl kinase. The deal had limited risk for Vertex. Novartis was to pay $15 million upfront, $200 million in research support, $400 million in fees and milestones, and a $200 million interest-free loan for development; Vertex was incentivized to innovate because the loan would be forgiven on compounds accepted by Novartis. However, the deal also had fairly low rewards: royalties on the small molecules issuing from the alliance, rather than coownership.*

Vertex used its alliance revenue to expand its technology with the $570 million acquisition of Aurora, which brought expertise in screening, assays, and cell biology. Because a major risk for technology firms is the commoditization of their platforms, they must continually update their technology portfolios.

---

* Alexander Wood, "Vertex and Novartis: the Kinase Collaboration," Windhover Strategic Alliances Conference, October 1, 2001.

Millennium: Networking Innovator

Founded in 1993, Millennium first operated in contract research, and its early deals were licensing agreements to discover gene targets for pharma partners. This funding allowed it to develop in seven years a "one-stop shop" technology platform.

The next step was the acquisition of drugmaking skills through the large Bayer, Aventis, and Abbott partnerships. In the future, the company plans to gain full product control and build its portfolio via more acquisitions than partnerships.

The substantial $1.8 billion earned from partnership revenues, together with equity raised from investors, funded acquisitions to fill technology gaps: lead research capacity from ChemGenics, medicinal chemistry from Cambridge Discovery Chemistry, and product pipelines from Leukosite and Cor.

TABLE 3.4 Millennium Bionetwork

Year	Collaborator	Economics ($M)	Subject
1995	Aventis	NA	Inflammation targets.
1995	Pfizer	$24M (excl. milestones and royalties).	Drug discovery (fungal diseases).
1995–1996	Eli Lilly	$8M equity, $61M upfront, R&D funding, milestones ($20M).	Drug lead discovery, technology transfer (atherosclerosis, cancer).
1996	Roche Bioscience	$70M equity investment and fees.	Small molecules (inflammation).
1996	ILEX Oncology	Millennium share sold to ILEX, 2001, $140M.	CAMPATH Mab (leukemia).
1996	AHP (Wyeth-Ayerst)	$90M (excluding milestones, royalties).	Drug discovery, technology transfer (CNS, bacterial diseases).
1997	Genentech	Up to $50M (equity plus milestones).	Product development (LDP-02/IBS).
1997	ChemGenics	$90M acquisition.	Lead research capability.
1997	Monsanto	$218M (fees, milestones, royalties).	Technology transfer (agriculture).
1997	Kyowa Hakko	Fees, milestones, R&D funding.	Drug discovery (inflammation).
1997–1998	Warner-Lambert	Equity, R&D, milestones, ex-U.S. royalties.	Target discovery (inflammation, HIV).
1998	Bayer	$465M equity, fees from partner.	Target by class (CVS, cancer, pain, etc.).
1999	LeukoSite	$635M acquisition (all-stock).	Lead research, product pipeline.
1999	Bristol-Myers Squibb	$32M, fees from partner.	Pharmacogenomics (cancer).
1999	Schering, Berlex, ILEX	Up to $30M from Schering plus royalties.	CAMPATH MAb marketing.
1999	Incyte, Lexicon	Database access.	Genomics databases.
1999–2000	Becton Dickinson	$70M (equity, fees, R&D, milestones, royalties).	Molecular diagnostics (cancer).
2000	Aventis	$450M equity investment and fees.	Codevelopment, copromotion; technology transfer (inflammation).

(continued)

TABLE 3.4 *Continued*

Year	Collaborator	Economics ($M)	Subject
2000	Roche Diagnostics	NA	Diagnostics (arthritis).
2000	Taisho	R&D funding, license fees, milestones.	Development (LDP-977, asthma).
2000	Cambridge Discovery Chem.	$50M acquisition.	Chemistry capability.
2000	Caliper, BiaCore, Abgenix, Morphosys	Technology transfer.	Human MAbs (Abgenix, Morphosys). Microfluidics (Caliper), arrays (BiaCore).
2001	Abbott	$250M equity investment, fees.	Codevelop, copromote (metabolism).
2001	ImmunoGen	$2M upfront, milestones ($41M per target).	Prodrug technology (cancer).
2001	Cor Therapeutics	$2B acquisition.	Cardiology product, salesforce.

Source: Millennium, Françoise Simon/SDC Group, 2002.

The keys to Millennium's transformation from genomic firm to bio-pharmaceutical were not only a seven-year technology investment, but also a willingness to assume increasing risk.

Millennium's earliest alliances, such as the Lilly and Wyeth deals in the mid-1990s, were technology-focused deals with full research funding but very little product ownership. By contrast, in the 2000 Aventis partnership, Millennium took on a new level of risk and potential reward. The inflammation component was a full cost-and-profit-sharing agreement, aiming to deliver annually 10 or more compounds into preclinical development. The 2001 Abbott partnership roughly applied the same 50/50 formula to the metabolism area. (See Table 3.4.)

TECHNOLOGY TRANSFORMERS: CELERA AND INCYTE

Driven by higher valuations, technology firms also want to move from plat-forms to products. Celera, helped by the $944 million it raised in a 2000 follow-on offering and by the resources of its parent Applera, announced the most radical change—from a genomic database firm to a biopharmaceutical.

The company had a tripartite structure (Applied Biosystems, Celera Genomics, and their joint venture, Celera Diagnostics) and further split the genomics unit into an online and a pharmaceutical business.

Celera planned to develop therapeutics in three forms: small molecules, therapeutic antibodies, and T-cell cancer vaccines. The 2001 acquisition of chemistry-based Axys brought in small-molecule screening capabilities. The growth of online business had slowed. Most importantly, Celera was reaching a scale where the growth expected by investors could not be sustained by subscriptions alone; products had to appear.[34]

By contrast, Incyte, once the archetypal platform company, was also moving downstream, but doing so within its core information business. It added in 2000 and 2001 several IT partners such as Corning, Agilent, and Motorola for DNA array development. It also gained proteomics expertise from the 2000 acquisition of Proteome and made equity investments in Iconix (chemogenomics) and Elitra (functional genomics). Biology alliances included Oxagen (joint genetic research on osteoporosis) and several universities.

Alliance Models: From Licensing to 50/50 Partnerships

Alliance models have shifted in two ways: Joint ventures have been largely superseded by 50/50 partnerships, and licensing has often been expanded into codevelopment and/or copromotion. Joint ventures have drawbacks: High setup costs, management complexity, difficulty in transferring and retaining staff, and culture clashes. The 50/50 partnerships have hybrid features: a more flexible format, but also a human capital comparable to that of a joint venture. The Millennium/Abbott alliance included 225 dedicated scientists, and 900 people were involved in the Millennium/Aventis deal. Joint ventures are still being formed, but they tend to link biotechs and pharmacos, as is the case for the Lilly/Icos deal. Biotechs have avoided them because of cost and scale requirements. (See Table 3.5.)

Full profit-and-cost-sharing deals have spread among biotechs. The increased risk can be mitigated by negotiating research funding, capping R&D expenses, and receiving equity investments.

Desirable deal features for licensers depend on their lifecycle stage. Startups in need of cash would want to maximize upfront payments and research funding, while avoiding pure out-licensing, which forgoes all product rights.

TABLE 3.5 Alliance Models

	Subscriptions	Licensing	Codevelopment and Copromotion	50/50 Partnerships	Joint Ventures	Consortia
Biotech/ Biotech	Incyte/ Genentech	Genentech/ Actelion (Tracleer, Veletri)	IDEC/Roche/Genentech (Rituxan)	OSI/Genentech/Roche (Tarceva)	Genzyme/GelTex (led to acquisition of GelTex by Genzyme)	Rat Genome Consortium (Celera, Genome Therapeutics, Baylor College of Medicine)
	Celera/Amgen	HGS/Medimmune				
Biotech/ Pharma	Celera/Novartis, Pharmacia, Pfizer	Vistagen/Pfizer (toxicogenomic assays)	Vertex/Novartis (kinases)	Bayer/CuraGen (target validation)	Lilly/ICOS (erectile dysfunction)	Human Proteome Organization (Celera, Roche, Proteome, Harvard, Scripps, University of Michigan, University of Utrecht, etc.)
		Neurogen/Pfizer (AIDD technology)	Celltech/Pharmacia (arthritis, Crohn's)	Millennium/Abbott (metabolism)		

Source: Françoise Simon/SDC Group, 2002.

A larger biotech needing commercial expertise would choose a 50/50 structure. By contrast, a pharma licensee would reduce risk by shifting payments downstream (more in milestones, less upfront).[35]

For licensers, several measures of deal attractiveness have been premium on equity investment, timing of milestones (as early as possible), R&D funding, codevelopment—but regulatory responsibility for the licensee. Several biotechs, ranging from Chiron to Genentech and Genzyme, have recently faced FDA delays, and the experience of a Big Pharma partner can significantly reduce approval risk. (See Table 3.6.)

BUILDING NETWORK EQUITY

Alliance performance has been tracked across industries. There has been little improvement over time. In 1993, a McKinsey study reported a long-term success rate of no more than 50 percent (measured in strategic and financial terms). From 1997 to 2000, PricewaterhouseCoopers biopharma surveys found a 30 to 65 percent failure rate, depending on research phase and type of partnership.[36] Because building a reputation as partner of choice is a key component of corporate brand equity, companies must formalize their alliance strategy—first benchmarking performance indicators, then codifying partner selection, and developing alliance metrics.

BENCHMARKING PERFORMANCE

Understanding performance variations by geography, value chain stage, and deal type helps companies determine their alliance portfolios:

- *Geography matters* because cross–border alliances fail more often than domestic ones (the highest failure rate belonging to U.S./Asia partnerships, followed by U.S./Europe deals, in cross-industry studies by Michael Porter and others).
- *Value chain stage* is another determining factor. Among others, a 2000 PricewaterhouseCoopers survey found that only 36 percent of discovery alliances met or exceeded expectations, compared with 40 percent for development partnerships and 43 percent of comarketing or copromotion agreements. This is to be expected, given the greater risk and cooperation needed in earlier stages.

TABLE 3.6   Alliance Drivers

	Licenser	Licensee	Win-Win Features
Subscriptions	• Assured but limited revenues; slowing database growth.	• Genomics/ proteomics databases best outsourced.	• Subscription fees plus low royalties (1 to 5 percent) on products from database.
Platform tech agreements	• Fee-for-service: short-term horizon. • Better: shared ownership of resulting products.	• Most flexible: nonexclusive fee-for-service (allows multiple partners).	• Best for both: fee-for-service payment combined with royalties and shared IP.
Pure out-licensing	• Low risk, high upfront: generate cash but lose control of development, reduce total payout.	• Most attractive (gain all product rights).	• Later-stage products give licenser higher payments and more security for licensee.
Codevelopment	• Gain clinical experience but decrease immediate cash flow.	• Reduce risk (shift cost from upfront to milestones, royalties).	• Upfront equity reduces licensee's cash outlay, raises licenser's value. • Define IP split, roles, goals.
Copromotion	• Higher payments than comarketing, high royalties.	• Expensive in short term (high upfront). • Broadest reach with joint salesforce.	• Ensure close strategic fit and coordination of two salesforces.
Joint ventures	• R&D, financial, marketing expertise needed; possible culture clashes.	• Need high investment, large staff, top management commitment.	• Due diligence to determine culture compatibility. • Projected revenue must offset high setup costs.

Source: Françoise Simon/SDC Group, 2002; Partly adapted from Datamonitor, *Creating Win-Win Biotechnology & Pharmaceutical Deals* (October 2000), pp. 14–17, 61, 77, 108–109.

■ *Deal type* has an impact, but there is no clear consensus in this regard. Most cross-industry studies ascribe the highest failure rate to joint ventures, but the PricewaterhouseCoopers biopharma survey found about the same high failure rate of 59 percent for joint ventures and cooperative agreements. One explanation may be that, in the pharma sector, joint ventures have been confined to large firms with the expertise to manage them.

No conclusion can yet be reached on large-scale 50/50 partnerships. The earliest of these was the Bayer/Millennium alliance in 1998, and others were not signed until 2000 and 2001. Because they are long term (5 to 17 years), it will take several years to determine their outcomes.

There is widespread agreement on overall failure factors. The top problems are culture, leadership, and strategy, rather than technology. A 1994 Conference Board survey of 138 firms across industries found "cultures too different" and "ambiguous/poor leadership" among the top three factors. In the biosector, PricewaterhouseCoopers also listed first culture, management commitment, leadership, and communications issues; technology failure was a distant fifth factor.[37]

SELECTING THE RIGHT PARTNER

Partner choice is critical to both pharmacos and biotechs; for pharmacos, a reputation as a preferred partner is key to winning competitive deals; and for biotechs, partner selection is crucial to timely development, product approval, and successful marketing. A 2000 survey of pharmaco reputations found that partnership status varied by deal type. For discovery alliances, Pfizer, Lilly, and Merck came first; the top three for clinical development were Pfizer, Merck, and BMS; for comarketing/copromotion, Pfizer, Merck, and BMS were again preferred.[38]

Rather than pick the highest bidder, biotechs should see financials as one component of a set of key partner attributes, at both the product and corporate levels.

Corporate Criteria Include:

■ *Global reach:* How broad is the worldwide sales and marketing infrastructure?

- *Strategic intent:* Is the firm independently strong, or will it need to offset patent expiries and portfolio gaps with acquisitions? Is it a takeover target?
- *Company values:* Are values aligned for the two partners?
- *Alliance track record:* What is the firm's experience with the type of deal considered, and what is its success rate?
- *Development effectiveness:* What is the company's attrition rate and speed at each development stage?
- *Regulatory experience:* What is the firm's approval and reimbursement record? How effective are its health economics studies and payer relationships?

Product-Related Criteria Include:

- *Category expertise:* What is the firm's knowledge and reputation in the relevant therapeutic area? What is the quality of its relationships with opinion leaders?
- *Marketing power:* What are the medical and consumer marketing resources? What is the track record in building blockbusters or targeted therapies? What is the quality of lifecycle management?
- *Sales power:* What is the sales force size and quality (as per independent ratings)? If a specialist salesforce is needed, how effective is it?[39]

For biotechs, it is important to assess all potential partners instead of the usual suspects. Most biologics are targeted therapies that require small specialist salesforces rather than Big Pharma's armies; for these products, *category depth* is more important than size, as it determines medical reputation, marketing power, and technical expertise.

Developing Alliance Metrics

Cross-industry studies around the world found that fewer than one in four firms had adequate alliance metrics. A key difficulty is the peripheral nature of alliances. Cost measurements are incomplete because of concealed expenses such as the value of management time; a large alliance could have up to 30 working teams and 300 members. Tracking benefits is also a challenge because of intangibles such as knowledge transfer, improved competitive positioning, and access to new markets.[40]

As a result, many alliance portfolios are a random assortment of tactical deals amassed over time. To move to an integrated portfolio aligned on corporate strategy, companies need to assess alliances in three ways:

1. At the *deal level,* each alliance should be regularly assessed to determine performance and possible remedial interventions.
2. At the *portfolio level,* companies should track patterns across franchises to uncover problematic deal structures, partner types, or operational tasks.
3. At the *corporate level,* companies should assess whether alliances support corporate strategy.

After signing, scorecards should be developed by each partner on four dimensions:

Dimension	*Metric*
Financial Health	
• Optimize revenue.	• Product sales growth (copromotion).
• Accelerate development.	• Technology milestones.
• Create growth options.	• New indications/new customers.
Strategic Health	
• Fit with partner portfolio.	• Priority rating by each partner.
• Increase market share.	• Market share growth.
• Enhance competitive position.	• Improved customer access.
• Transfer knowledge.	• Partner survey of best practices.
Operational Health	
• Fulfill operational goals.	• Milestone measurement.
• Effective decision making.	• Decision-making rating.
• Optimize alliance management.	• Time spent by team members, speed of conflict resolution.

(continued)

Dimension	Metric
Cultural Health	
• Build and maintain trust.	• Partner satisfaction survey.
• Communicate effectively.	• Communications rating by partner.
• Share time horizons.	• Speed of decisions.
• Define roles clearly.	• Governance structure rating.

The weight placed on each of these metrics depends on the type of deal and the value chain stage; discovery deals give top importance to milestones and technology transfer, whereas copromotion deals prioritize market share and competitive position.

Beyond rating all deals, companies should also analyze their portfolio-wide performance to answer questions such as these:

- Which deal types perform best and worst? Is it due to strategic fit or execution?
- Do problems occur at specific stages of the deal-making process?
- Are certain partner types better suited to the company culture and structure?

Finally, companies should periodically conduct a top-down review to prioritize alliances according to their relative contribution to corporate strategy.[41]

STRUCTURING ALLIANCE MANAGEMENT

The alliance formation process goes well beyond due diligence and deal structure:

- *Step 1* (before a partner search) prioritizes objectives and analyzes opportunities (range/quality of candidates) but also threats (potential counterbids).
- *Step 2* focuses on sourcing and screening partners, going beyond finance and technology to rate cultural fit and track record.

FIGURE 3.4   Key Alliance Steps

Define Objectives	Source and Screen Partners	Negotiate Contract	Implement and Monitor
• Assess needs Discovery, development, sales, and marketing • Analyze opportunity Quality of partners, technologies, and pipelines • Assess competitive intensity; projected competitor countermoves	• Identify and assess candidates • Conduct due diligence R&D/financial, risk assessment Culture fit and risk level Alliance experience Track record with products (licenser) and regulators (licensee)	• Jointly define mission/goals • Determine structure (licensing, equity, joint venture) • Set timetable, milestones, fee structure • Include conflict resolution, arbitration, and termination clauses • Define governance, allocate staff	• Finalize shared mission, priorities • Finalize teams, leaders, performance measures, and compensation • Integrate IT • Plan communications • Monitor partner satisfaction and alliance performance • Develop best practices database

Source: Françoise Simon/SDC Group, 2002.

■ *Step 3* is the actual contract negotiation and should include more than legal and financial terms. Partners need to jointly define goals and resource allocations (people as well as technology and money)—including "safety nets" such as reinsertion into each firm at the end of the project. Deal terms must also include conflict resolution, arbitration, and termination clauses.

■ *Step 4* monitors partner satisfaction and knowledge management (IT integration and best practices database). (See Figure 3.4.)

A consensus on success factors has emerged among experienced companies. P&G reviewed successes and failures and identified nine factors:

1. *Senior management commitment* (leadership by two senior executives).
2. *Accurate resource planning* (to ensure optimal allocation of funds and people).
3. *Aligned objectives* (single tracking plan for both partners).
4. *Clear responsibilities* (as set up by counterparts in each company).
5. *Multichannel communications* (meetings, joint reports, team Web spaces, and remote conferencing).
6. *Effective joint decision making* (agreement on timetable and risk acceptance).
7. *Disciplined improvement* (regular performance assessments).
8. *Integration of IT systems* (from e-mail to forecasting and quality assurance).
9. *Conflict resolution process* (led by the alliance general manager).[42]

More generally, alliance competencies were tracked in a survey of more than 100 biopharma executives. Ten percent emerged as top performers, and 30 percent were rated as underperformers. The greatest gaps between best and worst performers were in culture (compatibility, trust), communication, strategic alignment, and functional capability (allocation of high-caliber managers to alliance teams). This showed that operations and processes were no guarantee of success; culture and strategic fit played key roles.[43]

THE LONG VIEW

Research and consolidation trends yield several scenarios on industry structure and on the shape of future innovation. Technology firms are forecasting a "virtual R&D" scenario with decentralized innovation. Millennium and other protopharmas have based their strategies on a distributed R&D model; Glaxo has already disaggregated its research. By contrast, companies such as Merck contend that deep in-house research is vital to maintaining scientific assets and attracting biotech partners. A compromise might be category spinouts, whereby a large firm entrusts a therapeutic area to a biotech while retaining an equity interest; a precursor of this may be the large Millennium partnerships.

Industry structure also leads to speculation. A polarization scenario envisions a handful of megapharma marketing machines fed by a web of biotech satellites. Recent trends make this unlikely and support instead a

BUILDING ALLIANCE EQUITY: LILLY'S SYSTEM

Eli Lilly has developed a sophisticated alliance management system and it also has the longest track record. It started its core insulin business in the 1920s with a University of Toronto alliance, pioneered in the mid-1980s the first biotech drug (recombinant human insulin, licensed from Genentech), progressed to an oral antidiabetic (Actos/pioglitazone, from Takeda), and linked with Alkermes to develop an inhaled formulation.

After benchmarking alliances and surveying its own partners, Lilly set up an Office of Alliance Management (OAM) to serve as an advocate for alliances themselves rather than for one of the partners:

- To ensure *senior management commitment,* Lilly appoints a senior executive as the champion, supported by an alliance leader (usually from R&D) and an alliance manager (from a variety of functions).
- *To bridge cultures,* the alliance manager conducts a cultural assessment during due diligence. Initial meetings focus on shared goal definition rather than technical tasks and timetables.
- *Performance monitoring* is done through a Web-based Alliance Heath Survey tracking 14 dimensions ranging from strategy to culture and work processes.
- *Best practices* are codified with an online database and spread through training.*

Lilly now manages more than 140 collaborations—from a discovery alliance with Ligand to develop metabolic and cardiovascular products to a joint venture with ICOS for the erectile dysfunction treatment Cialis and a manufacturing alliance with Lonza Biologics to produce the sepsis drug Xigris.

Lilly also launched two venture capital funds: the $50 million e-Lilly fund for e-business startups and the $75 million Lilly Bio-Ventures for discovery technologies.

---

* Nelson Sims, Roger Harrison, and Anton Gueth, "Managing Alliances," *In Vivo* (June 2001), pp. 72–76.

three-tier structure: At the top, Big Biopharma ranging from Pfizer to Amgen, next, mid-cap firms, with strengths in category depth and marketing skills for midsize brands whose scale falls below the megafirms' thresholds, and finally, a third tier of boutiques serving as innovation engines for large IT and pharma players while developing their own discovery skills.

SUMMARY POINTS

✓ Declining productivity, the long payoff for postgenomic research, and the need to grow earnings are propelling Big Pharma and Big Biotech on a product quest; this has created a sellers' market for product-rich biotechs and has escalated late-stage product prices.

✓ M&As and alliances have turned into a high-stakes game. Merger scale has skyrocketed, and alliance partners are assuming more development risk.

✓ Power and independence are rising for biotechs, which are increasingly relying on one another's pipelines and merging within their sector.

✓ For pharmacos, vertical integration has had mixed results; in horizontal integration, key success factors are timing (first-mover advantage), leadership clarity (acquisition rather than "merger of equals"), portfolio fit, and rapid integration.

✓ Networking strategies vary according to company size and lifecycle stage.
—Large companies have built extensive bionetworks, giving IT players entry points though the value chain and offsetting pharmacos' declining productivity.
—Big Biotech is following suit, and the new generation of protopharmas is transforming into biopharmaceuticals via large-scale partnerships.
—Smaller biotechs are also moving from platforms to products through consolidation and pharma alliances.

✓ Building network equity is a key component of competitiveness; it is achieved through a systematic process, which includes benchmarking performance, selecting the right partner, developing alliance metrics, and structuring a stepwise alliance management process.

Part Two

LEVERAGING
THE POWER
OF BIOBRANDS

FORMULATING
BIOMARKETING

With the proliferation of new brands and endless brand extensions, more and more categories seem to be sliding toward commodity status. . . . What we don't get is a distinct message that helps consumers tell one brand from another.

Kevin Clancy and Jack Trout[1]

As biotechnology drives innovation in multiple sectors, biobrands cover an exceptionally broad range of product types, from industrial (environmental cleaners) to consumer-driven (functional foods). Among those, the highest value is in human health, and it is also the most rapidly evolving biosector.[2]

Over the past decade, escalating research cost and risk, as well as other factors such as consumerism, have driven a clear trend toward megabrands. In 2001, the Tufts Center for the Study of Drug Development placed the average development cost for a prescription drug at $802 million. When compared to its estimate of $231 million a decade earlier, it represented a 250 percent increase in inflation-adjusted terms. A Boston Consulting Group assessment was even higher at $880 million. The Tufts estimate included the expense of failed compounds, the opportunity cost of 10 to 15 years of development, and accounted for discovery, preclinical and clinical costs, attrition rates, and cost of capital.[3]

Postgenomic research and information technology will reduce development cost and time in the next decades, but they will also mandate an entirely different marketing approach. The industry is now at an *inflection point,* when the dominant mass-market strategy is starting to be challenged by the new paradigm of personalized medicine.

Addressing this fundamental change requires a rethinking of the concepts of health and disease, but also of drugs (shift from pills to integrated solutions, including diagnostics) and marketing models. As clinical practice is increasingly led by evidence-based medicine, biobrands will rely more and more on *evidence-based marketing*—that is, a clear differential advantage established, well before launch, by research data and hard clinical endpoints. As regulators and payers tightly link premium prices and superior clinical performance, and as Web-enabled consumers directly access clinical data, the tendency to overbrand "me-too" drugs will become unsustainable and a shift will occur from *experience-based marketing* to *evidence-based marketing.* Because biobrands have a wide scope, some categories such as functional foods will continue to follow consumer goods approaches. However, the higher value will belong to breakthrough biologics, marketed on the global niche model.

Beyond branding models, the current inflection point will impact definitions of disease and therapy, target segments, competitive spaces, and the business models of biopharma companies. This can be summarized as follows:

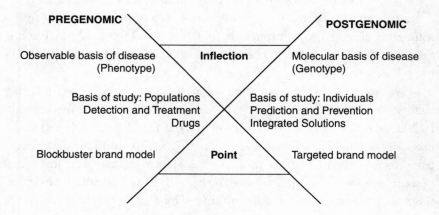

PREGENOMIC   POSTGENOMIC

Observable basis of disease   Inflection   Molecular basis of disease
(Phenotype)   (Genotype)

Basis of study: Populations   Basis of study: Individuals
Detection and Treatment   Prediction and Prevention
Drugs   Integrated Solutions

Blockbuster brand model   Point   Targeted brand model

It is only after companies reexamine their clinical and commercial paradigms that they can start to formulate a biomarketing strategy. This includes a triple transformation process: *shaping the market, the product, and the company* to effectively manage traditional products as well as the new therapies. New physician and consumer segments are emerging, such as genotypes and technographics (Web usage). Companies also have opportunities to leverage the new therapies to create new market space. As Pfizer launched Viagra (sildenafil), it created the erectile dysfunction (ED) market by renaming and destigmatizing the old concept of *impotence*.

This progression from an understanding of the new paradigms to the formulation of a biomarketing strategy is shown in Figure 4.1.

FIGURE 4.1   Formulating Biomarketing

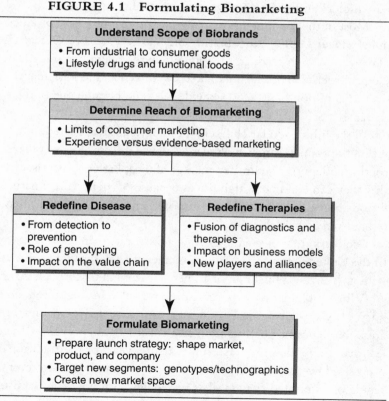

Source: Françoise Simon/SDC Group, 2002.

In addition to the costs of new technologies and the disruption of new paradigms, companies face added pressures from shorter time windows between competing products.

Hypertension pioneer Inderal (propanolol), launched in 1968, had a full decade on the market before a follower drug, Lopressor (metaprolol), appeared. By contrast, in the Cox-2 inhibitor category addressing arthritis, two drugs were launched within a few months of each other in 1999: Pharmacia's Celebrex (celecoxib), and Merck's Vioxx (rofecoxib). To offset this, the industry's motto in the past decade became: "The bigger and faster, the better." By 2002, over 50 drugs qualified as "blockbusters," with $1 billion or more in worldwide sales.

The blockbuster champion was clearly Pfizer. Its top 9 products ranged from over $1 billion to nearly $8 billion and covered almost every major therapeutic area, from hypertension to epilepsy. Pharmacia would add potential blockbusters in oncology and ophthalmology.

Most of the top brands are mass-market, primary care products such as lipid reducer Lipitor (atorvastatin) and antihypertensive Cozaar (losartan). However, biotech products are moving up the brand hierarchy. The top biologic, Procrit/Epogen, comarketed by Amgen and J&J for anemia, reached over $6.5 billion in 2002 worldwide sales and became one of the top three therapies. (See Tables 4.1 and 4.2.)

In the billion-dollar club, eight biologics have appeared, in addition to specialty products targeting low-prevalence diseases, such as Pfizer's Neurontin (epilepsy). The limited market of most biologics is offset by the fact that they can command high prices because of their critical nature. In addition, biotechs are starting to expand into primary-care areas such as asthma and arthritis.

Biologics are projected to grow at a faster rate than chemical compounds. In the United States alone, human therapeutics will be a key growth sector with an average annual rate of 12 percent from 2002 through 2012.[4]

While biologics have an increasing presence in the billion-dollar category, they do not necessarily have a time advantage. In life-threatening areas, biologics normally obtain fast-track FDA approval—which can be less than three months, versus more than a year for the traditional review process. However, several biotech approvals were delayed in recent years as regulators subjected first-in-class molecules with novel mechanisms of action to closer scrutiny.

TABLE 4.1 Top Pharmaceuticals (Worldwide Sales)

Brand	Company	Indication	Worldwide Sales, 2002 ($M)	Growth USD, 2001–2002 (%)
Lipitor (atorvastatin)	Pfizer	Hyperlipidemia	7,972	24
Zocor (simvastatin)	Merck	Hyperlipidemia	5,580	6
Prilosec (omeprazole)	AstraZeneca	Ulcers/GERD	4,623	(17)
Norvasc (amlodipine)	Pfizer	Hypertension	3,846	7
Zyprexa (olanzapine)	Lilly	Psychosis	3,689	20
Prevacid (lansoprazole)	Takeda/Abbott	Ulcers/GERD	3,157	7
Paxil (paroxetine)	GSK	Depression	3,083	15
Celebrex (celecoxib)	Pfizer/Pharmacia	Arthritis	3,050	(2)
Zoloft (sertraline)	Pfizer	Depression	2,742	16
Vioxx (rofecoxib)	Merck	Arthritis	2,530	8
Advair (fluticasone, salmeterol)	GSK	Asthma	2,447	101
Neurontin (gabapentin)	Pfizer	Epilepsy	2,269	30
Fosamax (alendronate)	Merck	Osteoporosis	2,250	38
Cozaar/Hyzaar (losartan)	Merck	Hypertension	2,190	21
Pravachol (pravastatin)*	BMS	Hyperlipidemia	2,173	NA
Risperdal (risperidone)	J&J	Psychosis	2,146	16
Effexor (venlafaxine)	Wyeth	Depression	2,072	34
Nexium (esomeprazole)	AstraZeneca	Ulcers/GERD	1,978	NA
Allegra (fexofenadine)	Aventis	Allergy	1,922	22
Premarin franchise (conj. estrogens)	Wyeth	Menopause	1,880	(10)

*Pravachol: 2001 Worldwide sales (BMS to restate financial data).

Source: Company reports (unaudited product sales), January/February 2003.

TABLE 4.2 Major Biologics (Worldwide Sales)

Brand	Company	Indication	Worldwide Sales, 2002 ($M)	Growth USD, 2001–2002 (%)
Procrit (Epoetin alfa)	J&J/Amgen	Anemia	4,269	24
Intron franchise (Interferon-alfa–2b)	Schering-Plough	Leukemia, hepatitis	2,736	89
Epogen (Epoetin alfa)	Amgen	Anemia	2,300	7
Neupogen (Filgrastim)	Amgen	Neutropenia, infection	1,400	2
Remicade (Infliximab)	Centocor	Rheumatoid arthritis	1,297	80
Rituxan (Rituximab)	Genentech	Lymphoma	1,200	42
Avonex (Interferon beta–1a)	Biogen	Multiple sclerosis	1,034	3
Humulin (Rec. Insulin)	Lilly	Diabetes	1,004	(5)
Humalog (Insulin lispro)	Lilly	Diabetes	834	33
Enbrel (Etanercept)	Amgen	Arthritis	802	5
Betaseron (Interferon beta)	Schering AG	Multiple sclerosis	741	15
Synagis (Palivizumab)	Medimmune	RSV	668	29
Cerezyme (Imiglucerase)	Genzyme	Type 1 Gaucher	619	9
Genotropin (Rec. isomatropin)	Pharmacia	Growth Failure	551	8
Rebif (Interferon beta)	Serono	Multiple sclerosis	549	45
Neulasta (Pegfilgrastim)	Amgen	Neutropenia	464	NA
Aranesp (darbepoetin alfa)	Amgen	Anemia	416	NA
Gonal-F (follitropin alfa)	Serono	Infertility	450	10
Herceptin (trastuzumab)	Genentech	Breast cancer	385	11
ReoPro (abciximab)	Lilly	Heart disease	384	(11)

Source: Company reports (unaudited product sales), January/February 2003.

Global speed to market is crucially important, given finite patent lives, and leading brands have demonstrated that a $1 billion sales level can be reached within one year. Viagra (sildenafil) reached more than 40 countries in its first year on the market. To increase the speed of their global rollouts and maximize their approval chances, biotechs have so far relied on pharma partnerships, but their top tier has started to expand its own global capabilities. Boundaries have blurred between the sectors, as Big Pharma generated (with some outsourcing help) a significant proportion of the top biologics. Their key attraction, besides their high prices, is their growth rates. Johnson & Johnson's Remicade (infliximab) had a worldwide growth of 80 percent in 2001 to 2002, and Eli Lilly's recombinant insulin Humalog grew by 33 percent in the second period. (See Table 4.2.)

While the highest-margin biobrands are human therapeutics, the category is broad and companies must understand its full scope before developing a biomarketing strategy. Products that, in a company's view, are unrelated, such as an osteoporosis drug and soy milk, are in fact part of the same decision set for a woman facing menopause.

LEVERAGING THE SCOPE OF BIOBRANDS

While biobrands range from ethanol to antiwrinkle creams, almost all categories have multiple target segments that require a hybrid marketing approach. Biofuels such as ethanol are industrial products, but their widespread diffusion depends on consumer acceptance. The neglect of public opinion caused great harm to the agbio sector when opposition to genetically modified organisms (GMOs) led to the demise of the "life sciences" concept and to the divestment of agbio units by AstraZeneca, Novartis, and others. Initial campaigns by companies such as Monsanto focused on farmers, rather than on the end users of GMOs. These products were perceived by consumers as "all risk, no benefit" and rejected accordingly. The second wave of GMOs includes products with high end value, such as a vitamin-A-enriched "golden rice," which would alleviate malnutrition in emerging markets—but they are facing a difficult turnaround situation.

Similarly, hospital and surgical products target professional purchasers but require some degree of consumer education. Diagnostics are complex, ranging from molecular tests for research laboratories to home kits such as glucose monitoring tests—the former typically have no patient input, while the latter are consumer-driven. (See Figure 4.2.)

While some categories (transplantation) are far removed from patient influence, and others (pain relievers) are consumer goods, their market success depends on two main factors: clinical evidence and hybrid marketing.

FIGURE 4.2 Scope of Biobrands

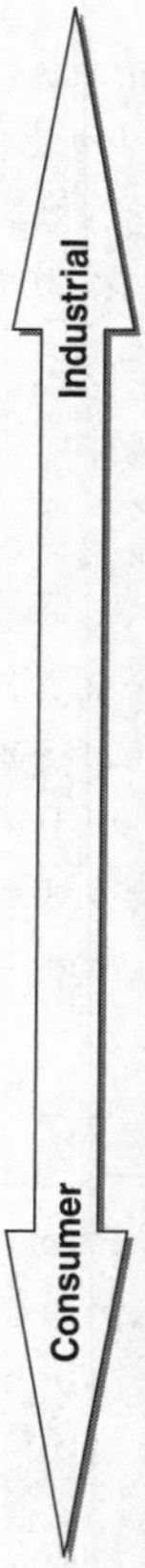

	Product Type	Category	Companies/ Brands	Targets
Industrial	Industrial Products	Biofuels / Agbio products, biodefense	ADM, ethanol / Vitamin A-enriched rice	Industrial customer (also consumers in energy, agbio)
	Hospital Products	Bioengineered tissue and organs / Drug-eluting stents	Organogenesis Apligraf skin	Surgeons/hospital purchasers
	Devices	Brain stimulators for Parkinson's disease	Medtronic, Activa	Physicians + consumer education
	Diagnostics	Molecular tests / Blood glucose monitors	Vysis, PathVysion / Roche, Accucheck	Pathologists / Consumers
	Specialty Drugs	Transplantation / Oncology	Wyeth, Rapamune / Genentech, Rituxan	Physicians, nurses, patients
	Primary Care Drugs	Hyperlipidemia / Arthritis	Pfizer, Lipitor / Merck, Vioxx	Professionals + Consumers
	Life-Enhancing Medicines	Erectile dysfunction / Obesity	Pfizer, Viagra / Roche, Xenical	Professionals + Consumers
Consumer	OTC Drugs	Analgesics	J&J, Tylenol / Bayer, aspirin	Consumers + Professionals
	Botanicals, Supplements	Depression / Vitamins	St. John's Wort / Wyeth, Centrum	Consumers + Professionals
	Medical Foods / Cosmeceuticals	Stanol-ester margarines / Retinoids	J&J, Benecol / Ortho, Renova	Consumers + Professionals

Source: Françoise Simon/SDC Group, 2002.

HYBRID MARKETING

In critical areas such as oncology, therapies are primarily judged on performance (efficacy, safety, and tolerability) and driven by professionals (physicians, but also oncology nurses). However, the opinion leaders who drive early adoption now include not only physicians, but also patient advocates. Many HIV and oncology drugs obtained fast-track approval largely because of patient activism. In this case, evidence-based marketing should target patients as well as physicians. Primary care drugs targeting mass markets are in transition. While there is a trend toward evidence-based marketing, some products can still be successfully marketed on a quasi-consumer goods model. Of the top 10 pharmaceuticals in 2002, several were either first-in-class (Prilosec, Procrit, Celebrex) or clinically superior (Lipitor). However, follower products such as Prevacid and Vioxx were also able to reach the multibillion-dollar sales level.

GROWING IMPACT OF RESEARCH

As pharmaceutical portfolios shift from palliative to targeted and curative medicines, the link between performance and market success will tighten. However, in consumer-driven categories, performance and image will continue to coexist. While major OTC brands prevail over generics on the strength of brand or corporate equity (Tylenol/J&J), others have vastly extended their lifecycles thanks to sustained research investment. Bayer Aspirin is more than 100 years old and still a category leader, in great part because clinicals demonstrated its cardiovascular prevention value and others now focus on its prevention potential in oncology and other areas. Accordingly, it continues to be promoted to physicians as well as to consumers.

As biotechs expand from niche to mass markets, they can learn from pharmacos' experience with their most consumer-driven products—life-enhancing medicines that affect physical or emotional quality of life.

LIFE-ENHANCING MEDICINES

This category is a small part of the U.S. prescription drug market, but it is expected to grow rapidly and account for a 10 percent share by 2010, as pipelines are brimming with nearly 400 compounds. Currently, Americans spend $33 billion annually on antiobesity/diet products and services alone, and the category has a potential U.S. consumer base of 58 million;[5] Europe shows similar trends. Other categories range from smoking cessation to anti-aging creams. While they reflect different levels of medical need, they face several challenges including limited reimbursement and high marketing costs, which may lead to lower margins than those of life-saving medicines.

VIAGRA: A CONSUMER-DRIVEN SUCCESS

With Viagra (sildenafil), approved by the FDA in March 1998, Pfizer grew a partly unreimbursed product to more than $1.7 billion in global sales in less than five years.[a]

REIMBURSEMENT CHALLENGES

Viagra was one-third of the cost of reimbursed invasive therapies, but the coverage was uneven. By 2000, only about half of U.S. plans had partial reimbursement.[b] After EU approval in September 1998, only Sweden and Ireland fully covered Viagra. In the United Kingdom, coverage was later allowed for certain conditions. In January 1999, Japan's approval in six months was the fastest ever but Viagra was not reimbursed.

SHAPING THE MARKET

Pfizer had a dual task: converting physicians and consumers. Around 150 million men suffered from erectile dysfunction (ED) globally, but less than 20 percent were treated. Physicians tended to think of ED as largely psychogenic and were not sufficiently aware of its medical basis and comorbidities. Most primary-care clinicians were uncomfortable with the condition, and some urologists feared an erosion of their practices. Pfizer researched epidemiology and publicized the 1993 NIH recommendation to shift terminology from *impotence* to *ED;* it also initially promoted Viagra only to physicians (direct-to-consumer promotion was not done until six months after launch). Pfizer then started consumer education, including sports sponsorships with on-site testing.

MARKET IMPACT

Viagra quadrupled the ED dollar market and boosted awareness—in the United States alone, the number of men seeking medical advice grew 75 percent in Viagra's first year.[c] However, diffusion varied, from success in Brazil to slow uptake in France.

NEW CHALLENGES

Upcoming competitors such as Lilly's Cialis (tadalafil) were striving to be consumer-centric with endpoints such as fast onset of action and long half-life—but they would have an uphill battle against Viagra's 5-year head-start and strong brand equity.

---

[a] This section draws on a personal communication to Françoise Simon by Neil Levine, Director and Worldwide Team Leader, Pfizer Pharmaceuticals Group, and on a presentation by Neil Levine at Columbia Business School, July 2002.
[b] Alison Keith, "The Economics of Viagra," *Health Affairs* (March/April 2000), pp. 147–154.
[c] IMS Health data, cited in Alison Keith, p. 154.

The Viagra case stresses the need for coordinated physician/patient education, but also the importance of efficacy and safety, because serious adverse drug reactions (ADRs) are not acceptable to prescribers and end users of life-enhancing medicines. This was shown after the withdrawal of Wyeth's Redux and Pondimin in September 1997—the U.S. antiobesity market lost more than 80 percent of its sales from April to year end.[6] Later products stagnated. Sales of Roche's Xenical (orlistat) were flat in 1999 to 2000, despite an annual DTC spend of $50 to $75 million, and sales decreased to $518 million in 2001. To better reach the medical community, Roche shifted Xenical's positioning from a lifestyle drug to a medicine for serious conditions. To this end, the Look AHEAD trial (Action for Health in Diabetes) included Xenical in June 2001 to determine the impact of weight loss in type 2 diabetes treatment.[7]

For consumer-driven products, the approval of physicians is critical because they can suppress demand—as they did for antiobesity drugs because of negative efficacy/tolerability trade-offs. Two segments are specific to this category:

1. *Proselytizers* are subsegments of relevant specialties such as dermatology. Despite its optional, unreimbursed status, Allergan's botulinum toxin Botox, approved for antiwrinkle injections, has booming sales because of a push-pull strategy: promotion and word of mouth among consumers, but also impact on practice economics (injections being vastly more lucrative than consultations).
2. *Skeptics,* by contrast, need hard medical evidence at the product and class levels. Companies need to communicate the need to treat; Viagra was helped by the fact that, unlike Botox, it addressed a serious medical condition, and the consultations men sought often uncovered serious disorders that would otherwise have gone undetected.

These examples demonstrate that the success of consumer-driven products depends on hard clinical data and on effective communications to physicians. Several factors are key:

- Proven safety for life-enhancing medicines.
- A good efficacy/cost ratio, in the face of lower-priced alternative treatments.
- Pharmacoeconomic studies to support some reimbursement.
- Early consumer and physician input allowing market-driven endpoints in clinicals.
- Physician segmentation leveraging proselytizers and converting skeptics.
- Identification of critical consumer touchpoints, from initial awareness to doctor's visit and prescription refill.
- Sustained medical and consumer education, especially when sales decrease.
- Close monitoring of consumer satisfaction, as well as loyalty incentives such as affinity programs for patients and sampling for physicians.

These principles also apply to the most consumer-driven biobrands, functional foods.

FUNCTIONAL FOODS

Functional foods, also called *medical foods* or *nutraceuticals,* are foods enriched with active ingredients that allow manufacturers to make "structural" or "functional," but not medical, claims. Since 1993, the FDA has approved claims such as "Low-fat diets rich in fiber may reduce the risk of some types of cancer." In the United States alone, foods with added

---

THE MARGARINE WARS: JOHNSON & JOHNSON VERSUS UNILEVER

A high-profile new class pitted a pharmaco against a consumer goods company, but neither achieved great success. In 1999, Johnson & Johnson's McNeil unit launched its cholesterol-reducing Benecol margarine, inlicensed from Raisio and sold in Finland since 1995. A debate with the FDA took place over the product's classification ("dietary supplement" versus "food"), but McNeil was able to market Benecol with a "proven to reduce cholesterol" claim; the packaging mentioned 20 studies in support of the claim. McNeil also had loyalty programs with its "Club Benecol," toll-free number, and Web site.

However, there were negatives: a direct competitor and a low efficacy/ price ratio. Shortly after Benecol's launch, Unilever's Lipton unit introduced Take Control, based on plant sterol esters, supported by a similar claim and less expensive. Both products had a steep price premium. Their efficacy was vastly weaker than that of prescribed statins such as Zocor and Lipitor. A 1995 Finnish study had shown that regular use of Benecol reduced cholesterol levels by 10 to 14 percent; Take Control, according to Lipton studies, produced a 10 to 17 percent decrease.* The statins were much more effective on LDL cholesterol and were also reimbursed. In addition, the companies had undermarketed this class to physicians, who largely failed to recommend it to their patients. Not surprisingly, neither product fully met expectations.

---

* "From Finland, One for the Heart," *BusinessWeek* (May 5, 1997), p. 8; Joseph Brown, "Benecol," *Med Ad News* (July 1999), pp. 3, 74–75.

vitamins and minerals are a $17 billion market, growing at 7 percent per year.[8] Competition is broad, ranging from pharmaceutical firms to food and beverage companies. Some categories are crowded and genericizing. In breakfast cereals, where most brands are fortified with a similar mix of vitamins and minerals, the additives have lost most of their differentiating power.[9]

While the market is growing on the strength of staples such as calcium-enriched orange juice, several initiatives have either failed or underperformed. Kellogg had to discontinue its Ensemble line because of weak demand.

DETERMINING THE REACH OF BIOMARKETING

LIMITS OF CONSUMER MARKETING

Across all industries, brands have reached unprecedented power, but that very power is what makes them increasingly vulnerable. In recent years, protesters have used brand power very effectively against multinationals, and companies that ignored them paid high prices. Monsanto's remoteness from consumer concerns led to boycotts and divestments. Coca-Cola's poor handling of a contamination episode in Belgium led to losses across Europe and contributed to the dismissal of its CEO. Nike's neglect of manufacturing standards turned its Southeast Asian supply network from a competitive advantage into its biggest liability, eroded the brand, and prompted heavy remedial expenditures.

Global consumer convergence is becoming a two-edged sword—a ready customer base for megabrands, but also a volatile community of Web-enabled critics. The latter is evidenced by a number of contrarian books, from Naomi Klein's *No Logo: Taking Aim at the Brand Bullies* to Jonathan Bond and Richard Kirschenbaum's *Under the Radar—Talking to Today's Cynical Consumer.*[10] Recent studies have shown a commoditization of major brands. A Market Facts/Copernicus survey polled U.S. consumers on their perception of brand differentiation for pairs of leaders across 46 categories. Only six of these increased or retained brand distinction. In the other 40, brands such as Visa/MasterCard, L'Oréal/Clairol, Nike/Adidas, and IBM/Compaq showed an increased perceived similarity. In the pharma OTC sector, even category leaders such as Tylenol and Advil were seen as beginning to converge.[11]

FROM EXPERIENCE TO EVIDENCE-BASED MARKETING

While the spread of the Internet and the U.S. legalization of DTC advertising led to the adoption of consumer marketing, the biosector needs to transcend it if targeted drugs become the gold standard. Even in the mass-market category, several factors are already driving a shift from *experience-based marketing* to *evidence-based marketing:*

- Regulators have less tolerance for "me-too" products.
- Payers are demanding pharmacoeconomic studies.
- Physicians are sensitized to drug recalls and want hard data on efficacy and safety.
- Web-enabled consumers have direct access to scientific information.

With 12 products in the $1 billion-plus class, Pfizer is the megabrand leader—and it has a clear strategy of science-driven marketing, stressing medical benefits and basing its product positioning on clinical research as well as marketing insights.[12] Among the most successful recent launches, Viagra and Celebrex were first in class, and Lipitor had clear evidence of superior performance.

Given the wide scope of biobrands, experience-based marketing will continue to coexist with evidence-based marketing. Their relative dominance depends on therapeutic areas. In critical areas such as oncology, evidence will prevail. In noncritical categories such as allergy, experience will continue to be effective—but only if it is complemented by hard clinical evidence. Novartis successfully repositioned its oral antifungal Lamisil (terbinafine) after an experiential patient-flow analysis. It showed a disconnect between physicians, who dismissed onychomycosis (toenail infections) as cosmetic, and patients, who took it seriously but were hesitant to discuss it with doctors. Novartis redirected its campaign toward enhanced education; consumer ads stressed the need for medical treatment, and medical promotion emphasized patient concerns—which led

FIGURE 4.3 Evidence versus Experience-Based Marketing

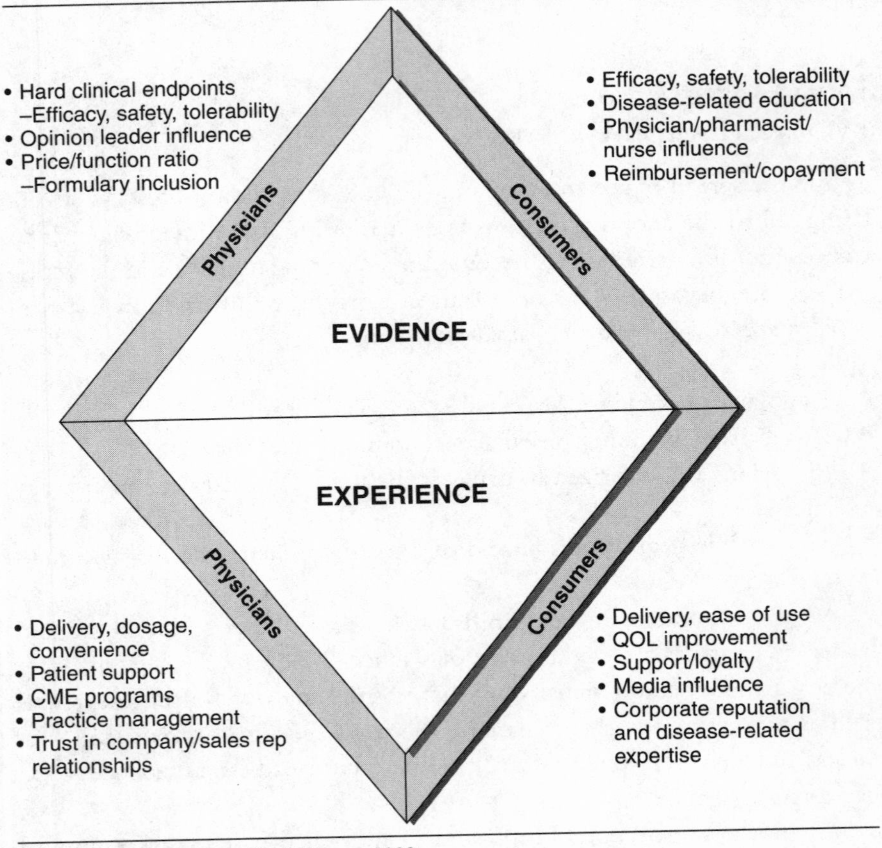
• Hard clinical endpoints
–Efficacy, safety, tolerability
• Opinion leader influence
• Price/function ratio
–Formulary inclusion
• Efficacy, safety, tolerability
• Disease-related education
• Physician/pharmacist/
nurse influence
• Reimbursement/copayment
Physicians
Consumers
EVIDENCE
EXPERIENCE
Physicians
Consumers
• Delivery, dosage,
convenience
• Patient support
• CME programs
• Practice management
• Trust in company/sales rep
relationships
• Delivery, ease of use
• QOL improvement
• Support/loyalty
• Media influence
• Corporate reputation
and disease-related
expertise

Source: Françoise Simon/SDC Group, 2002.

to a substantial share increase for Lamisil.[13] These two forms of marketing are shown in Figure 4.3.

Consumer trends support this dual marketing. Across major countries, consumers are driven toward hard evidence by several factors: brand proliferation and confusion, Internet access, negative publicity surrounding drug recalls, and interest in personalized medicine. A 2002 Harris Interactive Survey of more than 1,300 consumers found that, in Internet health-related searches, medical journals or research institutions were the first or second information sources in the United States, France, Germany, and Japan. Pharma Web sites came fourth in the United States, seventh in Germany, second to last in France, and last in Japan, after news media, government sites, patient groups, hospitals, and doctors.[14]

REDEFINING DISEASE AND THERAPIES

Postgenomic medicine is expected to evolve in two different ways: First, it will move from detection and treatment to prediction and prevention; second, its focus will shift from populations to individuals. These radical changes require a reorganization of the biopharma value chain, from discovery to manufacturing and marketing. They will also change markets and brands in a way that will put the current consumer marketing model on a collision course with the molecular reality of disease.

REDEFINING DISEASE: MOLECULAR SUBTYPES

In some areas such as oncology, the definition of a disease is fragmenting into molecular subtypes. While the molecular basis of some diseases has been known for some time, therapies did not follow. For instance, the molecular basis of sickle cell anemia was discovered more than 40 years ago but did not lead to a definitive treatment.[15] Therapies emerged only recently; in 1998, Genentech launched its monoclonal antibody Herceptin (trastuzumab) for a subset of metastatic breast cancer, characterized by Her-2 overexpression.

From Detection to Prediction

In addition to molecular subsets, a better longitudinal analysis of disease may be possible. The Millennium/Becton-Dickinson alliance included the development of a DNA-based test for melanoma, measuring expression levels of melastatin—a more accurate progression measure than tumor thickness, currently used by oncologists. Molecular diagnostics would also improve patient staging in large markets such as type 2 diabetes—which may begin with impaired glucose homeostasis and end in pancreatic failure after several stages characterized by different gene expression levels.[16]

The subdivision of diseases into their molecular types would lead to market fragmentation, but it would also optimize drug responses and minimize adverse events. A meta-analysis of 39 prospective studies from U.S.

BUSINESS IMPACT OF DRUG RECALLS

Drug withdrawals due to ADRs have multiplied in recent years. U.S. General Accounting Office records showed that 12 drugs were withdrawn because of ADRs in the 1979 to 1998 period. However, from 1998 to 2000 alone, as many as seven drugs were pulled from the market in areas as diverse as allergies (Seldane/terfenadine), cardiovascular (Posicor/mibefradil), analgesics (Duract/bromfenac), reflux (Propulsid/cisapride), diabetes (Rezulin/troglitazone), and irritable bowel syndrome (Lotronex/alosetron).[a]

The economic costs of drug recalls have skyrocketed because they include not only the opportunity cost of lost sales, but also the much higher liability costs. Wyeth took charges of $13 billion to cover claims related to its antiobesity drugs Pondimin and Redux, linked to heart valve and lung ADRs.[b] In August 2001, Bayer withdrew its statin Baycol (cerivastatin) because of reports of 52 deaths linked to rhabdomyolysis, a muscle-wasting disease. This ADR was more likely in patients combining Baycol and another cholesterol reducer, gemfibrozil—a fact that had been noted on the label. Baycol's 2000 sales were $558 million and, given the new statin guidelines expanding the market, it had peak potential of more than $2.5 billion. Bayer suffered a 17 percent share price drop on the day of the announcement and subsequently had to make large cuts in its workforce.[c]

---

[a] Lou Morris, "A Terrible Thing to Waste," *Pharmaceutical Executive* (June 2001), p. 146.
[b] Julie Earle, "Litigation-Hit AHP Reports $3.8bn Loss," *Financial Times* (January 26, 2001), p. 17.
[c] "Bayer: Will the Pillars Crumble?" *In Vivo* (October 2001), pp. 2, 8.

hospitals over 32 years showed a 6.7 percent incidence of serious adverse drug reactions (ADRs); for 1994, estimates were that more than 2.2 million inpatients had serious ADRs and 106,000 died—placing ADRs between the fourth and sixth leading causes of death.[17]

Diffusion of Genotyping

Linking disease subsets to patient genotypes and eliminating adverse reactants from clinical trials would greatly reduce drug withdrawal costs as well as their impact on corporate image. Both *pharmacogenetics* and *pharmacogenomics* aim to drive that process through two strategies. Genetics starts from disease populations to identify susceptibility genes, most of which are not drug targets; functional genomics then validates targets. By contrast, genomics starts from DNA databases to identify gene families based on their sequence homologies; these genes are then also validated through functional genomics.[18]

Pharmacogenomics (PGx) drives personalized medicine by linking drug response to individual genetic variations (SNPs and haplotypes, that is, patterns of SNPs). However, PGx may fragment the market and reveal ADRs that standard clinicals would not reveal—thereby compromising approval and possibly "tainting" the product with publicized side effects.[19]

Another barrier is the cost of PGx tests (some of which are priced at $1,000 to $2,000, whereas an entire clinical trial may be done at a cost of $1,000 to $6,000 per patient). For these reasons, PGx tests are not expected to be broadly used until 2005 to 2010. However, many biopharmas are now banking Phase III samples, which can be genotyped later.

The market itself may influence the diffusion of PGx. Physicians, consumers, and patient advocacy groups will increasingly demand better efficacy and safety; payers will be sensitive to the cost-effectiveness of targeted drugs—at least in high-cost diseases such as HIV and hepatitis. Interferon alpha costs $15,000 to $20,000 per treatment cycle, 40 to 60 percent of patients are nonresponders and side effects are substantial. Preselecting responders through PGx testing would be beneficial for payers.

The most likely scenario for the adoption of PGx is that it will evolve at different speeds, depending on the disease area. Both medical need and economic benefit are larger in critical areas such as oncology.

Economic Impact of Pharmacogenomics

A recent analysis of the impact of PGx on a chronic mass-market category such as hyperlipidemia concluded that PGx would grow the total market, but it would actually *decrease* revenues for the statins, as newer drugs would capture some of their sales. Starting from a $9.7 billion hyperlipidemia market in 2001 (including $9.3 billion for the statins), the analysis projected that the total market would grow to $17.2 billion by 2010 (including $16.8 billion for statins); this assumed 3 percent inflation and sales projections adjusted for compliance rates.

In an alternative scenario including PGx testing, the total market was projected to grow slightly more (to $18.5 billion), but the statin category would grow to only $15 billion, partly because new drugs would capture

$3 billion in sales—but also because of the loss of adverse reactants (18 percent of the market), which would be only partially offset by an increased compliance of 3 percent.[20]

Any decision to include genotyping in a drug's development would, therefore, benefit from assessing both the medical need and the economic potential of PGx. Categories with a high efficacy need and commercial potential range from oncology to HIV. Areas well served by current therapies include allergies and gastric reflux. Screening criteria should include:

- Level of unmet medical need for efficacy.
- Low tolerability of current drugs/frequency of ADRs.
- Percentage of nonresponders.
- Estimated time to market of PGx tests for a given disease.
- Size and growth of available market.

In the coming years, pharmacogenomics will become part of a molecular diagnostics tool kit—which is likely to be adopted faster by biotechs than pharmacos. Big Pharma has been slow to develop large molecules—even though these are expected to account for half of all drugs within 15 years. Most pharmacos still rely on in-licensing; Bristol-Myers Squibb, despite its core oncology franchise, has no large molecules, and its in-licensing of ImClone's Erbitux carried a very high price (nearly $2 billion) and an equally high risk (FDA's rejection of its application and request for more data).

Value Chain Restructuring

Increasing the macromolecule component of pharma portfolios entails a reorganization of the value chain:

- Time frames will have to be adjusted. Biologics have faster development time and lower attrition rates but potentially greater approval delays because of close regulator scrutiny of first-in-class therapies.
- Manufacturing is the most problematic stage because there is a shortage of protein production capacity and dedicated facilities must be developed early in the development cycle (they take four to five years to be fully operational). Enbrel (etanercept), jointly marketed by Wyeth and Immunex, encountered massive production shortages, which affected its

sales. Monoclonal antibodies will have the most acute supply problem because they are used in fairly high doses for long-term chronic diseases and there are hundreds of them in current pipelines, leading to more than 50 expected approvals in the next six to seven years. This requires a five- to six-fold increase in cell culture capacity—most of which will have to be provided by biotech companies.[21]

REDEFINING THERAPIES

The paradigm shift of personalized medicine involves a multistep approach: first, identifying the molecular cause of a disease; second, learning which patients have that molecular abnormality; third, linking genotypes and response to a candidate drug; and fourth, proving that the drug effects an actual molecular change.

This is prompting a second paradigm shift, that is, a fusion of diagnostics and therapeutics, with the joint development of tests and drugs based on the same molecular target. Genentech pioneered this concept with its monoclonal antibody Herceptin and its assay HercepTest, designed to identify and block Her-2 overexpression in metastatic breast cancer. Genentech partnered with diagnostic firm Dako to manufacture this dual product.

The integration of diagnostics into drug development prompted new structures such as Applera's Celera Diagnostics. Large diagnostics firms, like big pharmas, have been slow to commit to molecular therapies, but they are now increasing their investments. Roche Diagnostics has formed large teams to develop molecular markers, and Abbott Diagnostics has strengthened its genomics program with its Millennium collaboration to discover new diabetes markers. A significant advantage may belong to companies with dual drug and diagnostics units, such as Roche, J&J, and Abbott. J&J's advanced diagnostics group focuses on molecular oncology, which its pharma unit is addressing at the same time.[22]

The convergence of therapeutics and diagnostics will require a restructuring of two different business models. Discovery timelines, approval processes, channels, customers, and margins are all different in the two sectors. Dual salesforces will have to collaborate to reach labs as well as physicians, and consumer programs will be needed to ensure proper diagnosis and treatment compliance. Figure 4.4 shows the business implications of this shift from drugs to molecular solutions.

FIGURE 4.4   From Drugs to Integrated Solutions

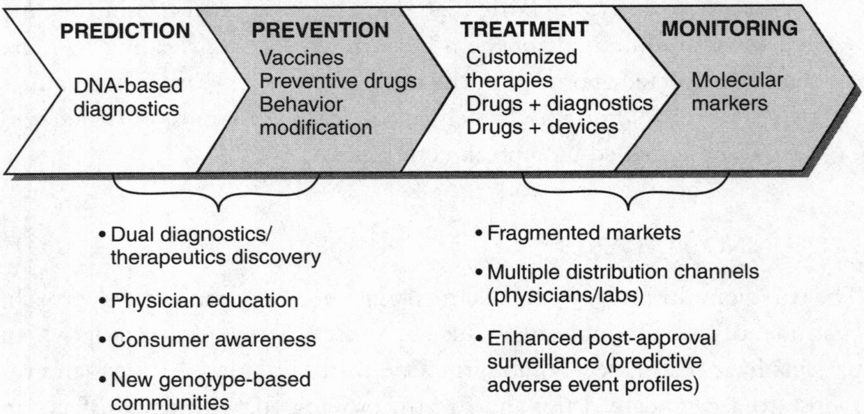

PREDICTION	PREVENTION	TREATMENT	MONITORING
DNA-based diagnostics	Vaccines Preventive drugs Behavior modification	Customized therapies Drugs + diagnostics Drugs + devices	Molecular markers

- Dual diagnostics/ therapeutics discovery

- Physician education

- Consumer awareness

- New genotype-based communities

- Fragmented markets

- Multiple distribution channels (physicians/labs)

- Enhanced post-approval surveillance (predictive adverse event profiles)

Source: Françoise Simon/SDC Group, 2002.

Drugs are now increasingly combined with devices, which will also impact business models. For instance, drug-eluting stents are now used in cardiovascular surgery, and new fields are emerging from the combination of drugs and electronic devices. Medtronic, the leading manufacturer of cardiac pacemakers, is now expanding into restorative neuroscience, which combines neurosurgery, neurophysiology, and biomedical engineering. In January 2002, the FDA approved for use in both sides of the brain Medtronic's Activa, a complementary treatment to the drug levodopa in advanced stages of Parkinson's disease. The intersection of electrical stimulation and biological therapy may have several applications: triggering angiogenesis in ischemic tissue, controlling gene expression, cardiac repair using cellular transplantation, and enhancing efficiency of gene uptake in targeted cells.[23]

FORMULATING BIOMARKETING

As personalized medicine prompts a redefinition of disease and drugs, it will also lead to a fundamental rethinking of marketing models, from segmentation and branding to pricing and communications.

Because of the innovative nature of molecular-targeted therapies, they need a coordinated effort to shape the market, the product, and the company several years before launch. Figure 4.5 illustrates this triple process.

FIGURE 4.5   Key Launch Components

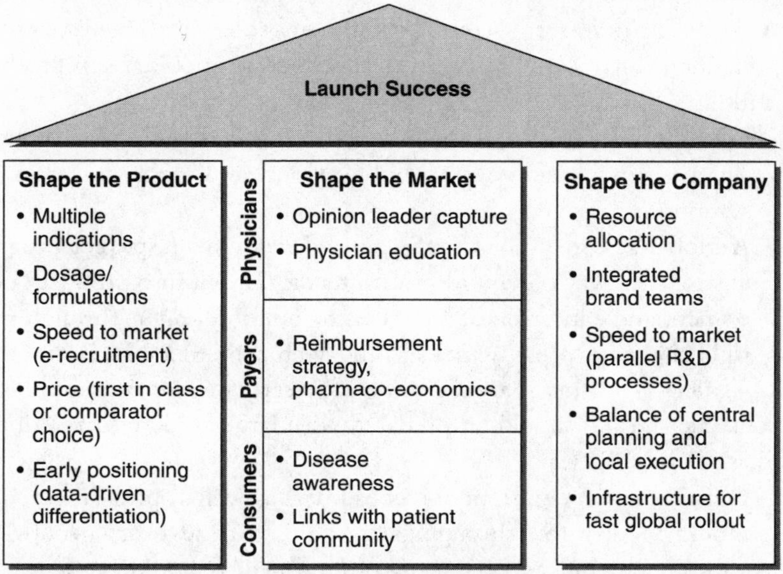

Source: Françoise Simon/SDC Group, 2002. Partly adapted from *Achieving World-Class Performance in Pharmaceutical Product Launches* (McKinsey, April 2002), p. 6.

Shaping the Product

Tight coordination between clinical and commercial development takes place as early as the preclinical stage:

- *Market input* comes from deep insights into unmet patient and prescriber needs, through consumer research including ethnographics (direct observation of consumer activities) and early identification and polling of medical thought leaders; this leads to preclinical positioning.
- *Economic input* is derived from a preliminary pricing study and, if the product is not first to market, the selection of comparators.
- *Clinical attributes* are mapped based on research performance and unmet market needs; for optimal lifecycle management, multiple indications, dosages, and formulations should start to be planned for Phase I and incorporated into Phases II and III clinicals.

SHAPING THE MARKET

- A *medical leadership strategy* is the most critical component of prelaunch activities; without it, even consumer-driven products will fail.
    - —Global clinical trials can be branded through the selection of investigators with "star power," publications, and global and regional symposia.
    - —A global advisory board and leader development/speaker program ensure two-way communications: medical input into product development and education of clinicians by opinion leaders through multiple channels (print, symposia, and Web conferencing).
- *Consumer education* is also key to ensure early disease awareness; early consumer insight should be validated with larger scale research during Phase II and III trials:
    - —Opinion leaders exist among consumers as well as prescribers; these should be identified through partnerships with advocacy groups, and coordinated online/offline communications should be started in Phase II.
    - —A dominant share of voice can be achieved with "smart" resource allocation, that is, full use of targeted, cost-effective media such as public relations and the Internet.

SHAPING THE COMPANY

- *Speed to market* is critical for economic and competitive reasons (a first-mover advantage was key to success in many product launches and helped Celebrex gain a leading position against Vioxx); this can be achieved by parallel development processes and Web-enabled trials but also through timely market and competitive input.
- *Multifunctional brand teams* must be formed as early as Phase I and must be globally coordinated to integrate country inputs into the development process, as world markets often differ greatly in their regulatory requirements, medical practices, and consumer preferences for specific formulations, dosages, and treatment regimens.
- A *seamless global infrastructure* must be built well before launch to ensure fast rollout:

—In marketing, global brand teams must ensure an effective transfer of best practices, not only to and from headquarters and subsidiaries, but also between countries.

—Salesforce strength differs by product type: For mass market drugs, size is key and can be bolstered with copromotion alliances—but for targeted therapies, knowledge is crucial in small specialist forces.

—Flawless execution comes from affiliate readiness to implement a global rollout, and conflicts between corporate and country management must be resolved before launch. (See Figure 4.6.)

FIGURE 4.6 Prelaunch Strategies

	Pre-clinical	Phase I	Phase II	Phase III	Launch
Clinical	• Assess unmet medical needs • Thought leader identification and input • Targets (indications, dosages) • Investigator recruitment (Phase I)	• Dosage and safety (human volunteers) • Trial investigator recruitment (Phase II) • Global advisory board • Leader development	• Safety and efficacy (patients with disease) • Opinion leader recruitment • Phase II conference presentations • Plan articles/ shape labeling	• Efficacy and safety in large studies • Early access programs • Phase IV planning • Publications • Global CME program	• Physician monitoring (attitude/ acceptance) • Start Phase IV clinicals (new indications) • Continue publications
Commercial	• Competitive comparators • Preliminary pricing study • Pre-clinical positioning/ initial attribute mapping	• Global brand teams • Early advocacy collaborations • Global payer assessment • Pharmaco-economics study • Early segmentation • Develop product profile	• Market needs: validate early insights • Refine physician and patient segmentation • Quantitative product profile • Competitive analysis • ROI modeling • Build communications	• Forecast and financials • Patient/ physician ad pretests • Advocacy program expansion • Final pricing/ reimbursement • Labeling/ monograph • Sales training/ complete communications	• Marketing ROI analysis • Assess positioning • Monitor advertising effectiveness • Monitor competitor response • Link with advocacy groups for Phase IV trials

Source: Françoise Simon/SDC Group, 2002.

TARGETING NEW SEGMENTS

Information technology and postgenomic advances are transforming consumer segmentation bases; this has already occurred for targeted therapies and is likely to spread gradually to mass-market products. Segmentation bases for physicians are also evolving in parallel.

TARGETED THERAPIES: GENOTYPE SEGMENTS

The starting segment for a targeted drug is a genotype. Rare mendelian diseases such as cystic fibrosis (CFTR gene) have single-gene mutations. More frequent are polygenic diseases such as Alzheimer's, which is related to a mendelian mutation (APP717) or, more often, to a susceptibility gene (ApoE4/4 homozygous genotype).[24]

In addition to genotypes, *technographics* are an influential segmentation base. A targeted drug for a life-threatening disease attracts an "Internet-positive" patient segment very early in its development—as soon as Phase I results were announced, in the case of Novartis' leukemia drug Gleevec (imatinib). Among these patients, a small but vocal group of *activist leaders* has emerged. In the HIV category, these were instrumental in accelerating product approvals and accessing drugs before launch through early access programs. Because all critical therapeutic areas have tight global patient communities, these activists and their "viral marketing" are a counterpart to powerful opinion leaders in the medical community.

Physician specialties relevant to targeted drugs also have tight global networks and are highly influenced by trial investigators and opinion leaders. These experts are the best awareness-builders for the drug, together with physicians participating in early access programs. (See Figure 4.7.)

MASS MARKET THERAPIES: DRUG RESPONSE SEGMENTS

Although mass-market drugs are not developed to target a specific gene mutation, patients' responses to them are affected by genetic polymorphisms that lead to new segments. Genes coding for drug-metabolizing enzymes (such as cytochrome P4502D6) have polymorphisms that produce the phenotypes of "poor metabolizers" or "ultrafast metabolizers." These

FIGURE 4.7   Segment Flow—Targeted Oncology Product

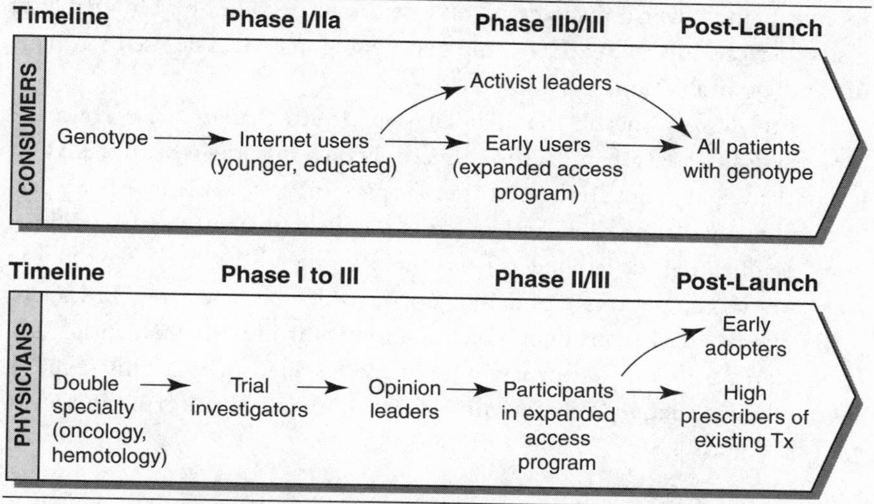

Source: Françoise Simon/SDC Group, 2002.

account for a sizable proportion of the population and for a significant share of adverse reactions, drug recalls, and high-cost litigation:

- *Extensive metabolizers* have normal-activity enzymes (75 to 85 percent of the population).
- *Intermediate or poor metabolizers* (5 to 15 percent) carry two decreased-activity or loss-of-function alleles.
- *Ultrarapid metabolizers* (1 to 10 percent) carry duplicated active genes.

These variations have serious consequences. Some antidepressants are toxic in poor metabolizers and ineffective in ultrafast metabolizers of CYP2D6. Antiarrhythmics can cause sudden cardiac death in patients with LQT 1–5 mutations on five genes coding for cardiac ion channels. These segments correlate with ethnicity in a "gene geography": The CYP2D6 loss-of-function alleles found in poor metabolizers occur in 5 to 13.5 percent of Whites, but 0 to 1 percent of Asians, for instance.[25] Several companies aim to produce chips useable in doctors' offices to identify these segments and select drugs appropriately.

Although pharmacogenomics is not routinely used yet to determine genotypes, their corresponding phenotypes (observable drug response) are well-known and include four groups: high and low responders, nonre-sponders, and adverse reactants. This last group becomes highly visible in case of serious adverse reactions, and genotyping may then be used for mandated drug restrictions.

Bristol-Myers Squibb found in the late 1990s that its drug Pravachol (pravastatin) treated atherosclerosis effectively only in patients with the B1 allele of the CETP (cholesterol ester transfer protein) gene—these were 85 percent of the population. For carriers of the B2 allelic variant, the drug did not work. Eliminating nonresponders from clinicals might have given Pravachol an edge over its competitors Lipitor and Zocor, which became category leaders.

For mass-market products, technographics is also an influential segmentation base—but less crucially than for targeted drugs. This segment subdivides into active Web networkers and more passive information seekers (see Figure 4.8).

FIGURE 4.8   Segment Flow—Mass Product (Statin)

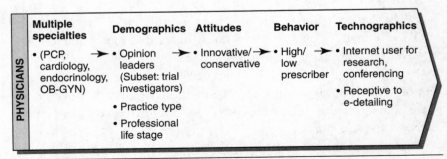

Source: Françoise Simon/SDC Group, 2002.

ATTITUDE CHANGES: THE PROACTIVE/PASSIVE RIFT

While consumers have always varied in their relative independence from medical authorities, the proactive and passive segments are now more clearly split, following the "Internet divide." This applies across countries: A 2001 survey of 1,500 consumers commissioned by McKinsey in Germany, the United Kingdom, and Italy showed that the proactive segment was growing fast but also subdividing. Key results were:

- 83 percent of respondents were confident in their ability to self-treat minor ailments.
- 67 percent made proactive lifestyle choices.
- 59 percent were willing to pay for additional products and services.
- 26 percent had requested specific treatments.

This shows that while Europeans are becoming clearly proactive, they still lag Americans in assertiveness at the physician's office; this reflects in part the absence of DTC in Europe, but it will change with the spread of the Internet.[26]

Broader segmentation bases can be summarized as follows:

Segment Type	Characteristics
Medical	
• Genetic basis	• Genotype, metabolism, drug response.
• Symptomatology	• Acute/chronic.
• Treatment	• Treated/untreated, responsive or not.
• Comorbidity	• Concomitant illness.
• Provider	• PCP, specialist, pharmacist.
Demographic	
• Age	• Metabolic maturity.
• Gender	• Hormonal effects/gender variance.
• Ethnicity	• Genotype prevalence.

(continued)

Segment Type	Characteristics
Psychographic	
• Attitude to health	• Proactive/passive.
• Attitude to risk	• Early adopter/risk-averse.
• Attitude to medicine	• Allopathic/alternative preferences.
Behavior/Technographic	
• Treatment regimen	• Compliant/noncompliant.
• Economic participation	• Willingness to pay.
• Technographic sophistication	• Web usage and involvement.

These changes have counterparts among physicians, as they diverge in their education, Web use, and attitudes. The diffusion and success of targeted therapies depend on extensive physician education about drugs and their diagnostic test protocols. Technographically inclined physicians are more receptive to e-detailing (electronic sales calling) and Web conferencing. Attitudes toward alternative medicine impact treatment. In the menopause category, the Women's Health Initiative (WHI) trial discontinuation because of serious ADRs for hormone replacement therapy (HRT) will lead to the adoption of different substitutes depending on physicians' and consumers' attitudes toward alternative therapies.

These segmentation bases entail specific planning steps. For targeted therapies, these are:

- Promote diagnosis of disease-related genotypes.
- Target medical opinion leaders via clinical trials and publications.
- Collaborate closely with patient activists and advocacy groups.
- Develop prelaunch awareness among physicians and patients.
- After launch, continue science-driven marketing with Phase IV clinicals.

For mass-marketed drugs, key steps include:

- If genotyping is not included in trial protocols, bank patient samples for retrospective testing in case of adverse reactions.

- Target medical opinion leaders via trials and publications.
- Segment patients by demographics, attitudes, and behavior.
- Develop awareness by collaborating with patient advocacy groups.

CREATING NEW MARKET SPACE

The fact that the biopharma sector is at an inflection point creates opportunities for companies to expand into the "white spaces" of the competitive map rather than fight for share in a crowded category:

- *Partnering across substitute industries* may yield a better competitive advantage than focusing on direct competitors. Pfizer broke new ground when it formed its Amicore joint venture with IBM and Microsoft to market medical practice software; because physicians' time is scarce for sales calls, Pfizer reps (already top-rated) may gain easier entry because of their expanded service portfolio.
- *Buyer groups* are also redefined by the rise of consumerism. J&J was the first company to launch a DTC campaign in a physician-driven category. Procrit was indicated for chemotherapy-induced anemia, a therapeutic area that does not easily lend itself to mass appeals—yet the multimedia campaign stressed consumer benefits in the form of a better quality of life. Partly thanks to this, Procrit sales grew 24 percent from 2001 to 2002.
- *Product scope* can be expanded. Targeted therapies such as Genentech's Herceptin are marketed with their diagnostic tests, but the highest value a company could provide might come from a product/diagnostic/service combination, including genetic counseling and support programs. At the other end of the biobrand spectrum, smoking cessation patches such as McNeil's Nicotrol are most effectively marketed in conjunction with behavior-modification programs that ensure better compliance.
- *Product focus* can also be creatively changed along the functional-emotional spectrum. Pfizer's DTC campaign for Viagra avoided a clinical tone and stressed instead relationships among couples of all ages.
- Finally, companies can create a first-mover advantage and *shape future trends* with a true breakthrough. Novartis's Gleevec was the first targeted small molecule, which translated into medical differentiation (much higher response rate than previous therapies) and consumer

TABLE 4.3   Creating New Market Space

	Complete Head-to-Head	Create New Market Space	Company Leaders
Industry	Focus on rivals.	Look across substitute industries.	• Amicore (Pfizer/ IBM/Microsoft)
Buyer Group	Focus on serving buyer group.	Redefine the buyer group.	• J&J/Procrit (DTC for biologic)
Product Scope	Maximize current product value.	Look for complementary products/services.	• Genentech/ Herceptin (Rx + Dx)
Functional– Emotional Focus	Focus on functional or emotional performance.	Rethink the functional-emotional spectrum.	• Pfizer/Viagra (ED concept)
Time	Adapt to current trends.	Shape future trends.	• Novartis/Gleevec (Rational drug design)

Source: Françoise Simon/SDC Group, 2002; partly adapted from Chan Kim and Renée Mauborgne, "Creating New Market Space," *Harvard Business Review* (January–February 1999), pp. 83–93.

benefits (convenience and tolerability). Table 4.3 illustrates these different ways to create new market space.

The scope of biobrands leads to discrepancies between manufacturer, physician, and consumer mindsets. While companies and clinicians tend to confine therapies to drugs, sprays, patches, or injections, patients have a broader view of the market.

Hybrid consumers wanting both high-tech and high-touch care became more visible to the medical community through David Eisenberg's surveys in the *New England Journal of Medicine* and *JAMA*; these showed that the use of alternative therapies had surpassed that of mainstream medicine in the United States.[27] Far from rejecting allopathic care, these consumers want the best of both worlds. They are the same shoppers who use Amazon to order a business book but browse offline for a gift item and who drove Schwab into online stock trading but also demanded retail stores with personal advisors. The "Webvan shoppers versus tomato squeezers" phenomenon also explains why online pharmacies such as PlanetRx did not meet expectations. While cost-effective for chronic diseases, online stores were not adequate for time-sensitive purchases such as antibiotics. Survivors were "brick-and-click" models such as CVS who could meet both types of needs.

Companies are now attempting to catch up with hybrid consumers and cover all bases with a full product range, from biologics to botanicals.

The menopause market is a striking example of the range of consumer demand. Even before HRT was impacted by the WHI clinical results, women feared it; they typically tried it only after exhausting other options and dropped out quickly (with a persistence rate of less than 40 percent after six months of therapy). By contrast, companies tended to keep a product-centered view of the competitive space—viewing hard therapies as most central and soft approaches as peripheral. (See Figure 4.9.)

FIGURE 4.9 New Space: Menopause Market

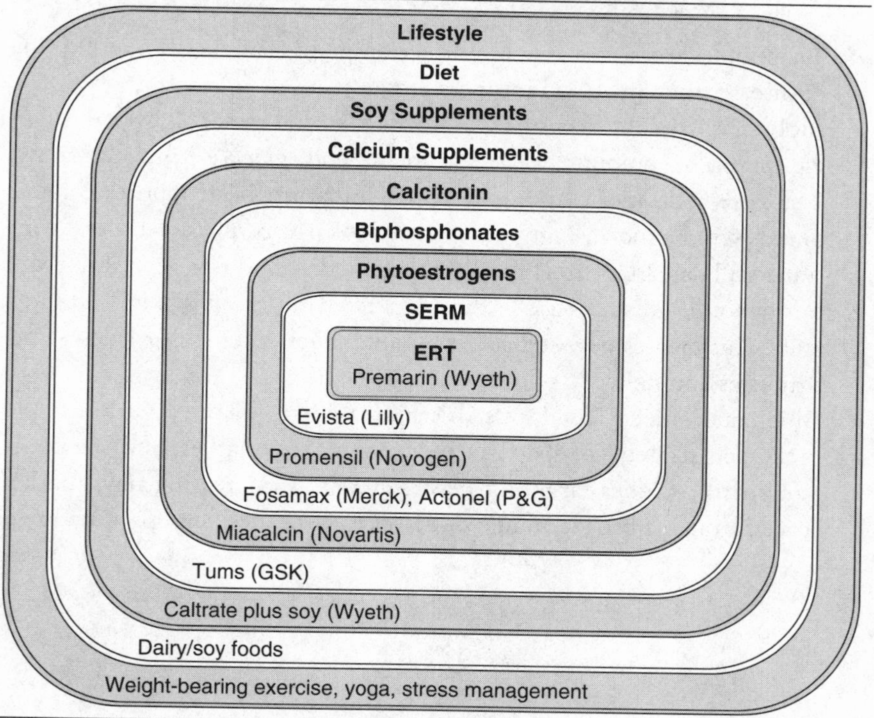

Source: Françoise Simon/SDC Group, 2002.

It is critical for companies to consider the entire range of therapy options. Accordingly, pharmacos are broadening their product lines. To round out its women's health franchise, Wyeth branched out into botanicals with its soy and calcium supplements. It also bought a German phytomedicine company, and J&J, Pfizer, Sanofi, and Fujisawa made similar acquisitions—all in Germany, where herbals are regulated and partly reimbursed. Botanicals are a $6 billion market in Europe and account for nearly $2 billion in the United States, where alternative medicine is a high-growth $27 billion sector.[28]

Across product categories, companies can optimize both product and corporate equity by looking at their competitive space through their customers' eyes and shifting from drugs to a broader range of healthcare solutions.

SUMMARY POINTS

✓ The biopharma sector is at an inflection point that entails a rethinking of disease, therapies, and business models.

✓ Biobrands have an exceptionally broad scope and require a hybrid strategic approach, combining *experience-based* and *evidence-based* marketing.

✓ The pure consumer marketing approach that has been applied to many brands will be increasingly unsustainable as payers, physicians, and consumers all demand hard clinical evidence and a good efficacy/price ratio.

✓ Postgenomic advances are leading to a redefinition of disease and therapies; this creates new structures as companies enter sectors such as diagnostics and delivery systems.

✓ Biopharmas need to address this increased complexity with a triple prelaunch strategy of shaping the product, the market, and the company; this includes targeting new segments and creating new market space through a broader range of partners, customers, and product lines.

BUILDING BIOBRANDS

A brand is a storehouse of trust that matters more and more as choices multiply. People want to simplify their lives.

Niall FitzGerald, chairman, Unilever[1]

The biopharma sector has increased its consumer marketing at the same time as it has come under attack for issues such as drug access and pricing. In this climate, large pharmaceutical companies run the risk of being perceived as marketing machines instead of innovation leaders. Product marketing has traditionally been disconnected from corporate campaigns, and the sector has only recently initiated industrywide efforts. There are signs that this fragmented approach carries risks and that a coordination of strategies across the "branding pyramid," from product to company and industry, might be more effective in the long term.

In the absence of such integration, some heavily branded products have become lighting rods for payers and consumers. In the United States, the antihistamine category has the highest adspend including DTC; and the three leaders, Claritin (loratadine), Zyrtec (cetirizine), and Allegra (fexofenadine), collectively reaped more than $5 billion in 2002 global sales. Their very success attracted the attention of payers. In July 1998, a petition was presented to the FDA by Wellpoint Health Networks, requesting that these second-generation antihistamines be switched to OTC status, despite the fact that they were all under patent. In 2002, a U.S. judge declared a Claritin patent invalid, and by 2003, Schering-Plough began selling it over-the-counter—hoping to transfer its prescription franchise to the successor molecule Clarinex (desloratadine).[2] This case may have created a precedent for similar actions by payers in categories where OTC switches are perceived as safe.

This chapter first reviews how companies need to redefine branding models; it then addresses how key success factors apply across categories, from targeted therapies to mass-market drugs; finally, it explores the best ways to extend this dual model globally. (See Figure 5.1.)

As issues ranging from biodefense, bioethics, and drug pricing keep the industry in the public eye, companies are reassessing their traditional strategy of branding products rather than corporations. Because many

FIGURE 5.1   Biobranding Strategy

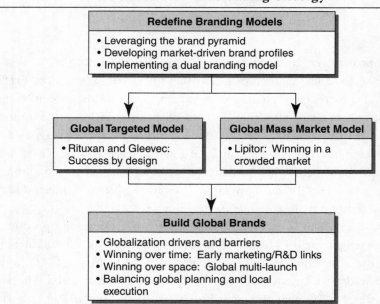

Source: Françoise Simon/SDC Group, 2002.

consumers are also investors, they are buying not only products, but also companies—as is the case for General Electric or IBM.

An intermediate step between the product and the corporate level, which can support both, is the category. A strong franchise facilitates a new product launch; expertise in a therapeutic area can also support corporate branding. For instance, Novartis has built a leading oncology franchise that differentiates it in the medical community and in patient advocacy groups.

Corporate campaigns have intensified for large pharmas. After 76 years, American Home Products changed its name to Wyeth to better reflect its pharma focus, as well as the brand equity of the Wyeth name among physicians. Pfizer started a "Tomorrow's Cures" series stressing its R&D scale and its expertise in areas such as Alzheimer's disease. Novartis adopted a "Think what's possible" theme featuring patient cases in areas such as oncology, and Bristol-Myers Squibb enlisted cyclist Lance Armstrong as a spokesperson for its core oncology franchise. Biopharma brand valuations were listed by Interbrand in its Top 100 Brand survey; Merck and Pfizer were ranked 28th and 30th, with respective brand values of $9.67 billion and $8.95 billion.[3] Merck has built equity with physicians as well as consumers through scientific initiatives such as its *Merck Manual* (now in online and offline versions) and its medical website.

The weakest equity component of biobrands is at the industry level. The Pharmaceutical Research and Manufacturers Association (PhRMA) only recently started advertising innovation, and the Council for Biotechnology Information promoted the consumer benefits of agbio, such as vitamin-enriched rice or corn to fight blindness and anemia in the developing world. However, this is insufficient, given the negative publicity surrounding the industry. Countering this situation involves a broad communication of industrywide tangible initiatives to facilitate drug access. It also entails a greater coordination of efforts among all levels of the branding pyramid. (See Figure 5.2.)

Unlike pharma companies, biotech firms have not widely engaged in corporate campaigns—in large part because of smaller budgets, but also because their products have so far targeted specialist audiences. In a recent survey of 900 business opinion leaders and financial influencers, Genentech was the only biotech named—but with the lowest familiarity ranking, although it was favorably viewed. Not surprisingly, the familiarity/

FIGURE 5.2   Branding Pyramid

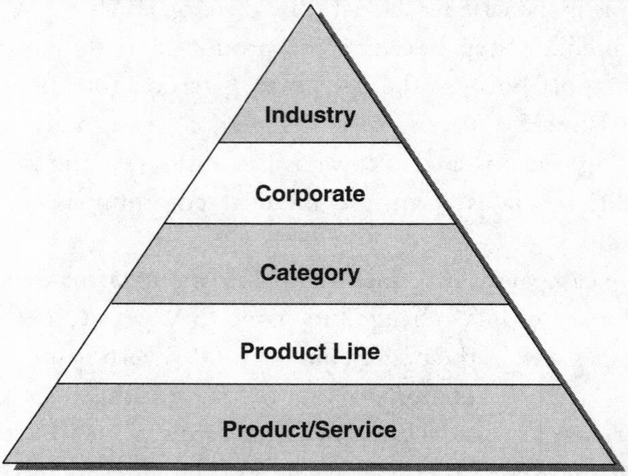

Source: Françoise Simon/SDC Group, 2002.

favorability winner was J&J, closely followed by other consumer/pharma hybrids such as P&G and 3M. Pfizer and Lilly were in a second tier, and Merck ranked high on favorability, but slightly lower on familiarity.

The three winning attribute clusters were *pioneering* (R&D leader, rapid developer, global, clear vision, high-quality management), *accountable* (ethical, responsible, sound investment, high-quality product/services), and *salient* (highly recognizable brand name, strong news presence).[4]

As biotechs expand into mass markets, they will benefit from a multi-tier branding strategy, proactively addressing their entire range of stakeholders, from consumer and physicians to payers, but also advocacy groups, investors, and regulators. (See Table 5.1.)

Corporate branding carries risk because a drug recall can erode the company image. But it also has clear advantages:

- Consistency of an umbrella brand, prevailing over product obsolescence.
- Influence over physician prescribing patterns, especially in new classes where clinical data can be effectively supported by trust in the manufacturer.
- Better differentiation in crowded categories such as hypertension.
- Enhanced consumer loyalty leading to brand resilience if a crisis occurs.

TABLE 5.1   Branding Tiers and Stakeholders

Stakeholders	Product	Category	Corporate	Industry
Consumers	+++	+	++	+++
Managed care customers	+++	++	+	+
Payers	+++	++	+	+
Physicians	+++	+++	++	+
Academia	++	++	++	+
Alliance partners	++	+	+++	+
Employees	++	+	+++	+
Advocacy groups	++	+	++	++
Media	+++	+	+++	+++
Stockholders/investors	+	+	+++	+++
Regulators/governments	+++	++	+	+++

+++ High influence
++   Moderate influence
+   Limited influence

Source: Françoise Simon/SDC Group, 2002.

The best-known example of brand resilience due to the manufacturer's reputation and good crisis management is the Tylenol U.S. poisoning episode. Johnson & Johnson, long known to the public through its baby care line, voluntarily and rapidly recalled the product and took a proactive stance in the media, with personal appearances by top management. As a result, the brand rapidly bounced back. (See Figure 5.3.)

DEVELOPING MARKET-DRIVEN BRAND PROFILES

Given consumers' growing influence on product diffusion, successful brands have combined in their positioning a clear clinical advantage and compelling customer benefits.

A good example is Pfizer's lipid reducer Lipitor (atorvastatin); despite a major initial handicap (reaching the market late, as the fifth product in its class), it was clearly differentiated by its superior clinical performance. This allowed Pfizer to gain payer approval and obtain broad reimbursement. At the service level, both customer types (prescribers and end users) received benefits beyond performance. Lipitor was initially marketed only

FIGURE 5.3   Biobrand Equity

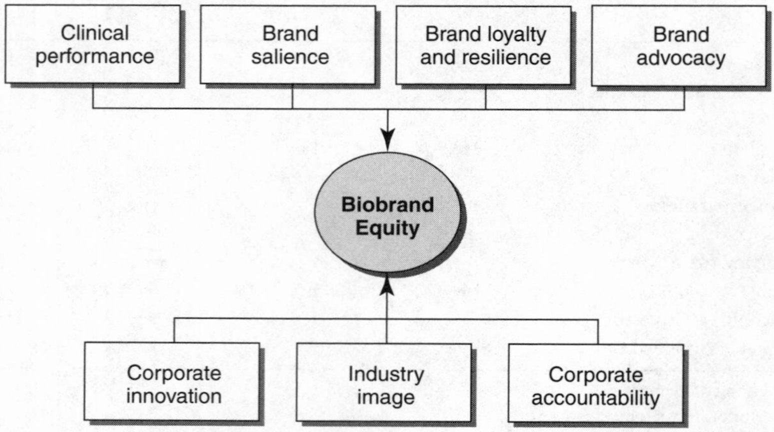

Source: Françoise Simon/SDC Group, 2002.

to physicians, and Pfizer's top-rated salesforce provided intensive information and support. In a second step, consumer programs included toll-free numbers and a dedicated Web site. The 2002 campaign theme of "Rewriting history" for patients with a family history of high cholesterol leverages the trend toward proactive consumers and stresses that they can gain control over their heredity by a combination of diet, exercise, and medication. Figure 5.4 illustrates this multilayer brand profiling.

This strategy also applies to biologics. Because they are often first-in-class products, they have a clear clinical advantage, but they also need to demonstrate their cost effectiveness to payers, given their high prices, and to convey to patients benefits that are specific to them, such as a better quality of life; that is what J&J aimed to do with its consumer campaign for Procrit.

IMPLEMENTING A DUAL BRANDING MODEL

While it is clear that targeted drugs will capture a much greater share of the market in the next decade, it may take longer for mass-market drugs to subdivide into their genotype-specific subsets.

Among large molecules already marketed, proteins such as recombinant insulin already account for more than $10 billion in global sales, and

FIGURE 5.4   Market–Driven Brand Profile: Lipitor

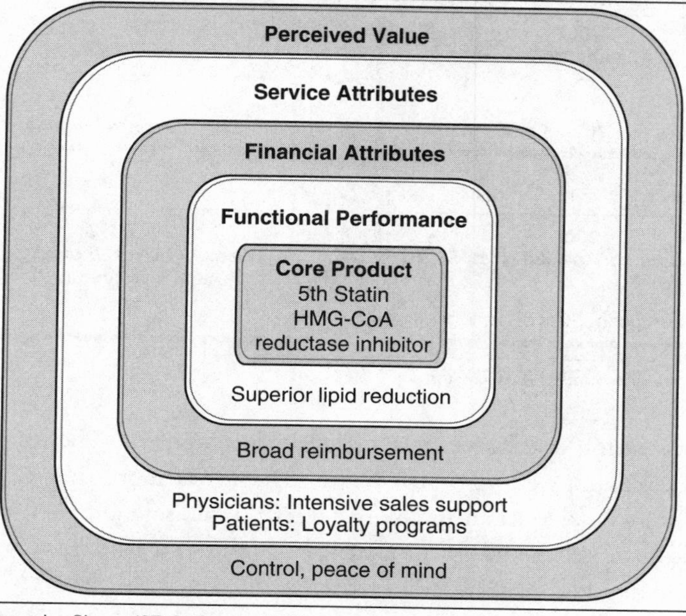

Perceived Value

Service Attributes

Financial Attributes

Functional Performance

Core Product
5th Statin
HMG-CoA
reductase inhibitor

Superior lipid reduction

Broad reimbursement

Physicians: Intensive sales support
Patients: Loyalty programs

Control, peace of mind

Source: Françoise Simon/SDC Group, 2002.

monoclonal antibodies bring in more than $5 billion; as most of these be-come fully humanized, they will reach even better tolerability and efficacy levels. In addition, recombinant vaccines may expand to large markets such as HIV. The fact that there are now hundreds of biologics in the pipeline makes it entirely possible, as some analysts predicted, that 100 biotech drugs could be marketed 10 years from now.

However, it is unlikely that mass–market drugs will evolve at the same speed. Current blockbusters may eventually lead to "blockbuster families," but manufacturers will try to retain their mass–market approach as long as possible, because subdividing a drug into its molecular subsets fragments the market. A major change driver would be mandated microsegmentation; as regulators develop a pharmacogenomic infrastructure, they may demand that genotyping be included in most clinical trials. (See Figure 5.5.)

In the short to medium term, two branding models will continue to coexist.

While they address global niches rather than large markets, targeted therapies can reach megabrand status because of their high margins, much

FIGURE 5.5   Evolving Biobrands

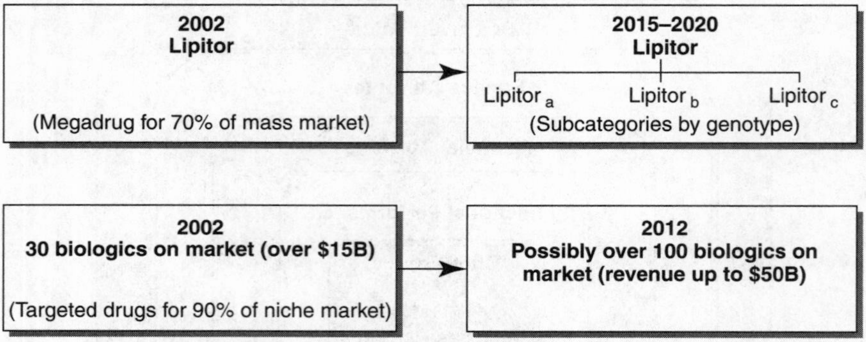

2002 Lipitor	2015–2020 Lipitor
(Megadrug for 70% of mass market)	Lipitor $_a$ Lipitor $_b$ Lipitor $_c$ (Subcategories by genotype)

2002 30 biologics on market (over $15B)	2012 Possibly over 100 biologics on market (revenue up to $50B)
(Targeted drugs for 90% of niche market)	

Source: Françoise Simon/SDC Group, 2002.

lower marketing costs, and more efficient development. The top protein, Amgen's and J&J's epoetin alfa, had 2002 sales of more than $6 billion, and the top monoclonal antibody, Amgen's Enbrel, sold over $800 million. It would have reached $1 billion if it had not been held back by supply problems. In addition, Enbrel is setting a new trend for biologics, because it is addressing a large global market (arthritis) and not a niche; therefore, it has full mass-market potential.

In development, the main advantages of targeted therapies are greater speed and lower attrition. While small molecules typically require two to four years for the development process, this can be significantly cut for biologics. In addition, about 1 in 10 small molecule candidates entering the clinic yields a marketed product, whereas among humanized monoclonal antibodies, 1 in 4 is generally successful.

Furthermore, targeted drugs have a higher marketing return on investment than mass products because their focused model is much more cost-effective:

- Physician audiences may be as small as 5,000 specialists worldwide and are reached with a very small, highly trained salesforce (fewer than 100 for most biologics in the United States, versus 4,000 for Celebrex).
- Patient pools are also small, highly motivated, and more effectively reached via the Internet than expensive mass media.
- Targeted therapies are often supplied directly to physicians or hospitals—thereby eliminating the wholesaler share of profits.

- Because customized drugs are largely breakthrough products, they can command high prices, have no generic or lower priced competition, and do not have great reimbursement barriers—although most provide free access programs for uninsured patients. (See Table 5.2.)

A recent study of marketing ROI for mass-market drugs concluded that current expenditure levels, which rival those of consumer goods, are becoming unsustainable. In the 1999 to 2000 period, the study found that one company achieved a better marketing ROI than competitors, and this was ascribed in part to shifting resources from DTC advertising to medical education.

There is increasing evidence of *overbranding* for mass-market drugs. Merck's marketing cost for its antiarthritic Vioxx (rofecoxib) reached record levels with $160 million in 2000. For the same year (first full year

TABLE 5.2 Dual Branding Model

	Targeted Brand	*Mass-Market Brand*
Product	Herceptin + Herceptest	Celebrex
Disease	Low-prevalence, gene-specific.	High prevalence.
Treatment protocols	Globally standardized.	Regional variances.
Patient targets	Disease-related genotype (Her-2-positive metastatic breast cancer).	Mass market (arthritis).
Physician targets	Double specialists (oncologists/OB-GYNs).	Generalists, rheumatologists.
Channels	Direct supply/wholesalers.	Wholesalers.
Pricing/reimbursement	High margin, high reimbursement (first in class/ no generics), patient access program.	Moderate-to-high margin, uneven reimbursement (lower-price NSAID competition).
Communications	Internet-led network effect (patient/physician leaders), small salesforce, science-driven message.	Large salesforce, DTC, hybrid message (evidence + experience).

Source: Françoise Simon/SDC Group, 2002.

on the market), sales were $1.8 billion. While detailing expenses were $74 million, DTC reached almost the same level (nearly $69 million).[5] While performing well, Vioxx had a first-to-market competitor, Celebrex, and fell short of its projected sales. The shortfall had two possible causes—namely, a report of cardiovascular adverse reactions and the impact of much cheaper competition (NSAIDs, or nonsteroidal anti-inflammatories such as ibuprofen). Both Vioxx and Celebrex had a weak efficacy advantage. Their main claim over NSAIDs was better GI tolerability—a benefit that ADR reports could quickly erode.

Future strategy should question whether there is a risk of overbranding; some resources could be shifted from DTC to R&D, because new indications are the surest way to expand in a competitive market. Parts of the targeted model also apply to a mass product:

- Evidence-based marketing (initial superior performance and new indications).
- Full use of network effects in the medical and patient communities (global web of opinion leaders and patient advocates).
- Partial shift of DTC spend from mass media to the Internet (especially for disease awareness and scientific education).

GLOBAL TARGETED MODEL: FROM RITUXAN TO GLEEVEC

RITUXAN: REBRANDING MONOCLONAL ANTIBODIES

Rituxan heralded in the late 1990s the biological age in cancer treatment, partly superseding the first-generation chemotherapy and facilitating the convergence of treatment protocols worldwide. Next would come the targeted age in the 2000s, with targeted drugs such as Gleevec. Beyond that, the personalized age projected for the 2010s would focus on preventive therapies and individual molecular profiles.

Changing Medical Perceptions

Approved in the United States in 1997, IDEC and Genentech's Rituxan (rituximab) was a breakthrough and played a significant part in the evolution of the oncology market. As early as 1986, the FDA had approved the first therapeutic monoclonal antibody, Ortho Biotech's Orthoclone OTK3 (muromonab CD3), indicated for treatment of steroid-resistant renal allograft rejection. Ortho pioneered at that time the science-driven clinical marketing, which has since been successfully used for targeted drugs.[6] However, the first generation of monoclonal antibodies (Mabs) was disappointing because they were largely murine (mouse-derived) and apt to be rejected by humans. When Genentech in-licensed Rituxan from IDEC, the prelaunch strategy had to start with a turnaround of medical perceptions about the product class. Genentech was a double pioneer in biotechnology: It had the first biotech IPO in 1980 and created the first recombinant DNA drug approved by the FDA (human insulin, launched with Lilly in 1982). The company had developed techniques to humanize monoclonals, and Rituxan was a chimeric Mab (i.e., partly humanized and better tolerated). It was the first to have an oncology indication. Its 1997 U.S. approval for the treatment of relapsed or refractory low-grade or follicular CD20 positive, B-cell non-Hodgkin's lymphoma (NHL) was followed by its EU approval under the MabThera name in June 1998.

Rituxan showed both high efficacy (overall response rate of 48 percent in patients who had had several prior courses of antineoplastic therapy) and tolerability (mild-to-moderate adverse events).[7]

Key Success Factors

Key success factors for Rituxan were high unmet medical need, first-to-market advantage, and strong clinical profile, which allowed Genentech to launch it with a pure evidence-based marketing approach. Approximately 1.5 million people worldwide had various types of lymphoma, and an estimated 300,000 died each year. In terms of incidence and death, NHL was the second fastest-growing cancer in the United States and the third-fastest growing in the rest of the world. Treatments ranging from chemotherapy to radiology temporarily stopped disease progression but did not lead to a cure. Rituxan had higher tolerability than the standard cytotoxic regimens.

Prelaunch Strategy

Genentech had three major objectives:

1. Change perceptions of the Mab class through a literature reprint series and other communications targeting specialists (medical oncologists and hematologists).

2. Create anticipation for Rituxan by publishing clinical trial results on an ongoing basis though the prelaunch period.
3. Shape Rituxan's identity with a prelaunch ad campaign in journals such as the *Journal of Clinical Oncology* and the *New England Journal of Medicine*; prelaunch ads were especially effective with their skeptical target audience because they were conservative and initially unbranded.

As a result of the premarketing campaign, awareness of Rituxan by launch time reached 80 percent among oncologists, leading to sales of $163 million in 1998, the first year on the market, rising to $280 million the following year.[8]

The launch message was "effective targeted monoclonal antibody therapy" for NHL, and key points were hard clinical data such as response rate, adverse event profile, and new mechanisms of action. In the following years, the message remained consistent.

In keeping with the specialty drug model, Genentech launched Rituxan with a small salesforce of about 60 representatives. Science-driven marketing continued with Phase IV trials leading to expanded uses. An announcement at the American Society of Hematology meeting of clinical results from the Groupe d'Etude des Lymphômes de l'Adulte reported the benefits of combining Rituxan with chemotherapy for aggressive NHL.[9] Sales grew by 59 percent in 2000 and were over $1 billion by 2002.

GLEEVEC: FIRST RATIONALLY DESIGNED SMALL MOLECULE

Gleevec (imatinib) represents an entirely new strategy for biopharma companies: It is the first small molecule to target a specific pathogenic molecule. It took Novartis decades to develop it, but it later broke several records. It had the fastest-ever FDA approval time (72 days) in the United States and was also approved in the EU and Japan in record time (November 2001 for both, after a May approval in the United States). Clinical trials themselves took only half as long as the standard development time; started in August 1998, they lasted only three years.[10]

New Product Class

Gleevec created a new class in bio-oncology, the signal transduction inhibitors; it was indicated for treatment of chronic myeloid leukemia (CML) after failure of interferon–alpha therapy. In 95 percent of CML patients, an abnormal "Philadelphia chromosome" was found; a translocation between chromosomes 9 and 22 formed an abnormal hybrid Bcr-Abl gene, which coded for an enzyme (tyrosine kinase) with increased activity; this in turn stimulated the growth of leukemia cells.[11]

Gleevec was a potent inhibitor of tyrosine kinase. It was the result of more than 30 years of cellular research in CML. When the Philadelphia chromosome was identified in the 1960s, it was the first instance of a genetic abnormality causally linked to cancer. In the 1980s, Novartis started a research program on Bcr-Abl kinase blockers. It took a decade to develop a compound, but it had weak efficacy. After two more years, Gleevec was identified as a potent and specific inhibitor—and more than made up for these delays with the speed of its clinical development.

Global Niche Market

Gleevec was addressing a small market with a high unmet medical need. CML patients accounted for 20 percent of all leukemias worldwide. In the United States, prevalence was 20,000, and incidence was about 5,000 cases per year. European incidence was similar, and Japan had about 1,200 annual cases. The physician market was also very small because it was a double specialty (hematology/oncology). There were about 5,000 oncologists in the United States, 6,000 in Europe, and only about 5,000 double specialists worldwide.

Clear Differential Advantage

The only curative therapy for CML was bone marrow transplant, but it was limited to 15 to 25 percent of patients because of age and donor availability, and it carried very high costs and mortality rates. The gold standard for CML chronic phase was interferon–alpha, marketed by Roche and Schering-Plough, which did not cure CML and had severe side effects. Pharmacia-owned Sugen had another signal transduction inhibitor in the pipeline, and another class (farnesyl transferase inhibitors) was in Phase I trials with compounds from Schering-Plough, BMS, and Janssen; they could potentially be combined with Gleevec.

Unlike older cytotoxics such as BMS's Hydrea (hydroxyurea), Gleevec had only mild side effects and a very high efficacy. In the Phase I trial, an unprecedented 100 percent of patients had had a complete hematologic response (drop in leukemia cells in blood), and one-third had had a complete cytogenetic response (disappearance of the Philadelphia chromosome). For chronic phase CML, Phase II trials had shown a hematologic response in 88 percent of patients and cytogenetic response in 49 percent.

Data-Driven Positioning

Gleevec's positioning stressed its unique targeted nature and its outstanding clinical data. The message was "precise targeting of the molecular abnormality that leads to CML," and key points were "outstanding hematological response," "unprecedented cytogenetic response," and "well-tolerated," as well as "convenient, once-daily, oral therapy."

As was the case for Rituxan, Novartis used an evidence-based marketing approach. Top opinion leaders numbered only about 15 worldwide, and many were trial investigators; in addition, a prelaunch expanded access program allowed trial of the product among nearly 7,000 patients worldwide.

Patient-Driven Demand

Unlike most other biologics, Gleevec was driven by patient demand from the earliest development phase. As soon as interim data were presented at the American Society of Hematology in December 1999, patient activists learned about them and aggressively lobbied for early access and fast-track approval. A key segmentation base was "Internet-positive" patients, who created a worldwide network and petitioned the company and regulators to accelerate approval. Advocacy groups such as the Leukemia & Lymphoma Society also had Web sites and facilitated global networking.

Comprehensive Access Program

Another unique feature of Gleevec's marketing approach was its innovative pricing strategy. The worldwide price was set at $2,200 per month, and treatment might continue indefinitely for patients who responded. Health economics studies in the United States and the United Kingdom aimed to show that Gleevec was cost effective compared with usual care, and a CML disease model was to be developed in the United Kingdom. A Global Assistance Program extended exceptionally broad discounting to uninsured patients. While most patient assistance programs addressed only the lowest income group, Novartis offered the following terms in the United States:

- Drug free of charge to anyone earning less than $43,000 per year.
- Drug cost capped at 20 percent of income for those earning between $43,000 and $100,000 per year.

This program reinforced the high share of voice gained from the product's innovativeness and earned Novartis broad and favorable press coverage.

New Challenges: Physician/Patient Education

As could be expected, Gleevec had a rapid sales uptake, reaching $615 million by 2002, and strategic objectives were to achieve sales of more than $1 billion by 2005. The goal was to establish Gleevec as the new gold standard treatment for CML and to expand usage to early chronic phase CML, first-line therapy, GIST (gastrointestinal stromal tumors), and other solid tumors. Gleevec was approved for GIST in 2002.

One hundred trials were underway to document survival rates, long-term endpoints, and new indications. Gleevec shared a key issue with other innovative therapies: physician education. Despite the fact that they were highly specialized, many physicians still did not know that the goal of therapy was cytogenetic response (rather than only hematologic results), and dosing was often suboptimal.

These issues should ideally have been uncovered through physician market research at the prelaunch stage, but the accelerated development time had not allowed it. Novartis later conducted an insight mining process and adjusted Gleevec's positioning to reflect these issues.

Gleevec had already made history as a double breakthrough—first targeted small molecule and first specialty product to be so strongly driven by patient demand.

GLOBAL MASS MARKET MODEL: LIPITOR

Launched in the United States and the United Kingdom in February 1997, Lipitor (atorvastatin) was a latecomer to the cholesterol market, as the fifth statin to be launched. Nevertheless, it went on to become the world's largest medicine, with 2002 global sales of nearly $8 billion. It accomplished this because of its superior clinical performance, science-driven marketing, and a powerful copromotion alliance between Warner-Lambert (WL) and

Pfizer—which evolved into the industry's first hostile takeover when WL threatened to merge with another company and take Lipitor along. Sales uptake was very rapid from the start, almost quadrupling from $649 million in 1997 to $2.3 billion in 1998.[12]

A CROWDED CATEGORY

The hyperlipidemia market was mature, highly competitive, and led by the statin class. Statins inhibited HMG-CoA reductase, an enzyme involved in the biosynthesis of cholesterol. They were already a 10-year-old class by the time of Lipitor's arrival. Launched in 1987, Merck's Mevacor (lovastatin) had a rapid sales uptake because of its greater efficacy and tolerability than existing treatments. Its successor, Zocor (simvastatin), introduced in 1992 in the United States, became the category leader. BMS's Pravachol (pravastatin) appeared in 1991 in the United States. Novartis' Lescol (fluvastatin) was launched three years later with a lower price but weaker efficacy and did not become a major brand.

DATA-DRIVEN DIFFERENTIATION

Given this competitive situation, WL designed its clinicals as head-to-head comparisons against the other statins and also obtained fast-track status with the FDA, thanks to a small South African trial showing its unique efficacy in a genetic disorder impairing cholesterol clearance. Trials showed that Lipitor had higher efficacy at lower doses in reduction of LDL (low-density lipoprotein), and unlike other statins, it also reduced triglyceride levels. However, Zocor and Pravachol both had demonstrated a reduction of morbidity and mortality among high-risk patients, and WL had no such data,[13] although Lipitor benefited from a positive class effect.

EVIDENCE-BASED POSITIONING

Positioning was data-driven and stressed Lipitor's high potency in LDL reduction and its triglyceride indication. It was also priced lower than Zocor—but price alone would not have triggered success. Bayer's Baycol (cerivastatin) was launched shortly after Lipitor as a lower-cost statin, but without a performance advantage; it achieved peak sales of only $550 million in 2000 and was later withdrawn because of adverse reactions.

Aggressive Prelaunch Strategy

A key part of Lipitor's success was its powerful premarketing. Because of a combined Pfizer/WL salesforce of more than 2,000 representatives, 86,000 U.S. physicians were visited before launch. In addition, an intensive journal advertising program emphasized Lipitor's power with a "Make it your goal standard #1" theme and quantified the product's performance.

Pfizer and Warner-Lambert also gained credibility by collaborating with the American Heart Association in a "Cholesterol Low Down Campaign" to promote national guidelines and educate consumers about the risks of hyperlipidemia. Marketing materials were science-driven, citing certain risk factors for heart disease before the American Heart Association officially communicated these in *Circulation* in September 1999. Pharmacists were also targeted with initiatives such as an alliance with CVS to provide screening and education about lipid management. Teaching the science behind the brand was done through a major medical education program.[14]

Key Success Factors

Key success factors identified by WL and Pfizer management were:

- Right starting dose and comparative trial data.
- Correct pricing and managed care strategy.
- Evidence-based positioning.
- High prelaunch investments.
- Solid manufacturing capability.
- Decentralization allowing quick decisions and implementation.

Remaining Challenges

Management recognized that two areas were suboptimal: WL was too slow in starting long-term morbidity/mortality studies, and some aspects of the global strategy were inadequate. The speed of geographic expansion broke records (20 countries in the first year on market and more than 50 by the second year), and good local partners were found in Italy and Spain—but it had a late launch in Brazil and France (April 1998). WL was also too slow in developing trademarks. As a result, Lipitor was marketed as Sortis in Germany, Tahor in France, and Citalor in Brazil.[15]

By 2002, Lipitor had become the world leader, not only in its class but also across all categories. However, the future was uncertain. AstraZeneca's second-generation statin Crestor was looming, with preliminary clinical results showing a superior performance, but it would take years before AstraZeneca could match Lipitor's cumulative clinical data. On the bright side, new 2001 guidelines by the National Cholesterol Education Program were expected to expand greatly the number of treated U.S. patients. Whatever its future, Lipitor remained a good example to follow for biotechs expanding into mass-market categories. Biopharma marketers could derive several key lessons from these examples:

- Hybrid marketing applies across categories, as consumers are increasingly knowledgeable and respond to data-driven differentiation.
- In critical therapeutic areas, consumers get involved and drive demand at the earliest development stage, as the Gleevec case showed; it is critical to leverage the power of patient advocates together with that of medical opinion leaders.
- For biologics and targeted small molecules, early insights from patients and physicians and a sustained education program are both critical; Gleevec demonstrates that, even with motivated patients and specialized physicians, issues such as response markers and appropriate dosing persist well after launch.
- Some mass-market success factors also apply to biotech products as they expand into primary care categories. Lipitor is a good example; its key differentiator was its superior performance, communicated in a well-timed sequence of prelaunch medical education and disease awareness campaign.

GLOBAL BRAND-BUILDING STRATEGIES

Both targeted and mass therapies need to gain a global scale to recover their research costs. Three principles that apply equally to both models are:

1. Winning over time.
2. Winning over space.
3. Balancing global planning and local execution.

Recent launches such as Viagra and Celebrex have shown that drugs that achieve the $1 billion level the fastest are also the ones that have near-simultaneous launches in the major global markets. There is also clear evidence that the key to reaching megabrand status is a very early interface of marketing and R&D. Finally, a balance needs to be struck between global and local brand components, given worldwide variances in treatments, physician attitudes, and consumer preferences.

DRIVERS AND BARRIERS OF GLOBAL BRANDING

Global branding is easier for targeted drugs. Their specialist audiences are tightly linked worldwide, and treatment algorithms tend to be standardized. They also have Web-enabled global patient communities. Pricing varies less for customized drugs because their use is mandatory in life-threatening diseases and they have no generic competition. One major issue for biologics is the global shortage of protein production capacity. Enbrel lost as much as $200 million in sales in 2001 because of a production shortfall, and its new plant will not be operational until 2003. While nearly 100 biologics are in late development stages, new dedicated plants cost $300 million to $500 million and may take five years to build. Contract manufacturers such as Lonza Biologics and Boehringer Ingelheim now supplement major producers such as Amgen, Biogen, Genentech, and IDEC, and production volume is projected to grow by 200 percent in the next four to five years, but this may not be adequate. In addition, manufacturing issues have caused not only supply delays but also approval delays; Wyeth and Aviron's FluMist spray, Xoma/Genentech's psoriasis drug Xanelim, and IDEC's NHL drug Zevalin were all delayed because of FDA concerns about manufacturing.[16]

By contrast, mass-market drugs generally have no availability problems but face other globalization barriers. Government payers are restricting reimbursement on "me-too" drugs. In addition, categories such as allergy or menopause have wide variances in treatment protocols and consumer attitudes.

A controversial issue is the profit impact of globalization. On the positive side, speed to global markets is directly related to reaching the billion-dollar level. A negative factor is the fact that global consistency in packaging and trademarks may increase parallel imports. The argument that high launch expenditures ($150 to $350 million) are more efficiently spent on global campaigns does not hold—DTC is restricted to the United States, and medical marketing needs to be partly localized, which offsets the potential cost savings from a global approach. The key benefit of global branding is *scientific consistency*—uniform clinical profile and opinion leader influence in shaping the brand's identity. Figure 5.6 illustrates these drivers and barriers of globalization.

WINNING OVER TIME

The current group of megabrands has a time to peak sales that is three to five times faster than that of the previous generation: Celebrex reached a record $1.5 billion in its first year on world markets. This can be achieved only by an extensive premarketing process, starting as early as five years

FIGURE 5.6   Global Branding: Drivers and Barriers

	Targeted Drug	Mass Market Drug
Drivers	← Clinical Profile Consistency →	
	← E-trial management →	
	← Opinion leader management →	
	←Simultaneous registration →	
	Global treatment algorithms	Converging protocols
	Global specialist community	Global top tier physicians
	Global Web-enabled patient community	Global disease awareness via Internet
	←Revenue impact of fast globalization →	
Barriers	Pricing less problematic (breakthrough drugs)	Reference pricing/ reimbursement constraints
	Availability/protein production shortage	Few supply problems
	Technical complexity prevents parallel trade	Risk of parallel imports
	Low variance in prescribing (critical therapeutic areas)	Variance in prescribing patterns and consumer preferences

Source: Françoise Simon/SDC Group, 2002.

before launch. The combination of faster development, premarketing, and a global rollout is key to a rapid product uptake. When Celebrex was launched, nearly 90 percent of U.S. primary-care practitioners were aware of it. Prelaunch planning is also critical to extend the lifecycle: Phase IV clinicals leading to new indications and new patents are the most solid way to expand the market continuously.

Medical Leadership Strategy

The key to a seamless lab-to-market process is an alignment of marketing outreach and development efficiency. For both targeted and mass-market drugs, the crucial players are opinion leaders. Currently, 20 percent of the marketing budget is spent, on average, before launch—this is likely to increase in coming years; up to half is spent on development of opinion leaders because these experts have a unique ability to create medical brand equity for a new therapy.

As early as the preclinical stage, they can communicate unmet medical needs and shape the design and endpoints of Phases I and II clinical trials. Thought leaders should also be segmented at that stage. First, a global advisory panel provides epidemiological and attitudinal input from key world markets. Later, regional thought leaders should participate in Phase III trials. Closer to launch, national leaders can be part of a speaker program.[17]

Clinical trials are the most credible and powerful form of marketing in the prelaunch period. As investigators present findings at key conferences, they help establish global treatment algorithms and, if results support it, shape a drug's identity as the new gold standard. Large-scale Phase III trials also create a sizable body of early adopters. Merck conducts 35 percent of its trials outside the United States and enrolled 8,000 patients in 40 countries for its Vioxx trials—thereby creating significant preawareness. Opinion leaders also drive the second-most crucial premarketing component, that is, publications. There is a close correlation between successful launches and aggressive publication programs. Category leaders such as Pfizer's antibiotic Zithromax (azithromycin) and the BMS anticancer drug Taxol (paclitaxel) had significantly more published articles than their competitors.

Salesforce Strategy

Another premarketing feature of blockbusters is their early share of detail voice. Lipitor promotion to U.S. primary-care practitioners started six months before launch, and it reached a 30 percent share of voice at launch. Specialty drugs have an advantage at this stage because their salesforces are vastly smaller. While 3,000 representatives are the minimum in the United States alone for a blockbuster, a specialized drug targeting transplantation surgeons can be effectively launched with 15 salespeople. Given global communications within the medical community, it is important that sales-forces of any size receive globally standardized training and incentives.

Consumer Outreach

It is increasingly clear that DTC is not necessary for the early success of bio-pharma products. While Celebrex and Vioxx had some of the heaviest DTC adspend, consumer advertising did not start until six months after launch. Lipitor's early success resulted entirely from its performance and ex-tensive medical marketing; DTC did not begin until 18 months postlaunch.

An area of divergence between targeted and mass-market drugs is mar-ket research. While a specialty market can be viewed through the eyes of opinion leaders, extensive consumer research is needed for high-prevalence diseases, as well as when a new market is created. Before the launch of the Novartis antidiabetic Starlix (nateglinide), more than 10,000 people were screened in Europe and the United States, and 10.4 percent were found to have a glucose spike after meals—a key differentiator for Starlix was the control of these glucose spikes. For its irritable bowel syndrome drug Zelmac/Zelnorm (tegaserod), Novartis also did large-scale surveys of physicians as well as consumers leading to attitudinal segmentation (e.g., preference for medical treatment versus lifestyle change).

WINNING OVER SPACE

Across industry sectors, the challenge of global marketing is the trade-offs it presents between central efficiency and local responsiveness and between scale economies and market focus. Companies tend to reconcile these by fo-cusing resources on key markets and by ensuring coordination through global brand teams. Figure 5.7 illustrates global tradeoffs.

While biotechs and pharmas share a need for global scale, their geo-graphic expansion strategies differ because of their respective resource lev-els and because of the nature of their products. Because biologics are subject to central registration in Europe, they gain EU approval in one

FIGURE 5.7   Global Marketing Trade-Offs

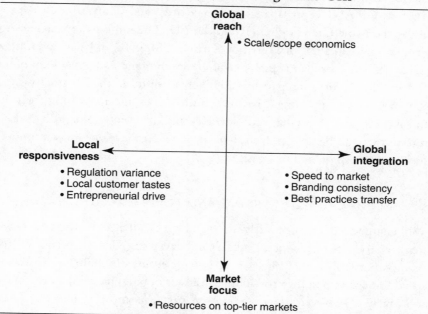

Source: Françoise Simon/SDC Group, 2002.

step. Recent drugs such as Amgen's second-generation anemia drug Aranesp (darbepoetin alfa) were explicitly developed as global products and gained fast approvals in major markets. In 2001, Aranesp was approved in the United States, most European countries, Australia, and New Zealand for the treatment of anemia associated with chronic renal failure.

Amgen: Toward a Global Strategy

While Amgen operates as a global company, other top-tier biotechs such as Genentech delegate ex-U.S. sales to marketing partners. Many of these alliances have led to underperformance in non-U.S. markets. As biotechs become global category leaders in areas such as oncology, they need to assume more direct control over their cross-border marketing.

Most top-tier biotechs are still U.S.-dominated—with exceptions such as Serono and Celltech.

In its early years, Amgen focused on the U.S. market and formed a successful joint venture, Kirin-Amgen, with Japan's Kirin in 1984, in order to address ex-U.S. markets. Neupogen (filgrastim) is marketed by its developer Kirin as GRAN(R) in Japan, Taiwan, Korea, and China and by Roche under the name Granulokine (R) in the EU. The same pattern applies to Epogen (epoetin alfa), marketed by Kirin as ESPO(R) in Japan and China and by J&J in other countries. This difference in brand names does not build global brand equity, and partners are likely to differ in their marketing approaches. However, Amgen has now built a sales and marketing force in Europe, Canada, Australia, and New Zealand. It recently bought back European rights to Neupogen from Roche, and it has developed new products such as Aranesp on a global basis.[18]

BALANCING GLOBAL PLANNING AND LOCAL EXECUTION

While targeted drugs have fairly uniform target audiences worldwide, mass-market products face widespread cultural variances. The main tradeoff for them is between global integration (which ensures branding consistency, speed to market, and the cross-border transfer of best practices) and local responsiveness (which reflects regulation variance and differing customer tastes and also supports the entrepreneurial drive of country managers).

A consensus has emerged on the marketing activities that should be centrally planned versus those that can be locally adapted. Brand positioning (including clinical performance, major differentiator, and key messages) is centralized—but based on a clinical profile developed with early input from the main markets worldwide. While packaging varies, components that support the brand identity, such as symbol, logo, and trademark, are standardized—but uncontrollable factors often arise concerning the trade name. While companies begin a name search as early as Phase I or II, it is increasingly difficult to find candidates that are not high-risk or already taken in at least one major market.

Another difficulty is that the FDA does not approve names until late in the development process, which results in last-minute changes. Astra had to change the Losec name for its antiulcerant omeprazole to Prilosec to avoid confusion with Lasix (furosemide). Lilly also had to change the name of its sepsis drug Zovant (drotrecogin) to Xigris in the United States.[19] Other aspects of global marketing that vary because of market conditions are pricing, channels, and media mix (DTC through mass media in the United States but only disease awareness via the Internet in other countries). This variance is shown in Figure 5.8 with the Prilosec case.

FIGURE 5.8   Global Scope—Prilosec Case

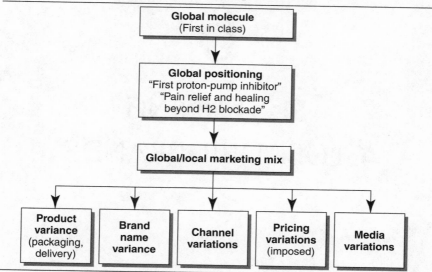

Source: Françoise Simon/SDC Group, 2002.

SUMMARY POINTS

Key biobranding success factors are:

✓ Adopt evidence-based marketing for targeted drugs and also use it to support the clinical profile of mass-market drugs.

✓ Include genotypes, technographics, and attitudinal traits such as proactiveness in segmentation bases.

✓ Retain a mass-market model for drugs targeting high-prevalence disease areas but support it with science-driven marketing.

✓ Accelerate time to peak sales with early marketing input into the development process.

✓ Increase speed to global markets with simultaneous registrations and multicountry launches.

✓ Balance centralized branding components (strategic positioning, key message) and localized components (advertising execution, packaging, channels).

SUSTAINING
GLOBAL BIOBRANDS

If you are fortunate enough to have a product on the market, you have a duty to maximize it.

Thomas Ebeling, CEO, Novartis[1]

For a while, the industry could patch the time between cycles. Now, the cyclical nature of the industry is more visible.

Jean-Pierre Garnier, CEO, GlaxoSmithKline[2]

After sailing through many decades of what appeared to be a bulletproof insulation from business cycles, the biosector is now facing an unprecedented triple squeeze: declining productivity from traditional R&D, long time frame for a postgenomics payoff, and a flood of patent expirations. Pharmaceuticals generating nearly $33 billion in U.S. sales are projected to lose their market exclusivity in the 2002 to 2007 period, and the impact of this trend is already rocking the industry.[3] Merck faces a wave of patent expirations from 2000 to 2005, eroding its cardiovascular and gastrointestinal franchises.[4]

This is a sharp escalation from earlier patent expirations, which themselves destroyed companies: After Syntex lost exclusivity on its analgesic naproxen, it was taken over by Roche in 1994—and Roche itself had been badly shaken by the patent expiry of its best-selling Valium (diazepam). Entire franchises are now at stake. For Schering-Plough, the Claritin family represented one-third of net sales in 2001, and it decreased by more than 40 percent in the 2001 to 2002 period.

On the biotech side, the first generation of blockbuster products is maturing, and companies are now feeling a sharp need to renew their portfolios. Unlike pharmaceuticals, biologics are not currently exposed to generic competition. In the United States, the Hatch-Waxman Act of 1984, facilitating approval for generic drugs, did not include provisions for biologics because these were largely undeveloped at that time. The Food and Drug Administration (FDA) is not recommending regulatory changes, given the difficulty of showing equivalence between macromolecules, but U.S. legislators are starting to examine this area. A bill was introduced to open the way for generic biotechs; these are already sold in Eastern Europe and Asia. Companies such as Ivax and Israel's Teva sell generic biologics ex-U.S. or expect to do so. This matters to many first-generation biotechs, whose patents on drugs worth more than $10 billion a year are set to expire in 2002 to 2006.[5]

However, the uptake of biogenerics will be slowed by entry barriers such as high manufacturing and approval costs, as well as high marketing costs to promote product safety to physicians and consumers.[6]

In the next five years, top-tier biotechs are expected to sustain a high level of growth in earnings per share. Only Pfizer is projected to match their rates among Big Pharma firms.[7] To maintain growth, large biotechs will need not only sustained innovation, but also aggressive *portfolio, franchise,* and *brand management.* In these areas, they can learn a lot from Big Pharma and its enduring brands.

This chapter focuses on sustaining strategies at these three levels. (See Figure 6.1.)

MANAGING PORTFOLIOS AND TIMELINES

Among value-sustaining strategies, the highest return comes from portfolio management; as diversification decreases the risk of dependence on one or two therapeutic areas, franchise management is also critical because

FIGURE 6.1   Sustaining Biobrands

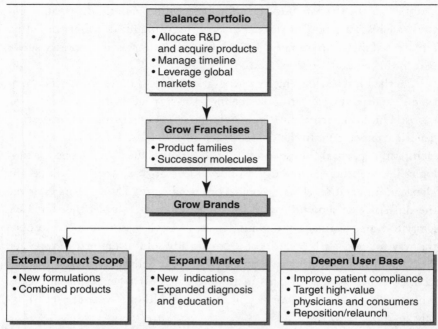

Source: Françoise Simon/SDC Group, 2002.

well-timed successor products can seamlessly transfer brand equity from first- to second-generation molecules.

At the brand level, it is possible to optimize a product's life span with a combination of better diagnosis, new indications and formulations, and a deeper user base. The best example of this is aspirin, launched over 100 years ago and still a category leader. The optimization of a product's life span is shown in Figure 6.2 on page 156.

While few compounds have aspirin's therapeutic scope, it is possible to maximize most of them by integrating three tiers of *brand, franchise,* and *portfolio strategies.* Whereas the risks of undiversified portfolios are clear, many companies are still struggling with the "one-drug" syndrome. It is unavoidable for early stage biotechs but not viable for larger firms. The long-term answer is balanced research, but a shorter term measure is licensing. Genentech is an aggressive in-licenser in the biosector. To offset the slowing growth of its cardiovascular business, Genentech built an oncology franchise by sourcing Rituxan from IDEC and Tarceva (a small

ASPIRIN: THE UR—BIOBRAND

The longest life span on record belongs to aspirin. Its chemical precursor, salicin, was first described some 5,000 years ago in Sumerian clay tablets as a willow bark extract to treat rheumatism, and it was later used by Hippocrates to treat headaches and fever. In 1897, Bayer chemist Felix Hoffmann managed to acetylate the phenol group of salicylic acid, and aspirin was launched as the first truly synthetic drug—and the first mass-marketed brand. For its introduction, Bayer sent product information to 30,000 physicians, and by 1914, aspirin was a sizable brand. Even though foreign rights were confiscated as part of Germany's reparations after World War I, the product continued to thrive and Bayer paid $1 billion to win it all back in 1994. By then, aspirin was the number two product in the world in volume terms (after acetaminophen). In 1995, Bayer relaunched it in the United States, and the brand thereafter gained a leading category share. The key to the brand's durability was a sustained *investment in clinical studies* yielding new indications.[a]

In the 1980s, a key five-year study of male physicians showed a 44 percent reduction in heart attacks for those on aspirin therapy. The FDA expanded aspirin's labeling to include four areas: acute myocardial infarction, stroke prevention after transient ischemic attack, primary prevention of a first heart attack or stroke, and low-dose aspirin in stroke prevention. By 2002, 26 million Americans were taking aspirin for cardiac prevention, and low dose aspirin accounted for nearly 23 percent of the market. Studies linked aspirin use to a lower incidence of several cancers, including prostate, colorectal, and esophageal. Aspirin also showed promise in atherosclerosis and Alzheimer's disease.[b]

---

[a] "An Aspirin a Day Keeps the Doctor at Bay," *The Economist* (August 9, 1997), p. 69; "Comeback," *Med Ad News* (June 1996), pp. 3, 24–25; Taren Grom, "The Wonder Drug," *Med Ad News* (January 1999), pp. 26–27.
[b] "Aspirin: The Oldest New Wonder Drug," *Newsweek* (May 27, 2002), pp. 64–65.

molecule tyrosine kinase inhibitor) from OSI to supplement its own breast cancer therapy, Herceptin.[8]

In addition to portfolio management, franchise management is the key to long-term protection of brand equities. At first, this relied on developing product families such as Lilly's insulin franchise. It also included product transfer, as Pfizer did when converting customers from Procardia

FIGURE 6.2   Optimized Biobranding

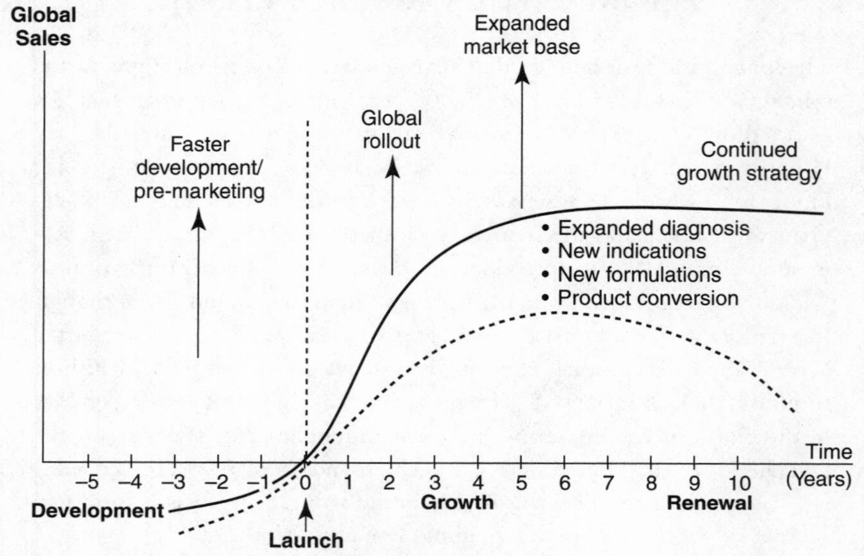

Source: Françoise Simon/SDC Group, 2002.

(nifedipine) to Norvasc (amlodipine) to extend its cardiovascular business. Franchise management now also includes equity transfer from the original to a successor molecule (single isomer or active metabolite). Aventis transferred its antihistamine Seldane's user base to Allegra (fexofenadine) after Seldane was withdrawn because of side effects.

At the brand level, growth strategies range from product extension (new formulations) to market expansion (new indications) and deeper user base penetration (improved compliance). (See Figure 6.3.)

An analysis of each strategy reveals that key success factors are flexibility and timing.

BALANCING PORTFOLIOS

Proactive portfolio planning is more effective and less costly than a defensive approach. Many firms have long relied on one or two dominant products and taken remedial actions only when these were nearing the end of their patent lives.

FIGURE 6.3   Value-Sustaining Strategies

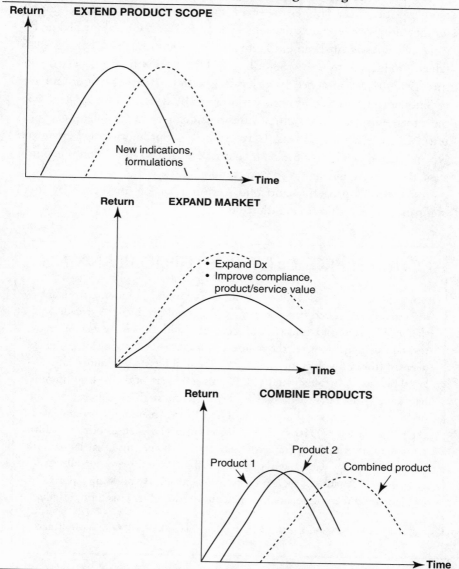

Source: Françoise Simon/SDC Group, 2002; partly adapted from R. Findlay, "A Compelling Case for Brand Building," *Pharmaceutical Executive* (February 1998), p. 78.

Defensive, late-stage in-licensing continues to be very expensive, and mergers—often the last resort—even more so. After two mergers partly prompted by key patent expirations such as Zantac's, GlaxoSmithKline became an aggressive in-licenser to remedy a genericization problem. By 2005, Glaxo products with nearly $8 billion in U.S. sales will face generic exposure. By 2001, it had signed 10 major deals with partners ranging from Bayer to Shionogi. In part to replace its withdrawn IBS drug Lotronex, Glaxo outbid others with its $270 million offer to Adolor for a late-phase gastrointestinal drug. In osteoporosis, Glaxo signed a copromotion agreement on Roche's ibandronate, but took a higher risk with a $150 million preclinical stage deal with Unigene on an oral compound.[9]

By contrast, proactive portfolio planning can be done even by small companies as the Cubist case illustrates.

CUBIST: PROACTIVE PORTFOLIO PLANNING

Among small biotechs, Cubist has shown flexibility in moving from anti-infective discovery to drug delivery and natural products. A decade ago, the need for new anti-infectives became clear with the emergence of drug-resistant pathogens. After the failure of three early collaborations, Cubist licensed from Lilly daptomycin, a Phase III antibiotic; after launch was delayed because of stricter standards, Cubist used part of the $140 million it had raised in 2000 to diversify. It partnered with Emisphere for an oral formulation of daptomycin and started work on an oral version of Rocephin (ceftriaxone), Roche's $1 billion intravenous antibiotic. In addition, Cubist acquired TerraGen Discovery on the premise that its natural products libraries were likely to yield antibiotics and were not subject to competition because of their process complexities. By building a portfolio of niche products and technologies, Cubist reduced its risk substantially.[*]

---

[*] Jeffrey Dvorin, "Cubist: The Virtues of Pipeline Diversification," *In Vivo* (April 2002), p. 100.

Leveraging Ex-U.S. Markets

Ex-U.S. markets can also be used for creative sourcing, as midsize pharma company Forest has done. After in-licensing antidepressant Celexa (citalopram) from Denmark's Lundbeck and launching it in the United States in 1998, Forest copromoted it at first with Warner–Lambert (WL). After WL's acquisition, it went solo with an expanded salesforce. Celexa is now the fastest growing selective serotonin reuptake inhibitor (SSRI), thanks to its better tolerability and 20 percent price discount over competitors. To offset the fact that Celexa now accounts for almost 70 percent of revenues, Forest has licensed other drugs from European firms, including compounds for hypertension from Italy's Recordati and for alcohol addiction from Merck KGaA's subsidiary Lipha. Given Celexa's 2005 patent expiration, Forest developed its successor Lexapro (escitalopram) on the basis of an efficacy advantage.[10]

VALUE-SUSTAINING GROWTH STRATEGIES

Long-term sustainability involves early planning as well as a full range of strategies. In addition to portfolio and franchise management, brand strategies have two distinct forms, pre- and postpatent expiry. In the growth phase, new formulations and new indications have the highest long-term value because they bring new patents. Market expansion can help, especially in underdiagnosed areas such as osteoporosis. Product combinations also offer new patents; Glaxo Wellcome pioneered HIV therapeutics with the 1987 launch of Retrovir (zidovudine), which peaked in 1996 at $472 million in sales. In 1995, Glaxo launched Epivir (lamivudine), which soon led its class and reached sales of $668 million by 1997. That same year, Glaxo combined them into Combivir, a twice-daily single tablet that was more effective than either drug in monotherapy. While the first two products would lose market exclusivity in 2005 and 2009, the combined form extended the franchise to 2012. Two years later, Combivir achieved better sales than either of its parent molecules (more than $700 million)—but it also cannibalized both, especially Retrovir. The franchise was later expanded with a triple combination branded as Trizivir.[11] Figure 6.3 illustrates these growth strategies.

MANAGING TIMELINES

In addition to portfolio strategies, *early planning* is critical to sustain ability. The consensus is that value protection strategies should start at least five years before patent expiry, and some approaches, such as multiple

DIVERSIFYING AMGEN'S PORTFOLIO

When Amgen bought Immunex, it was counting on Enbrel's $3 billion peak sales potential. To Amgen, however, Enbrel was not just a product, it was a *franchise anchor* and a *pipeline*. The FDA had approved it for psoriatic arthritis in January 2002, and it had a potential for multiple indications. It would also complement Kineret (anakinra), FDA-approved in late 2001 for rheumatoid arthritis and acquired with Synergen in 1994.

In addition to this new inflammation business, Amgen planned to rejuvenate its older franchises with two successors, Aranesp (darbepoetin alfa) and Neulasta (pegfilgrastim). The original molecules, Epogen and Neupogen, reached combined global sales of $3.7 billion in 2002.[a] Epogen was approved in 1989 for anemia-related chronic renal failure, and Neupogen, a recombinant G-CSF (granulocyte colony-stimulating factor), was launched two years later to treat chemotherapy-induced neutropenia. Their successor molecules had a longer serum half-life and could be administered less frequently—but would face strong competition. Since the 1985 partial license of epoetin alfa to J&J, the two brands were restricted to different U.S. markets. Aranesp had no such restrictions and would compete directly against Procrit and its marketing machine—a salesforce doubled to 600 and heavy promotion, including nearly $80 million in DTC advertising since 1998.[b] Neulasta also faced competition from Novartis and Chugai products.

Amgen was relying on alliances and expected half of its future therapeutics to be externally sourced. The most recent partners included Isis (antisense drug discovery), Acadia (small molecules), and Hyseq (development of Amgen's clot-dissolving Alfimeprase). This would supplement internal R&D; research expenditure reached over $1 billion in 2002, or 20 percent of revenue.[c] For Amgen, the upside was a $3 billion potential for each of three major franchises.

---

[a] Amgen press release, "On an Adjusted Basis Amgen Reports 4th Quarter EPS Increase 17 Percent," January 23, 2003.

[b] Arlene Weintraub and Amy Barrett, "Up from Biotech," *BusinessWeek* (March 18, 2002), pp. 71–72.

[c] Amgen press release, "On an Adjusted Basis Amgen Reports 4th Quarter EPS Increase 17 Percent," January 23, 2003.

indications, should be started during development. Because clinicals are needed to obtain exclusivity, even an OTC switch should be planned at least three years ahead.[12] The risks involved in delays are illustrated in a high-profile example, Schering-Plough's megafranchise Claritin.

This case demonstrates the importance of timing. Whereas SP had developed its line extensions early and well, it was late on strategies such as combined products. A partnership with Merck on a combination of Claritin and Merck's asthma drug Singulair was initiated only in May 2000. By

A DEFENSIVE APPROACH: THE CLARITIN SAGA

To protect its core franchise, Schering-Plough (SP) engaged in protracted legal maneuvers, but it was ultimately forced to switch Claritin to OTC status in a reversal of its earlier position. SP had fully used line extensions, from Claritin Syrup to RediTabs; the line generated 2001 sales of nearly $3.2 billion, or a third of revenues. Claritin's metabolite Clarinex could extend patent protection to 2014 (for rights licensed from Sepracor) and to 2019 (U.S. formulation patent).

However, quality control problems in manufacturing had delayed the approval of Clarinex. SP had never sought approval for two dosages of Claritin, which would have allowed an earlier OTC switch (with dual Rx/OTC marketing), and it had not done new clinicals that would have secured three years of OTC patent protection.

Some insurers had stated that they might not reimburse Clarinex once OTC loratadine was available, because clinicals showed only a slight efficacy improvement for the metabolite.

Wellpoint Health Networks had also petitioned the FDA to classify Clarinex as an OTC drug. This posed a threat to the entire category. SP's approach also impacted its corporate image. At a 2001 FDA meeting, it had testified that an OTC switch would pose "a major health risk"—only to reverse itself less than a year later when it filed an sNDA (supplementary new drug application) in March 2002 to cover all five formulations of Claritin for all indications.*

---

* "Schering-Plough's About-Face on OTC Claritin," *In Vivo* (April 2002), pp. 3, 8.

January 2002, Phase III trial results did not show sufficient added benefits in the treatment of seasonal allergic rhinitis.[13]

For optimum value protection, all applicable strategies should be pursued in parallel, starting well before launch:

- Multiple indications and patents—development stage.
- Market expansion (disease awareness/detection)—before launch.
- Reformulations, successors, combined products—five to seven years before patent expiry.
- OTC switch clinicals (if applicable)—at least three years before patent expiry. (See Figure 6.4.)

Costs/Benefits of Key Strategies

On a cost versus return basis, *portfolio and franchise management* clearly scores highest of all strategies—if undertaken in a timely manner.

At the brand level, the best ways to add value are *new formulations* and *multiple indications*—but new formulations have an edge because they can lead to dual patents (e.g., compound and device patents for an asthma nebulizer), and a family of line extensions adds an "umbrella equity." Because basic safety and efficacy data are known, new trial costs range from only

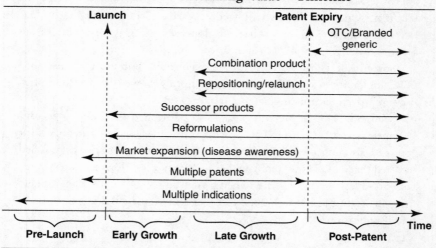

FIGURE 6.4　Sustaining Value—Timeline

Source: Françoise Simon/SDC Group, 2002.

$10 million to $50 million. Potential returns justify the cost: Extended-release Procardia XL brought Pfizer an additional $8 billion in the 1990 to 1998 period, for instance.

Multiple indications are most effective when planned early (Phase III clinicals, if possible, and Phase IV in any case). They also have a high return because they lead to new patents and expand the market base—but other products may be prescribed off-label for the same indications. *Combined products* also lead to new patents, but their return is lower if one of the products is externally sourced because partners share the profits.

Deeper penetration of the user base is possible by increasing service value or improving patient compliance (less than 50 percent in asymptomatic diseases).

FIGURE 6.5   Value Protection Strategies—Cost/Benefit

	Time needed	Cost	Technical/ legal feasibility	New revenue generation	Long-term return	Applicability across categories
Portfolio management	●	●	◑	●	●	●
Franchise management/ product conversion	●	◕	◑	●	●	◑
Multiple indications	●	◕	◑	◕	◕	◕
New formulations	◑	◑	◑	●	●	◕
Combined products	◔	◑	◑	◑	◑	◔
Deeper penetration (compliance, service)	◔	◔	◔	◔	◔	◔
Patent maximization	◔	◔	◔	◔	○	◑
Status change (OTC, generic)	◑	◑	◑	○	○	○

Low ——— Medium ⟶ High

Source: Françoise Simon/SDC Group, 2002; partly adapted from *Countdown to Patent Expiry,* Datamonitor (July 2000), p. 101.

Patent maximization is the most controversial strategy. Again, early planning is key, as a broad initial patent portfolio may cover compounds as well as processes and methods of use. The next chapter addresses this strategy. Figure 6.5 summarizes the cost/benefit profile of these approaches.

An in-depth look at how biotechs and pharma companies have used these strategies further pinpoints their key success factors.

GROWING FRANCHISES

Biopharma companies can optimize lifecycles by growing their original franchises. Lilly provides an example of franchise extension over an exceptional time period.

LILLY: THE FIRST BIOTECH FRANCHISE

The first and most durable biotech franchise is Lilly's endocrinology business. It grew over nearly 80 years to reach more than $3 billion in sales by 2002.

Lilly's diabetes care business started in 1923 with the launch of Iletin, the world's first insulin product, sourced from Frederick Banting and Charles Best of the University of Toronto. A second breakthrough occurred in 1982 with the launch of Humulin, a human insulin sourced from Genentech—and the first therapeutic using recombinant DNA technology. Humulin reached peak sales of more than $1 billion before its U.S. patent expired in 2001; before that, Lilly had started to switch its user base to Humalog (insulin lispro), a fast-acting insulin analog with greater dosing convenience and improved glucose control. From 1998 to 2002, Humalog sales grew from $130 million to over $830 million, and a new formulation (Humalog Mix 75/25 Pen) was launched in 2000. Humalog was patent-protected in the United States until 2013. Lilly also licensed oral diabetes drug Actos (pioglitazone) from Takeda in 1999, yielding by 2002 a $392 million share of revenues to Lilly; it was patent-protected until 2006. Whereas Lilly did not have another diabetes blockbuster in its pipeline, a related product was a protein kinase C beta for diabetic retinopathy and macular edema, expected to be launched in 2004 to 2005. Other endocrinology products were Evista (raloxifene), with 2002 sales of $822 million, and Fortéo (teriparatide). In 2002, the endocrinology business accounted for more than $3 billion in global sales.[14]

Lilly's neuroscience franchise was still dominant with more than $4 billion in 2002 global sales. While the Prozac franchise had lost more than 60 percent of its sales revenue in 2001 to 2002, antipsychotic Zyprexa (olanzapine) was the first-ever neuroscience brand to pass $3 billion in worldwide sales and had reached nearly $3.7 billion by 2002.

Lilly's late-stage pipeline included 10 potential new products in 2002 to 2005. R&D spending reached more than $2 billion in 2002, that is, 19 percent of sales, and in-licensing continued with several molecules externally sourced.[15] This growth potential had alleviated the loss of the U.S. patent for Prozac, which led to a sharp sales erosion.

The implication for marketers is that portfolio and franchise management can mitigate brand problems. Lilly's R&D investment and growth in the endocrinology and oncology franchises had alleviated the loss of the U.S. patent for Prozac.

GROWING BRANDS

Successful biobrands, from Neupogen to Lipitor, have maintained strong growth through three main strategies:

1. *Extending the brand scope* with new formulations or combined products.
2. *Expanding the market base* with new indications and better awareness/detection.
3. *Deepening the user base* with improved compliance, high-value segmentation, and, if applicable, repositioning or relaunch.

EXTENDING BRAND SCOPE: NEW FORMULATIONS

Reformulations are a high-cost, high-reward approach. Together with successor brands, they offer long-term revenue protection but need substantial time and investment. Their cost/benefit profile is as follows:

	Benefits	*Requirements*
Time	Long-term added exclusivity (10 years from new patent).	Trials to begin five years before patent expiry.
Market	Drug improvement may expand share in new segments.	Need to prove unmet therapeutic need.
Return	Multibillion dollar level for a blockbuster.	Cost of clinicals in $10 to $50 million range.
Impact	Strengthens and renews franchise.	May cannibalize original molecule.

Reformulations often do not reach their full potential because of *timing errors*. Given the minimal one-year time frame needed for a conversion, clinicals should start about five years before patent expiry—but they may be done at a fraction of the cost of a new product. Again, evidence-based marketing applies, and the reformulation has to fulfill a true unmet need and offer tangible benefits in terms of efficacy, tolerability, ease of use, compliance, or cost.

A new delivery system may meet a true therapeutic need, but it carries some risk. Pfizer's Procardia XL, based on an extended-release delivery system, had an improved uptake and convenient once-daily dosing.[16] However, delivery systems are also open to legal challenges.

Sandimmun (cyclosporin), launched by Sandoz in 1983, was a breakthrough therapy for transplant rejection, but 50 percent of patients were poor absorbers and blood levels of the drug had to be constantly monitored. As its patent was expiring in the United States, a new formulation, Neoral, was approved in 1995. Its improved bioavailability filled a true need, due to a microemulsion technology that was patent-protected until 2010 in the United States. The company succeeded in switching about 90 percent of its patient base within 18 months, which was helped by a price advantage. Global sales reached more than $1.3 billion by 1999.

However, the FDA ruled in 1998 that Neoral was not a microemulsion, which allowed generic maker SangStat to claim bioequivalence for its own cyclosporin. Despite litigation by Novartis, generics from SangStat and Eon were approved in 2000. By 2002, Neoral sales had dropped 12 percent over the prior year, but growth ex-U.S. partly countered a decline in the United States, and global sales were still more than $1 billion. The product had two indications (transplantation and autoimmune diseases) and a wide range of formulations, from a capsule to an oral solution and intravenous infusion. Simulect (basiliximab), a complement to Neoral designed to prevent early graft rejection, contributed to the franchise with a significant rise in sales—albeit from a small base.[17]

COMBINATION PRODUCTS

The most ambitious initiative in this area was the May 2000 creation of Merck/Schering-Plough Pharmaceuticals to codevelop and comarket in the United States two combinations: Zocor (simvastatin) and Zetia (ezetimibe) for cholesterol management and Singulair (montelukast) and Claritin (loratadine) in the respiratory area.

The high stakes justified the expense of creating a separate entity. Zocor was a multibillion dollar brand, and the cholesterol-management market was one of the world's largest, with total sales projected to exceed $30 billion by 2007.

New U.S. guidelines from the National Cholesterol Education Program (NCEP) could almost triple the treatment-eligible population, from 15 to 36 million.[18]

While Zocor faced U.S. patent expiration in 2005, Zetia was patent-protected until 2015. In December 2001, Merck/SP filed a U.S. application for Zetia as monotherapy and in coadministration with a statin. Human clinicals started in 2001 for the combination, with an FDA submission planned for late 2003.[19]

EXPANDING THE MARKET: NEW INDICATIONS

Many best-selling biobrands, from Rituxan to Paxil, have built and maintained growth because of *sequences of new indications*. Multiple indication programs are a high-cost approach, but they expand the market as well as extend brand life. Their cost/benefit profile is shown in the following table:

	Benefits	*Requirements/Risks*
Time	Long-term added exclusivity (method of use patents).	Multiple clinicals, several years before patent expiry.
Market	Expand total market, bring in new patient segments.	Off-label drug use by competitors may erode the financial return.
Franchise Impact	Strengthen franchise, increase physician and patient loyalty.	May divert resources away from R&D for entirely new products.

Whereas new indications have a life extension potential equivalent to that of reformulations, because they garner new method of use patents, they may have a lower return due to the off-label use of competing products. As multiple indications are now often built into prelaunch development, their potential to prolong brand life at later stages will diminish, but they remain highly valuable.[20]

This is the case for Novartis' Gleevec, which was approved in February 2002 for its second indication in nine months—the treatment of gastrointestinal stromal tumors. Other studies are underway for solid tumors, prostate cancer, and other indications.[21]

New Indications: Growth Driver for Biologics

Genentech's Rituxan continues to achieve high growth rates. By 2002, sales passed the billion-dollar mark. It remains the only monoclonal antibody approved for non-Hodgkin's lymphoma (NHL)—a disease affecting about 300,000 people in the United States alone. Phase III clinicals for intermediate and high-grade NHL have a 2004 planned completion date.[22]

For earlier blockbusters, the key to sustained growth was also a steady stream of indications. Eleven years after its launch, Amgen's Neupogen reached sales of $1.4 billion in 2002, an 8 percent increase over 2000. It had obtained several new indications, including a new one every year in the 1993 to 1996 period: bone marrow transplant, severe chronic neutropenia, peripheral blood progenitor cell transplant, and acute myeloid leukemia.[23]

Impact of Publications

The direct impact of a *publication stream* supporting new indications can be documented, not only for biologics, but also for mass-market products. Merck's statin Zocor had 86 publications in the two years before its 1991 launch and reached 116 in the two years after. *Trial quality*—not just quantity—is what drives prescriptions. Merck generally delivers few flagship studies, but they tend to be the first in their class. In its landmark 4S study (Scandinavian Simvastatin Survival Study), Merck showed that high-risk individuals with heart disease and high LDL-cholesterol treated with Zocor experienced fewer deaths from heart disease and all causes after five years than those given a placebo. This was the first proof that a statin not only lowered cholesterol but also saved lives. Recent years have seen an escalation of publications, especially in crowded categories such as cardiovasculars. Introduced five years after Zocor, antihypertensive Cozaar (losartan) had more than 200 publications in its 1995 launch year and has collected nearly 3,000 since then. By 2002, the Cozaar family led its category with more than $2 billion in global sales.[24]

Multiple Indications: Differentiation Driver

Multiple indications can also protect equity by giving a brand a *unique position*. Among SSRIs, SmithKline Beecham's Paxil (paroxetine) came third to market in 1993, behind Prozac and Zoloft. Its clinical profile was not compelling, but it gained a unique position in 1996 with the first claims in its class for anxiety and OCD. SmithKline also undercut competitors on price, scaled up its salesforce, signed a copromotion with Janssen in the United States, and leveraged ex-U.S. markets. The publication strategy was aggressive, with more than 200 articles in the two postlaunch years versus about 100 for Zoloft. By 2002, Paxil was the category leader with more than $3 billion in global sales against $2.7 billion for Zoloft and only about $700 million for generic-eroded Prozac.[25]

Lipitor: A Full-Growth Portfolio

The most aggressive trial and publication strategy may belong to Lipitor. Pfizer's success came from a three-prong approach: initial clinical differentiation, follow-on studies for multiple indications, and massive sales and marketing investment. It had a very fast uptake, reaching more than $2 billion by its second year, and later sustained that growth. Zocor sales grew 48 percent from 1999 to 2001, but Lipitor rose by 67 percent in the same period.

The scale of its Phase IV trials is massive—a probable half-billion dollars—which is justified by Lipitor's patent protection until at least 2009. At launch, Lipitor showed superior LDL cholesterol reduction, but could not match competitors' long-term studies. Pfizer therefore invested from the start in mortality and morbidity studies. Over 180 clinicals involving more than 100,000 patients worldwide will be conducted over the next several years to assess Lipitor in stroke prevention, osteoporosis, and Alzheimer's, as well as usage by diabetics and the elderly. Leaving no stone unturned, Pfizer is also testing a Lipitor/Norvasc combination.

Finally, Pfizer is taking full advantage of the stricter NCEP guidelines to step up its already-intense *sales and marketing effort.* In addition to its 5,000-strong, top-rated salesforce, Lipitor has consistently been one of the most promoted brands in medical journals. Pfizer also started in late 2001 a new consumer campaign supported by the lipitor.com Web site to propel 30 million Americans with untreated high cholesterol to their doctors' offices. The campaign has a branded component targeting patients diagnosed with high cholesterol but untreated, and the unbranded part addresses high-risk consumers who have not yet been diagnosed. It is supported by professional education programs emphasizing the new guidelines.[26]

Fosamax: Creating a Market

Whereas Lipitor entered a mature market as the fifth statin in its class, Merck's Fosamax (alendronate sodium) was first in class, but osteoporosis was plagued with low awareness. Fosamax had a fairly slow uptake, passing the billion-dollar mark by 1999 after a 1995 launch; energized by a new formulation, it reached over $2 billion in worldwide sales in 2002.[27] Merck's three-prong strategy focused on:

1. Expanding diagnosis.
2. Obtaining multiple indications.
3. Developing new formulations.

In-licensed from Italy's Istituto Gentili, Fosamax was a first-in-class amino-biphosphonate, FDA-approved in 1995 for the treatment of post-menopausal osteoporosis (PMO). The market was vast (nearly $5 billion worldwide) and growing by 17 to 26 percent annually. A 2000 study showed a prevalence of 30 million among women over age 50 in the United States, the EU "Big Five," and Japan. Of these, only a third were diagnosed and 22 percent were drug-treated.

However, there was no globally accepted disease definition; some physicians defined PMO by fracture, others by low bone mass. Treatment patterns varied widely. Calcitonin and vitamin D were well entrenched in Japan, while fluoride was widespread in Germany and an older biphosphonate, P&G's Didronel, was the U.K. market leader. PMO was underdiagnosed: Outside the United States, few sites had equipment to measure bone mineral density (BMD)—and it was not reimbursed in countries such as France and Spain. Fosamax itself was reimbursed only for PMO with fracture in France, Italy, and Australia.

To develop the U.S. market, Merck had taken equity positions in BMD equipment manufacturers. Merck also funded and managed the National Osteoporosis Risk Assessment program, the largest-ever patient registry including more than 150,000 women over age 50 with no prior PMO diagnosis; early findings suggested that roughly half had low bone mass. This had results: In 1995 to 2000, BMD sites had grown tenfold, to more than 7,500 nationwide. Lower-cost scanners had appeared ($25,000 to $35,000 range), the cost of a test had dropped to less than $30 for pDEXA technology, and a 1998 new Medicare benefit standardized BMD test coverage.

Merck had also obtained approval for three *new indications*. In addition to the initial 1995 approval of PMO treatment (10 mg) and Paget's Disease (40 mg), they were:

	U.S. Launch	Ex-U.S. Launch
PMO Prevention (5 mg)	2Q97	4Q97
Glucocorticoid-induced osteoporosis (5/10 mg)	3Q99	4Q98
Male osteoporosis (10 mg)	4Q00	4Q98
Once weekly formulation (35/70 mg)	4Q00	2Q00

The most effective growth strategy had been the November 2000 launch of a once-weekly (OW) formulation of 35 mg/70 mg. It carried the same price as the daily tablet, and it had immediately cannibalized the daily formula, but it had also grown overall Fosamax sales. While the original molecule patent would expire in 2008, Fosamax OW was patented until 2018. By 2002, it had been approved in more than 50 countries. New avenues arose with the doubts cast on HRT by the Women's Health Initiative Study, and Merck seized the opportunity in its DTC advertising and through increased salesforce emphasis on OB/GYNs.

Merck had managed the Fosamax timeline well, launching new indications and formulations well before patent expiry. However, competition was intensifying. Another biphosphonate, P&G's Actonel (risedronate) launched its own once-weekly formulation in 2002. In addition to its SERM Evista, Lilly had a first-in-class product, Fortéo (teriparatide), with a high efficacy but low tolerability. Pfizer expected to launch another SERM, lasofoxifene, in 2004, and Novartis, Roche, and Wyeth had pipeline candidates. Fosamax faced other challenges:

- Relatively low ex-U.S. sales.
- Delayed consumer marketing (branded DTC had started only in 2001).
- Low long-term compliance.
- Mixed class image due to reports of GI side effects (eased by the OW formula.
- Low franchise equity in women's health.
- Low diagnosis and treatment rates.
- Continued low diagnosis and treatment rates.

Demographic trends and the partial invalidation of HRT presented a good opportunity for Merck to continue building Fosamax brand equity worldwide—but this required a sustained investment in clinical development and marketing power.

DEEPEN THE USER BASE

While new formulations and indications are by far the best ways to add long-term value, another growth strategy is to expand the physician and patient base.

Compliance improvement, in particular, is one of the most underutilized approaches. It completes the continuum of consumer loyalty that starts from awareness and diagnosis and ends with the monitoring of treatment

FIGURE 6.6   Deepening the User Base

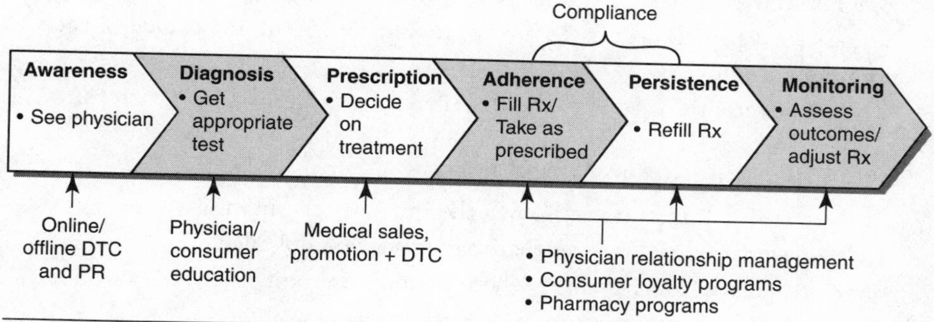

Source: Françoise Simon/SDC Group, 2002.

outcomes. It consists of *adherence* (filling an initial Rx and taking it as prescribed) and *persistence* (refilling the Rx as needed for chronic disease). Figure 6.6 describes this continuum of care.

From Market Share to Compliance Metrics

A key performance indicator for biobrands is *market share,* that is, the percentage of prescriptions sold for a product within its category. However, this tracks only one fraction of the care continuum and misses most of the brand value for chronic diseases, from diabetes to arthritis.

Market share metrics borrowed from consumer goods are inadequate for biobrands, which present a unique paradox: While a Jacuzzi or a heating pad is a one-time purchase and can be measured as such, a prescription for an antiarthritic drug requires *compliance* over time, that is, many repeat purchases and discipline in taking the product despite frequent side effects— and all this from a consumer who thoroughly resents being a "patient" and whose natural tendency is to deny her disease—especially when it is asymptomatic, such as osteoporosis. This leads to notoriously low compliance rates for most chronic categories. A study by the Brigham and Women's Hospital and Harvard School of Public Health focusing on cholesterol-reducing drugs showed that only 41 percent of patients were largely compliant during the first six months of therapy, and even fewer—30 percent—were compliant in the second six months.[28] In other studies, osteoporosis and HRT had an equally dismal compliance rate of 36 percent at 12 months.[29]

This disconnect between market share metrics and the cumulative value of compliance is especially important for high-price biologics. An arthritis patient who stays on Enbrel or Remicade for 12 months may generate more than $12,000 in prescription revenues. The fact that many biologics have small user bases further magnifies the annuity value of each retained patient.[30]

Patient retention strategy should, therefore, include these six steps:

1. Measure patient adherence and persistence.
2. Determine "stress points" with the greatest termination risk.
3. Uncover product features that may hinder compliance.
4. Understand "touchpoints" where patients are best reached.
5. Allocate resources to compliance programs.
6. Develop integrated physician and patient communications.

Permission Marketing: A Compliance Prerequisite

For this strategy to succeed, a prerequirement is permission marketing. Many compliance programs have proved ineffective or alienated physicians and consumers. A worst-case outcome was a class-action lawsuit against a pharmacy chain that had sent unsolicited refill reminders to its customers— many of whom saw it as an invasion of privacy.

While compliance always has limits, a degree of success comes from co-operation and integration:

- Measuring compliance is most effective via *alliances with managed care groups* because they have incentives to keep patients on medication— for antidepressants, the National Committee for Quality Assurance requires health plans to report persistence at three and six months.[31]
- *Stress points* appear in data from payers, pharmacy benefit managers (PBMs), and physicians. A first drop-off point, one month after an initial prescription, may be due to side effects.
- *Uncovering product features* that may prevent compliance is vital. Nebulizers and inhalers have a much lower compliance than pills, which could be countered by consumer education.
- *Understanding touchpoints* where patients may be reached is also critical to avoid alienating the user base. These are likely to include physicians' offices.
- Finally, *shifting some resources* from medical and DTC promotion to compliance programs should lead to a substantial long-term return.

LIFESTYLE SEGMENTS
AND COMPLIANCE

To explore why hypertension control rates had declined, a medical study sampled more than 700 hypertensive patients and showed a covariation between compliance and healthy lifestyles. Fifty-nine percent of respondents had made lifestyle changes, and nearly three-quarters were on long-term therapy, but 12 percent had stopped or decreased medication without consulting a physician. A full drug range was used, from diuretics (43 percent) to beta-blockers (25 percent) and angiotensin receptor blockers (3 percent).

An information gap was evident. While 87 percent felt "very knowledgeable" about hypertension (HT), 29 percent thought that they could self-diagnose it. Cluster analysis identified four subgroups: Group A (39 percent) combined medication and a healthy lifestyle and had the best outcomes (lower diastolic blood pressure and lowest body mass index or BMI). Group B (16 percent) relied on medication but was less likely to exercise. Group C (22 percent) was less compliant and less likely to diet and exercise and, predictably, had the highest BMI. Group D showed the least compliance and diet control and—although younger than other groups—had higher systolic blood pressure.

The study recommended different clinical management strategies for each group:

- Group A (compliant and active) should receive positive reinforcement.
- Group B (compliant but not active) should get aggressive management, such as a smoking cessation program.
- Group C (less compliant and active) should have more frequent office visits and simpler medication schedules.
- Group D (least compliant and diet-conscious) could benefit from frequent contacts with case managers and simpler medication schedules.*

---

* Matthew Weir, E. Maibach, G. Bakris, et al., "Implications of a Health Lifestyle and Medication Analysis for Improving Hypertension Control," *Archives of Internal Medicine,* vol. 160 (February 28, 2000): 481–490.

This type of physician-directed compliance program is likely to be more acceptable to patients than pharmacy reminders and other marketing moves. In the late-growth or mature phase of a therapeutic, the user base can also be optimized with a repositioning or even a full relaunch; this particularly applies to brands that have been undermarketed and face increased competition.

Diovan: A Successful Relaunch

Novartis had launched its antihypertensive Diovan (valsartan) in the United States in February 1997 as the second brand in the new AIIA class of angiotensin receptor antagonists. Merck's Cozaar (losartan) had pioneered the class in 1995, and two major competitors, Bristol-Myers Squibb's Avapro (irbesartan) and AstraZeneca's Atacand (candesartan) had closely followed Diovan in 1997 to 1998. In addition to the forthcoming and possibly more effective AIIA olmesartan, the class might soon face new categories such as vasopeptidase inhibitors. The older ACEs were also becoming genericized.[32]

The antihypertension market was large and growing (50 million hypertensives in the United States alone, including 36 million untreated patients), but the AIIA class was small and crowded (8 percent of the U.S. market in 2001, versus 24 percent for beta-blockers and ACEs and 21 percent for calcium channel blockers). Diovan was patent-protected in the United States until 2012, versus 2009 for Cozaar, 2011 for Avapro and Atacand, and 2007 for the word's best-selling antihypertensive, Pfizer's CCB, Norvasc. By late 1998, Diovan had settled as a follower brand, but Novartis then started investing to support a five-step relaunch strategy:

1. Compete out-of-class with ACEs and CCBs for first-line use.
2. Differentiate from other AIIAs on efficacy and selectivity.
3. Pursue new indications, dosages, and combination products.
4. Support all of the above with the most extensive trial program in its class.
5. Increase share of voice in medical publications.

Because the AIIAs were perceived as a second-line therapy, Novartis helped reposition the entire class—renaming it ARBs (angiotensin receptor blockers). Diovan had only a modest clinical advantage (same efficacy as the leading ACE and CCB and better tolerability), but this was exploited in its new global position, stressing that Diovan was "protective, effective, and selective."

However, given cardiologists' focus on clinical evidence, repositioning alone would not improve Diovan's ranking. Novartis initiated an aggressive Phase IV clinical program to support new indications and formulations. *New indications* included congestive heart failure (2002), postmyocardial infarction (2005), and high-risk hypertension (2005).

New formulations included a starting dose of 160 mg to enhance efficacy, as well as other strengths. *Combination products* planned were Diovan plus Norvasc (2006) as second-line hypertension treatment and Diovan plus Zocor (2006) for management of comorbidity.

To support this, Novartis started clinicals involving more than 40,000 patients. First among these was the 5,000 patient VAL-HeFT (Valsartan Heart Failure Trial), which found that Diovan significantly reduced the combined endpoint of mortality and morbidity and led to an FDA approvable letter for congestive heart failure.[33]

Other megatrials were to be completed in 2003 to 2006, and Novartis planned to brand them through extensive publications. In addition, the company started to outspend Merck's Cozaar and Pfizer's Norvasc in marketing and sales for Diovan. The strategy began to pay off: Global sales increased 49 percent in 2002, to nearly $1.7 billion, and Diovan became the fastest growing of the top brands; by November 2001, it had passed Cozaar in U.S. share of new prescriptions. The downside was, as in many other cases, *timing*. The morbidity/mortality trials were late, and underinvestment had impacted publications (242 for Diovan versus 2,892 for Cozaar).[34] Novartis was planning 50 publications on the VAL-HeFT trial alone but would remain in catch-up mode, especially because competitive megatrials would fuel their own publications—at the same time as new players would enter the market.

SUMMARY POINTS

✓ Biobrand growth strategies are critical because pharmacos face a wave of patent expirations, and biotechs (while protected now) may be exposed in the future to generic competition.

✓ The highest long-term value comes from portfolio and franchise management; diversification is the best protection against patent losses, and product conversion extends the value of original molecules over time.

✓ Managing timelines is essential; value protection strategies should be initiated as early as the development phase.

✓ At the brand level, extending product scope with new formulations yields the highest return; other options are to expand the market with new indications and to deepen the user base with improved compliance and a focus on high-value customer segments.

RENEWING BIOBRANDS

This industry is making the same mistake it's made forever: they get a new product approved, they get some large number of years of patent life, and they wait till the end of that patent life to wake up. And then they say, "Oh. My patent's expiring three years from today. What do I do now?" . . . Research is a risky business. You've got to spread your risk. But few of them do it.

Joseph Riccardo, senior managing director, Bear Stearns[1]

Traditional lifecycle management assumed that, like people, products eventually die. There are many proofs to the contrary—not only in consumer goods, where brands like Coca-Cola and Ivory Soap are more than 100 years old, but also in pharmaceuticals. Xylocaine/lidocaine, the most widely prescribed anesthetic agent worldwide, was launched by Astra in a dental formulation in 1948 and maintained leadership because of a multitude of new indications and formulations—from surface anesthesia to antiarrhythmia (Xylocard in 1969), and from ointment (1949) to epidural injection (1968), suppositories (Xyloproct, 1969), dental cartridges (1974), pump spray (1990), and patch (1993).[2] The Xylocaine family was still reaping more than $200 million in global sales by 2001. With careful planning several years before launch and well beyond patent expiry, it is possible to *manage beyond the lifecycle* with renewal strategies at the franchise and brand levels.

RENEWING FRANCHISES

At the franchise level, companies started to extend businesses by building product families such as Eli Lilly's insulin line. In addition, franchises can now be extended with product conversions from the original molecules to their successors, as AstraZeneca did with its GI therapy Prilosec (omeprazole) and its isomer, Nexium (osomeprazole).

At the product level, companies are renewing brands by maximizing patents; to be effective, this should be planned early by building patent portfolios at the development stage. Later patent defense strategies, ranging from pediatric extensions to litigation, are either short-term or controversial.

Another brand renewal strategy is a change in product status. Branded generics have a mixed record but can be profitable if the company has the relevant competencies, as is the case for Novartis. When appropriate, a switch to over-the-counter (OTC) status can yield long-term equity, as Wyeth's Advil line (ibuprofen) demonstrates.

These strategies have been extensively applied to pharmaceuticals, but they are also relevant to the first generation of biologics, which have begun to gain new life through successor brands. Lilly's Humulin, launched in 1982, was followed by Humalog in 1996; and Amgen's Epogen and Neupogen got their own successors more than 10 years after their 1989 and 1991 launches.

This chapter first analyzes franchise renewal strategies, then assesses brand renewal strategies as they relate to patents and status changes. (See Figure 7.1.)

EXTENDING FRANCHISES WITH PRODUCT FAMILIES

An example of a durable franchise is Schering-Plough's (SP) family of interferon products. Started in 1986 with the launch of Intron A (interferon alfa-2b), licensed from Biogen, it made SP the world leader in therapies for hepatitis C, which affects more than 10 million people in major markets—only 10 to 15 percent of whom have been treated.

Intron A also had oncology indications, including adjuvant to surgery and malignant melanoma. An addition to the franchise was Rebetol (ribavirin), sourced from ICN; combined with Intron A, it improved virologic

FIGURE 7.1   Brand Renewal Strategies

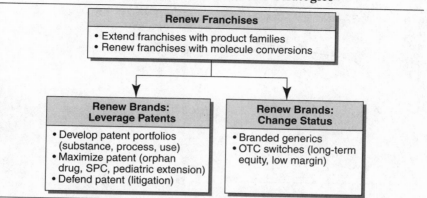

Source: Françoise Simon/SDC Group, 2002.

response rates in chronic hepatitis C. The combination was introduced in the United States as Rebetron in 1998. Intron A plus Rebetol was approved in Japan in 2001 as the first combination therapy for hepatitis C.

In January 2001, the franchise was strengthened with PEG-Intron, a longer-acting form of interferon alfa using technology licensed from Enzon. A combination (PEG-Intron plus Rebetol) was approved in the United States for chronic hepatitis C. Beyond building product families, companies can maximize patents and change product status to sustain brand equity beyond patent expiry. (See Figure 7.2.)

In addition to new forms, transfer of equity to new product is fruitful—especially when the timing is right, as was the case for Pfizer and its transfer from Procordia (nifedipine) to Norvasc (amlodipine).

RENEWING FRANCHISES WITH MOLECULE CONVERSIONS

By the late 1990s, renewal strategies were increasingly dominated by molecule conversions. Sepracor had surprised the industry by obtaining patents on several drugs' metabolites or isomers, which forced innovators to obtain rights to the successors. By 2002, companies included these molecules in their initial patent portfolios. However, they had a mixed record. Lilly had returned Prozac's isomer to Sepracor. In 2002, the FDA rejected Soltara, an active metabolite of Hismanal (astemizole), an antihistamine developed by

FIGURE 7.2   Sustaining Value—Renewal Options

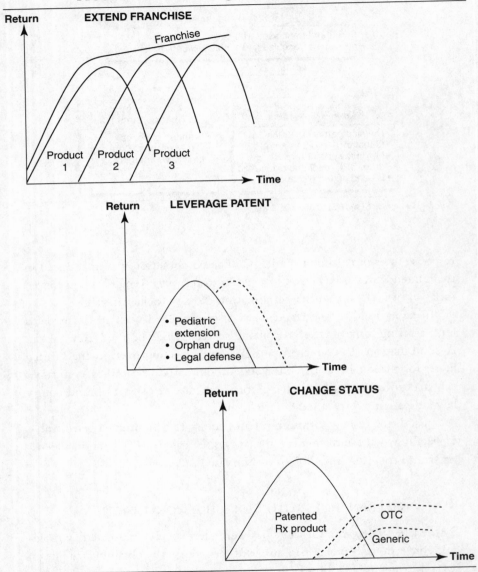

Source: Françoise Simon/SDC Group, 2002; partly adapted from R. Findlay, "A Compelling Case for Brand Building," *Pharmaceutical Executive* (February 1998), p. 78.

PROCARDIA TO NORVASC:
A SUCCESSFUL TRANSFER

Pfizer's cardiovascular franchise passed the $10 billion mark in 2000. In addition to the $7.9 billion Lipitor, Norvasc reached more than $3.8 billion in global sales by 2002. The franchise was spearheaded by the Procardia launch in 1982. Its patent began to expire in 1991, but Pfizer had introduced two years earlier the extended-release Procardia XL, based on Alza's Oros delivery system (patent-protected until 2007). Switching was helped by a Procardia XL price discount to the original molecule, which was soon completely cannibalized. A generic XL version was not introduced until 2000, when Pfizer settled a patent challenge by agreeing to manufacture the product for Mylan against royalties. By that time, Pfizer had successfully switched its user base to Norvasc, launched in the United States in 1992. Through the 1990s, Norvasc steadily replaced Procardia XL.

In addition to hypertension, Norvasc obtained two angina indications. While the calcium channel blocker (CCB) class had come under attack for side effects, Norvasc had prevailed because of its clinical profile: long acting, once daily, and fewer side effects due to its slow onset. Norvasc was also the only CCB to be pronounced safe by the FDA in patients with congestive heart failure.* Its growth had slowed by 2002 (7 percent over 2001) and angiotensin receptor blockers (ARBs) were a threat, but this was mitigated by the need for multiple therapies in hypertension. Norvasc's patent was due to expire in 2007, and Pfizer sued in 2002 two generic companies (Mylan and Dr. Reddy's) for patent infringement, which would delay the launch of generics.In addition, a Lipitor/Norvasc combination was expected in 2004.

---

* *Pharmaceutical Branding Strategies,* Datamonitor (October 2001), pp. 75–77, 110; Robert Coakley, "Defending Norvasc," *Med Ad News* (January 2003), p. 31.

Janssen and withdrawn in 1999 because of adverse reactions.[3] So far, isomers or metabolites had tended to show better tolerability, but only a marginal efficacy improvement. If this trend persisted, these successor molecules risked being classified as "me-too" products and not reimbursed. The biggest gamble against this trend was AstraZeneca's 2001 conversion of its megadrug Prilosec into Nexium.

Prilosec to Nexium: A Battle of Marketing and Managed Care

Prilosec (omeprazole) was a proton pump inhibitor (PPI) that suppressed acid secretion in the gastric parietal cell. It had made history with its launch in the late 1980s, which had successfully depositioned the formidable Zantac, Pepcid, and Tagamet with its theme, "Beyond the H_2 Blockade." Prilosec had amassed a wide range of indications, from dyspepsia and peptic ulcer to gastroesophageal reflux disease (GERD), erosive esophagitis (EE), both approved in the United States in 1995, and eradication of Helicobacter pylori (1996 in the United States).[4] Despite some patent expiries, sales still reached nearly $5.7 billion in 2001.

This posed a portfolio problem for AstraZeneca (AZ): By 2002, only one other AZ brand, antihypertensive Zestril, was in the billion-dollar category, and the forthcoming statin Crestor was still an unknown entity. AZ also had a short time window to make the conversion. Nexium was FDA-approved in late February 2001, and Prilosec's U.S. patent expired in early October 2001 after a six-month pediatric extension. The following month, U.S. regulators approved an ANDA (abbreviated new drug application) by Andrx for generic omeprazole, but AZ sued in December for infringement of Prilosec's secondary patents—which temporarily blocked generics. In October 2002, a district court in New York ruled that another company, Kremers Urban (owned by Schwarz Pharma) did not infringe Prilosec's patent, and its generic was FDA-approved the next month.

Nexium's target audience was large—in the United States alone, 20 million adults suffered from GERD. Given its crucial role in AZ's survival, the company pulled all the stops in its launch campaign. It offered Nexium at a 4 percent discount to Prilosec's average wholesale price and included free sampling in its DTC ads. In 2001, it was the third most-promoted drug in medical journals, with the theme "We captured the essence of Prilosec . . . and created Nexium." Covering all bases, AZ made Nexium the most promoted brand to managed care groups in 2001 and also invested in e-health initiatives: electronic clinical recruitment, e-detailing with iPhysician Net and ePocrates, and online continuing medical education (CME) programs with the University of Texas.

Early results were positive: Nexium generated $580 million in sales in 2001 and reached nearly $2 billion worldwide in 2002. By the end of 2001 Nexium had been launched in 38 countries. Whether Nexium could prevail in the long run remained uncertain. The main risk was the market entry of generic omeprazole. The Prozac episode had demonstrated that even massive brand awareness was no match for aggressive price discounts and managed care activism.

A related uncertainty was the acceptance of Nexium by the medical community. A Brand Institute Study showed that, in late 2001, fewer than 6 percent of U.S. physicians recognized Nexium, versus 34 percent for Prilosec and nearly 15 percent for Prevacid (lansoprazole), another PPI.[5]

Opinion leaders were unlikely to be impressed by Nexium's clinical profile. On the main trial endpoints (EE healing at four and eight weeks) and on speed of healing and heartburn control, studies promoted by AZ showed superiority for Nexium. However, one trial comparing omeprazole and esomeprazole *at the same dose (20 mg)* revealed no statistical difference, and another showed only a slight improvement. Thereafter, the AZ-sponsored studies used only Nexium 40 mg in comparisons with Prilosec 20 mg. No studies compared the two drugs at the 40 mg dosage.[6] This "apples and oranges" approach did not allow the evidence-based marketing that had supported megadrugs such as Lipitor.

There were precedents of marketing successes with weak clinical bases—including Glaxo's Zantac (ranitidine), which had zoomed to the top of its category despite an FDA science rating showing no clinical superiority. However, tolerance was fast decreasing for high-priced "me-too" products, and the future remained uncertain for Nexium.

Preliminary lessons can be derived from these brand conversion stories:

- Multiple conversion strategies are most effective (i.e., new formulation plus new entity for Procardia > Procardia XL > Norvasc).
- Timing is the key success factor.
- Successor molecules have not shown so far a greatly improved clinical profile.
- Heavy marketing for clinically weak successors worked in the past but may be less viable in the coming years.

RENEWING BRANDS: LEVERAGING PATENTS

Recent years have seen an escalation of patent optimization strategies—by both biotechs and pharma companies. These are clearly a double-edged sword: They can provide a high return, but it is generally short term and carries a significant risk.

At one end of the time spectrum, early development of broad patent portfolios is likely to deliver longer term benefits. At the other end of the timeline, postpatent litigation against generic makers is expensive and unpredictable. Litigation may add some short-term profits at the brand level; but may also create long-term damage at the corporate level, as it alienates consumers and regulators. Most importantly, the time and money required by legal actions are diverted from innovation. Pfizer did not make heroic efforts to defend its Feldene franchise, generating more than $600 million, when its patents expired in the early 1990s—judging that new product development was a more effective use of company resources than the protection of dwindling annuity assets.

In addition to their inherent risks of resource diversion, erosion of corporate image, and unpredictability, patent leveraging strategies are now scrutinized by regulators. The U.S. Federal Trade Commission (FTC) and the Antitrust Division of the Department of Justice started investigations of innovator–generic competition, including:

- Proliferation of overbroad patents and the threat it may pose to biotech competition and innovation.
- Patent settlements between innovators and generic firms and the anticompetitive potential of last-minute infringement suits or secondary patent listings.

As patents issued by the U.S. Patent and Trademark Office (PTO) rose from 66,000 in 1980 to 175,000 today, regulators want to determine whether this reflects true innovation or an increase in "blocking patents" that prolong profitability.[7]

DEVELOPING PATENT PORTFOLIOS

While biopharma firms now strive to obtain full patent portfolios, the solidity of patent classes varies widely:

- *Product patents* are the most defensible; they apply to new chemical or biologic entities and to medical devices, including drug delivery systems.
- *Formulation patents* are more susceptible to legal challenges.

- *Process patents* refer to the manufacturing process for a given product and are less protective because several methods may be used to produce the same compound.
- *Method of use patents* cover different indications and are the least protective because competitors may be prescribed off-label for the same uses.

Prilosec's Patent Portfolio

One of the broadest portfolios was assembled by AstraZeneca (AZ) for Prilosec, covering not only the basic substance, but also its elements, formulations, processes, and indications, extending the patent expiries from 1999 to 2014.

In a first step, AZ obtained supplementary protection certificates (SPCs) in most European countries to extend the 1999 expiry dates and was granted a six-month pediatric extension in the United States to October 2001; the latter could mean more than $2 billion in additional revenues and—more importantly—gave AZ more time to switch its user base to Nexium, approved in February 2001 in the United States. A U.S. metabolite patent was obtained with a 2005 expiry. The system used to produce the tablet form was patent-protected, and two U.S. patents also covered the H.pylori indication until 2014. Although process and formulation patents are generally less defensible than those relating to substances, AZ had a solid case because achieving sustained release might be impossible without infringing its multilayer technology. Figure 7.3 summarizes Prilosec's patent scope.

However, the very breadth of these patents spurred an investigation by European regulators in May 2000. A finding of anticompetitive behavior could entail fees up to 10 percent of worldwide revenues and possible restrictions on patents. In addition, AZ had embarked since the mid-1990s on a flurry of infringement lawsuits—most of which had managed to delay generic entry but were ultimately rejected. By 2000, the company had more than 50 ongoing suits in markets ranging from the United States and Canada to Germany, Scandinavia, and Australia. One last option that had been planned for Prilosec was an OTC switch. In December 1997, Astra Merck and Procter & Gamble had formed a codevelopment and copromotion alliance for an OTC formulation in the United States. P&G would handle the marketing, against upfront and royalty payments to Astra Merck.[8] No further action was taken then because AZ was focusing on patent defense.

FIGURE 7.3   Prilosec—Timeline

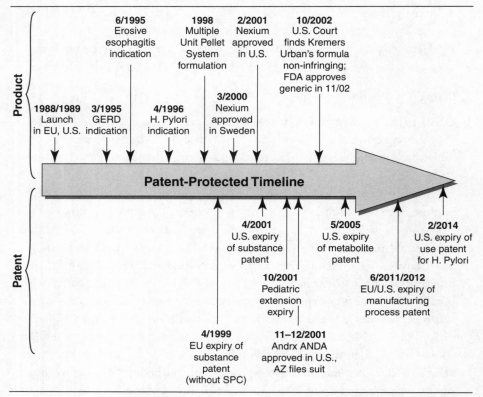

Source: Françoise Simon/SDC Group, 2002; partly adapted from *Countdown to Patent Expiry*, Datamonitor (July 2000), p. 127.

MAXIMIZING PATENTS

Without resorting to litigation, biopharma companies can extend patent lives for up to 10 years with regulatory extensions.

Orphan Drug Status

The United States and Japan introduced orphan drug legislation in the early 1980s, and the EU drafted guidelines in 2000 with similar criteria:

- Disease with low prevalence (0.04 percent to 0.07 percent of population).
- Unmet therapeutic need (absence of effective therapies).
- Development costs not expected to be recovered from drug sales.

This status applies to biologics and chemical entities. Protection varies:

United States	European Union	Japan
• 7-year exclusivity. • May be shortened if: −Supply problem. −Innovator consents to similar product's launch. −More effective drug found for same indication.	• 10-year exclusivity, except: −Availability not guaranteed. −Innovator consents to similar product's launch. −Drug no longer meets its approval requirements. −More effective drug found.	• Preferential treatment for reexamination (10 years vs. standard 4 to 6 years): −Innovator must collect efficacy and safety data while protected. −Competitor with similar drug must have extensive NDA data.

While orphan drug status is highly beneficial to niche therapies, *market exclusivity may be shortened* because of the superiority of a new entrant. For multiple sclerosis, which affects fewer than 400,000 Americans and fewer than 350,000 people in the EU Big Five markets, orphan drug status was granted to the method of use rather than to products. The pioneer was Schering AG's Betaseron (interferon beta 1b), launched in the United States as an orphan drug in 1993. Only three years later, the FDA granted Biogen's Avonex the same status because it was made with a different expression system and it slowed disease progression. Avonex was expected to share exclusivity with Betaseron until 2003, but the FDA approved Serono's Rebif in 2002 because a pivotal study (contested by Biogen) showed fewer relapses for Rebif versus Avonex over a 48-week period.[9]

Supplementary Protection Certificates

SPCs were introduced in the United States and the EU to offset delays during the review process. The U.S. Waxman-Hatch Act of 1984 had a Roche/Bolar provision permitting generic makers to start development while brands were still under patent; the *quid pro quo* was up to five years of added exclusivity for innovators who had suffered delays. The EU followed suit in 1993. These SPCs have benefited many brands including Lundbeck's Celexa (citalopram), launched in Europe in 1990 and introduced eight years later in the United States by licensee Forest. Celexa's basic patent expired in 1997, but it was granted five additional years, from 1998 to 2003, to offset regulatory delays. Its high selectivity and low drug interactions, combined with discounting and sampling, propelled Celexa to more than $700 million in global sales by 2001.[10]

Pediatric Extensions

The FDA Modernization Act (FDAMA) enacted in 1997 and extended in 2002 to 2007 allows a six-month extension to companies that voluntarily conducted pediatric studies on products offering:

- Significant improvement over existing pediatric therapies.
- Annual volume of more than 50,000 pediatric prescriptions.
- Treatments targeting unmet therapeutic need among children.

The FDAMA covered chemical entities and biologics. It allowed companies to start nearly 400 pediatric studies in four years, yielding extensions for about 40 products. With clinicals estimated by the NIH to cost between $1 million and $8 million and legal filings requiring less than $1 million, pediatric studies have a very high return, especially for blockbusters. For an additional six months of exclusivity on Claritin, Schering-Plough gained $975 million in added sales. Time frames for the United States and the EU are:

United States	European Union
• 1997 FDA Modernization Act–*voluntary* pediatric studies. • 1998 Final Pediatric Rule (effective 2/2000)–*required* pediatric trials if applicable. • Best Pharmaceuticals for Children Act (1/2002)–NIH funds pediatric studies. • FDA review of Pediatric Rule (2002).	• No legal provisions for pediatric studies; over half of existing therapies untested on children. • EU health ministers asked European Commission for action in December 2000. –Proposal to require pediatric studies as part of approval, added market exclusivity. –Proposal to fund pediatric research.

Although the EU proposed the same mandated studies as the United States, this raised objections because some therapies have too little market potential to warrant pediatric trials. The FDA has not used its mandate so far and announced in March 2002 that it would review this policy. On the other hand, some groups have criticized what they see as abusive pediatric trials—namely, those covering diseases uncommon in children, such as hypertension, arthritis, and Type 2 diabetes.[11]

Submarine Patents

A submarine patent focuses on elements of a therapeutic not covered in its initial filing. This approach was successfully used by GlaxoSmithKline (GSK) for Augmentin (amoxicillin clavulanate), the world's top antibiotic with 2001 sales of more than $2 billion. Developed in the 1960s, amoxicillin was enhanced by clavulanic acid, a beta-lactamase inhibitor that prevented it from degrading. SmithKline had used a full range of strategies, from new indications to new dosages and formulations. Augmentin was launched in the United Kingdom in 1981 and held a composition patent, which also protected the manufacturing process—requiring special fermentation equipment and safety measures because clavulanic acid was highly combustible (this in itself was a generic barrier).

Before the original patent was due to expire in 2002, GSK filed a submarine patent on Augmentin, covering components including its acid and a new oral solution. GSK was granted a new patent in 2000 that could extend to 2017—but in a surprising move, in 2002 a U.S. district court invalidated the three patents that had been challenged by generic makers Geneva, Teva, and Ranbaxy; GSK planned to appeal this ruling and previous invalidations of the patent extension, but sales declined by 13 percent in 2002. This demonstrates once more the unpredictability of patent litigation.[12]

DEFENDING PATENTS THROUGH LITIGATION

The most controversial patent strategy is *litigation,* especially when started at the eleventh hour to squeeze in more profits or buy time for a brand conversion. What the Generic Pharmaceutical Association calls "systemic mischief" is under congressional scrutiny in the United States and includes:

- *Infringement suits* against ANDAs to obtain a "30-month stay."
- Last-minute *secondary patents* on everything from a formulation to a metabolite.
- *Collusion* between innovators and generic makers.

This maneuver is under attack. Starting in May 2001, 29 American states sued Aventis and Andrx because of an Aventis cash settlement to Andrex to delay a generic version of cardizem CD (diltiazem). The FTC also concluded that their agreement had blocked generic entry.[13] Aventis and Andrx were ordered in early 2003 to pay an $80 million settlement to compensate consumers, insurers, and states, and they had previously settled for $110 million with wholesalers over the same case.

AMGEN VERSUS TRANSKARYOTIC

Amgen waged for five years a battle against Transkaryotic (TKT) and its partner Aventis, which involved 18 claims. Amgen held five patents on Epogen (one of which was to lapse in 2004) and claimed rights on its production in all vertebrate cells. TKT asserted that this claim was too broad. A January 2002 U.S. decision favored Amgen, but a U.K. appeals court ruled in July that TKT's production method did not infringe Amgen's patent.

Biologics are likely to encounter legal challenges—because patents apply not to natural substances, but to their method of use or manufacturing process. The PTO may reject a claim as "not enabled for its entire scope." If it concerns the delivery of cloned DNA to a cell through a viral vector and the submission refers to a single vector, the PTO may reject the claim as not enabled to all viral vectors. Another risk is the PTO requirement that, when filing, starting materials (ranging from cell lines to hybridomas) be placed in a depository such as the American Type Culture Collection, where they can be accessed under the Rules of Practice in Patent Cases.* This implies that biotechs need *early and extensive legal counsel* to navigate approval and prevent later challenges.

---

* Amgen SEC Form 10K (2001), pp. 27–28; Debra Anderson, "Clearing the Path," *Pharmaceutical Executive* (May 2002), pp. 94, 96; "TKT: Victory At Last," *In Vivo Europe Rx* (September 2002), pp. 17–18.

Litigation has been a major strategy for Bristol-Myers Squibb (BMS). Taxol (paclitaxel), the cornerstone of its oncology franchise, was the object of a convoluted legal saga. Launched in 1993 and strengthened by a mix of new indications, dosages, and delivery systems, it reached nearly $2 billion in global sales by 2001. Starting in 1997, BMS filed several suits against generic makers. In March 2000, Ivax won a decision over parts of Taxol's patent, but American BioScience claimed its own patent on a dosage form (to which BMS had a license option) and led BMS to list it in the FDA Orange Book. The FDA argued that the patent was invalid because of contradictions and timing issues. The patent was delisted, and Ivax launched its generic in October 2000. More than a year later, a federal appeals court surprisingly reversed the delisting—but in June 2002, 29 state attorneys general sued BMS for improperly blocking generic entry, which led to a $135 million settlement.[14]

Citizen Petitions: The Premarin Bioequivalence Defense

Under 1977 federal rules permitting anyone to question the safety of a medication, companies may file *citizen petitions,* which often delay generic approvals. The FDA has received more than 70 industry petitions since 1990, and fewer than 20 percent of the processed requests were granted. An unusual case was that of Wyeth's Premarin—a $1.9 billion franchise in 2002. Approved in the United States in 1942, it had obtained a new indication (osteoporosis) in 1988 and had launched the Prempro/Premphase line extensions in 1994 and 1995, with a Prempro patent until 2006. However, Prempro was negatively impacted by the Women's Health Initiative (WHI) discontinuation of its HRT study arm in 2002 because of serious adverse effects.

To defend Premarin, Wyeth's approach was a controversial bioequivalence defense. In 1994, Wyeth filed a citizen petition challenging generic filings for synthetic conjugated estrogens. As an equine-originated blend of 10 estrogens, Premarin had an ingredient (delta 8, 9 dehydroestrone) missing from the synthetics. Wyeth submitted data documenting its activity, and the FDA acknowledged two years later that it had potential effects on bone metabolism. In May 1997, the FDA ruled that until Premarin's active ingredients were sufficiently defined, a synthetic generic could not be approved. When Duramed filed for approval of its synthetic estrogen Cenestin, Wyeth challenged it with another citizen petition in May 1998. Cenestin

BUSPAR: THE METABOLITE DEFENSE

Approved by the FDA in 1986, antianxiety drug BuSpar (buspirone) faced the potential loss of more than $700 million in sales when its patent was due to lapse in November 2000. BMS countered it with legal maneuvers. The *metabolite defense,* which first appeared in the mid-1990s, has never won a case but continues to be used to buy time. BMS retested BuSpar's metabolites in the late 1990s and claimed to have discovered one (6-hydroxy-buspirone) with therapeutic properties. BMS was granted on November 21, 2000 (the last day of BuSpar's patent), a method of use patent for *swallowing the metabolite.* Generic makers including Mylan immediately sued, and the attorneys general of 29 states and Puerto Rico soon filed a similar charge of improperly blocking generic competition. A U.S. district court ruled against BMS in March 2001, and Mylan launched its generic at a 13 percent discount; generics had captured two-thirds of BuSpar's share by late June.

BMS had gained five months (or about $200 million in sales), but the district court ruling allowed states, generic makers, and consumer groups to proceed with their own suits. In June 2002, BMS settled one suit by paying Watson $32 million, and also cited a total settlement of $535 million to resolve claims related to BuSpar.★

★ BMS Annual Report (2001), p. 45; Gardiner Harris and C. Adams, "Drug Makers Step Up Attacks That Slow Down Generics," *Wall Street Journal* (July 12, 2001), p. A10; Julie Appleby, "Bristol to Pay $670M to Settle Antitrust Suits," *USA Today* (January 8, 2003), p. 2B.

was approved in 1999—but as a different product and based on a new drug application.

Wyeth's actions had protected Premarin, but had also alienated consumer groups, and the legal defense had diverted resources from innovation and market expansion. A missed opportunity had been ex-U.S. markets, which accounted for only 14 percent of sales in 2002.[15]

In conclusion, litigation trends are negative and likely to get worse. Companies should consider the following points:

- Early portfolio development and patent maximization (orphan drug, pediatric extensions) are worthwhile approaches.

- Litigation is under attack and defensible claims (bioequivalence) are rare.
- Most antigeneric infringement suits fail.
- Buying time via litigation leads to short-term high returns, but possible long-term image erosion and alienation of consumer groups.

Figure 7.4 summarizes the benefits and risks of the main patent strategies.

FIGURE 7.4   Leveraging Patents—Key Strategies

	STRATEGY	ADVANTAGES	RISKS/LIMITATIONS
DEVELOP	Develop broad patent portfolio	• Value protection from substance, method of use, process, and other patents	• Should be started in early development stage • Abuses under investigation
MAXIMIZE	Obtain orphan drug status	• 7-year extension (U.S.), maximum 10 years (EU)	• Applies only to rare diseases
	Obtain SPC (supplementary certificate)	• Maximum 5-year extension in U.S. to offset regulatory review delays	• Applies only if regulatory delays can be proven
	Pediatric extension	• 6-month extension in U.S. • Fairly low cost of new clinicals, low filing costs	• Does not apply to all diseases
	Submarine patent	• Additional patents for elements of compound not previously covered	• Under investigation by regulators
DEFEND PATENTS	Bioequivalence defense	• Blocks generics due to non-bioequivalence	• Applies to few drugs • Alienates consumer groups
	Patent infringement lawsuit	• "30-month stay" in U.S. blocks generic entry during litigation	• Litigation is unpredictable • Pending legislation to eliminate multiple stays
	Citizen petition with FDA	• Questioning safety or bioavailability of generics can delay their approval	• FDA has upheld only 4 of 51 citizen petitions since 1990
	Lobby government for direct legislation or addition to unrelated bill	• May lead to a multi-year extension (to offset delays in approval process)	• Increasingly ineffective

Source: Françoise Simon/SDC Group, 2002.

RENEWING BRANDS: CHANGING PRODUCT STATUS

Whereas renewal strategies such as brand conversion yield the highest returns, it is possible to leverage postpatent brands, either with a branded generic or OTC switch.

BRANDED GENERICS: A MIXED RECORD

As biotechs may face generic competition in the future, they can benefit from the experience of their pharma counterparts.

Because of cost containment, generics will continue to gain share in major markets. In the United States, they had reached 43 percent of all prescriptions by 2001—and this would increase with future patent expirations.[16] The U.S. market was especially attractive because the first generic maker to file an ANDA was granted six months of exclusivity after approval. In Japan, the Supreme Court allowed in 2000 prepatent expiry development work by generic firms.

In Europe, Germany had a significant generics market. France was underpenetrated because of relatively low brand prices and a lack of price sensitivity in patients who were reimbursed. However, France allowed generic substitution in 1998. Some innovators had leveraged the local preference for branded generics; SmithKline had launched its own generic amoxicillin to win back some of the share lost by its reference drug.[17]

The generic strategies of innovator firms had evolved in three distinct waves:

1. Acquisition or internal development of generic businesses (1980s to early 1990s).
2. Divestment of most generic operations (late 1990s).
3. Intensified litigation against generics (post–2000).

Two scenarios could unfold: continued litigation or a shift to a mixed pattern—litigation in case of clear infringement and collaboration when the product warranted it. By 2002, litigation looked precarious because of proposed stricter legislation in the United States. The six-year old

European Medicines Evaluation Agency (EMEA) was preparing for similar actions when its own patents neared expiry.[18]

Generic acquisitions had largely failed because of widely divergent business models. Whereas innovators offset R&D and marketing costs with very high margins, generic makers worked with equally low R&D costs and margins and distributed products through pharmacy contracting rather than expensive salesforces. Hoechst had bought a 51 percent share of generic maker Copley in 1993 for $546 million, and Marion Merrell Dow had purchased Rugby that same year for $300 million. Postmerger, Aventis divested both as fast as it could.

One exception was Novartis, whose predecessor Ciba-Geigy had pioneered branded generics. Novartis continued to invest in its generic business, which generated nearly $1.5 billion in global sales in 2001—two-thirds of which were generic drugs and one-third industrial products. In 2001 alone, Novartis had made several acquisitions:

- In the United States, BMS's Apothecon for nearly $40 million in cash.
- In Europe, BASF's generic business in six countries and Lagap in the United Kingdom.
- In Argentina, Labinca SA.

Generic sales were up by 26 percent in local currencies from 2000 to 2001. In the United States, subsidiary Geneva had obtained six months of exclusivity on fluoxetine 10mg (Prozac). Other launches included antibiotic Curam/Clavamox (amoxicillin and clavulanic acid), Loratadin for allergies, and Ciprofloxacin from subsidiary Azupharma.[19]

Other innovators had engaged in postpatent collaborations with generic firms, as was the case for BMS and its antihypertensive Capoten in Germany.

In future years, a shift from relentless litigation to some degree of innovator/generic collaboration may be facilitated by the blurring of boundaries between the two sectors. A hybrid generic model is emerging with companies such as Andrx.

While Andrx is an aggressive litigator, it tends to add some innovation to the patents it targets. In its dealings with Aventis over Cardizem CD, Andrx reformulated it for its ANDA approval; this was novel enough to prompt Aventis to abandon its infringement claim—which gave Andrx

CAPOTEN—GENERIC STRATEGY IN GERMANY

Bristol-Myers Squibb's Capoten (captopril) had pioneered the ACE inhibitor class with its 1980 launch. It had reached peak global sales of more than $1 billion in 1996. After its U.S. patent expired that year, sales rapidly fell to less than half by 1999. In Germany, BMS and Schwarz Pharma held almost 50 percent of the ACE market with Lopirin and Tensobon, their two captopril brands. Almost a year before the German patent was due to lapse in 1995, BMS partnered with Azupharma and Schwarz to launch two other captopril brands at a 26 percent discount. These gained a preemptive share of the generics market and still held a value share of more than 80 percent almost two years after patent expiry. Had BMS not signed this agreement, it would have lost most of its profits. After patent expiry, competition was so intense that generics were soon selling at a 75 percent discount to the original brands.*

---

* *Countdown to Patent Expiry,* Datamonitor (July 2000), pp. 81–82.

added exclusivity. Andrx plans to step up internal R&D, acquire niche products, and build its own salesforce to market these.[20]

The dynamics of innovator-generic relationships yield several suggestions:

- Generics are here to stay, and legislation will increasingly support them globally.
- Generic purchases by innovators have largely failed because of different economics.
- Generic firms may evolve toward hybrid models with a degree of innovation.
- Innovator/generic collaborations may be productive on a case-by-case basis.

OTC SWITCHES: LONG-TERM EQUITY

A postpatent strategy with a relatively high return is *a switch from Rx to OTC status.* This extends brand equity but is limited to the few areas where consumers can safely treat themselves. Many biologics will never be candidates, but products targeting diseases such as asthma, psoriasis, and arthritis may in the future qualify.

Public and private payers have powerful incentives to encourage OTC switching. A U.S. study estimated that sales of OTC drugs led to savings of $20 billion—60 percent of which came from switches. In Sweden, a study of 16 switched drugs estimated savings of $30 million to the health-care system.[21] Many European governments followed Denmark's example, which dereimbursed 79 ethical drugs in 1989; many of these became available over the counter.

In the United States, the Hatch–Waxman Act incentivized switches by providing three years of market exclusivity if additional trials were submitted to the FDA. Switch criteria were well defined:

- Can the condition be self-diagnosed and self-treated?
- Can the patient understand the product label to ensure proper use?
- Is the product safe and effective when used as recommended?
- Can the patient monitor treatment outcomes and identify adverse events?
- Is the dosage form safe and easily administered?

These criteria explain why additional trials may be required: Studies of label comprehension and actual-use trials simulate conditions in which drugs are taken without medical supervision. A 2002 survey found that one-third of U.S. consumers exceeded recommended doses of OTC medications. The social rationale for switches can be summed up as follows:

Benefits	Risks
• Increased drug access.	• Inaccurate self-diagnosis.
• Decreased physician visits.	• Failure to follow label, adverse
• Improved consumer autonomy.	reactions, drug interactions.
• Decreased costs to payers.	• Increased costs to patients.[22]

Keeping these risks in mind, the FDA rejected proposals to switch categories such as antivirals and asthma drugs.

In addition to social factors, OTC switches have powerful economic drivers:

- Long-term revenue and brand equity.
- Acquisition of new customers (non-Rx users).
- Growth of entire category through new OTC indications.
- "Halo effect" sustaining loyalty for both Rx and OTC products.

In the United States alone, consumers spend more than $20 billion annually for OTC therapies, and switches have higher growth rates, lead their categories, and drive OTC portfolios. More than 50 percent of Wyeth's OTC business comes from switched products, mainly Advil (ibuprofen), switched in 1984 and still the biggest success to date. The top 25 OTC products included 13 switches in 2000, many of which led their classes, from Advil to Pepcid AC (heartburn), Nicorette/Nicoderm (smoking cessation), and Benadryl (cold/allergy). A primary care drug with annual Rx sales of $750 million and an adspend of $100 million could achieve OTC sales of nearly $600 million in its first two years as an OTC medication.[23]

However, Rx-to-OTC switches also have a downside:

- Lower profit margins (20 percent, versus up to 80 percent for ethical drugs).
- High DTC promotion costs.
- Possible cannibalization of the Rx version.

Cannibalization may happen because converting customers mandates that a switch be made several years before patent expiry. Many switches also lead to a *dual status* whereby the Rx and OTC forms have different strengths, indications, or formulations. The dual status may reinforce overall brand equity, but may also lead to Rx erosion.

Key success factors include timing and *dual promotion*. Advil's success came because it was first to market, clearly positioned ("Advanced Medicine for Pain"), and promoted to physicians as well as consumers (dedicated salesforce and $100 million DTC launch adspend). By contrast, later entrants Nuprin and Medipren never had effective positions. J&J feared that Medipren would cannibalize Tylenol and gave it a narrow position (body aches only) with a fuzzy slogan, "New Medipren-From the Makers of Tylenol"; not surprisingly, it was eventually discontinued. These factors also drove the H_2 blocker switch in 1995 to 1996.

Timing includes early planning, first-to-market position, and rapid distribution:

- Optimal planning starts before the launch of the Rx molecule: Incorporating OTC end points into Phase III clinicals is more cost-effective than addressing them at a late stage.
- The value of being first to market has been demonstrated by many successful switches, from Advil to Pepcid AC.
- Prompt execution is also critical at launch: Advil was in U.S. stores within four days of its OTC approval.

Clinical differentiation is a key asset, as in Rx marketing:

- A switch that satisfies an *unmet need* can create a new market; this was the case for smoking cessation therapies such as Nicoderm and Nicorette.
- *Safety* is a primary concern; for Pepcid AC, Merck conducted actual-use trials to determine whether patients could safely self-diagnose and treat heartburn.

Multiple-track promotion is critical to ensure acceptance. Medical detailing educates physicians about dual dosages or new indications and generates referrals; pharmacist sampling and retailer promotion help at the point of sale, and managed-care outreach may lead to partial reimbursement. For all tracks, a dominant share of voice is needed—at least 25 percent of category ad spending for consumer promotion.

Consumer-specific benefits also help gain and maintain OTC leadership:

- Convenience may be increased by new delivery systems such as quick-dissolving tablets. Pre-switch, new Zantac formulations were launched in 1995 (effervescent tablets and easy-to-swallow soft gelatin capsules).

Finally, sustained investment is needed for the OTC brand to evolve and maintain dominance: Clinical trials have led to new indications for aspirin.

In conclusion, maximizing biobrands involves the *early and sustained use* of a full portfolio of growth and renewal strategies. Table 7.1 summarizes these at each stage of a brand's evolution.

PEPCID VERSUS ZANTAC:
THE HEARTBURN EXPRESS

When the H$_2$ receptor antagonist class was switched in 1995 and 1996, its leaders enjoyed a strong ethical heritage, and the new OTC indications of acid prevention and heartburn helped grow the market. Again, *speed* was the key to success. Merck and partner J&J managed to switch Pepcid (famotidine) in June 1995, with a six-week lead over SmithKline's Tagamet HB (cimetidine) and nearly a year before Glaxo's Zantac 75 (ranitidine) in April 1996. Lilly's Axid AR (nizatidine) was launched last in May 1996 and was undermarketed—it remained a minor player. Despite the fact that Pepcid had the longest patent life (expiry in 2000 versus 1997 for Zantac), Merck chose to launch it first and gained a preemptive share.

Pepcid achieved leadership despite the fact that it had the least heritage: Zantac led the class and Tagamet had pioneered it. Adspend for the OTC launch was similar for Pepcid and Zantac and double that of Tagamet HB. All three brands had dual status, with lower OTC dosages. Merck and J&J later invested in a *triple combination product,* Pepcid Complete, including active ingredients from their own Mylanta (magnesium hydroxide) and from Glaxo's Tums (calcium carbonate). It was sold at double the price of Pepcid AC or Zantac 75 and triple the price of generic famotidine. By 2001, Zantac continued to lead the Rx category, but Pepcid AC had maintained its OTC lead.*

Marketers could draw several lessons from this episode:

- *Switch your brand first and well ahead of patent expiry.*
- *Use a novel indication* to grow the market and create a clear identity for the switched product.
- *Use the ethical heritage* to support the switch, but do not assume that Rx dominance guarantees OTC leadership.
- *Invest to grow the brand* with new indications or formulations.

---

* *Patent Protection Strategies,* Datamonitor (July 2000), pp. 76–79.

TABLE 7.1 Growth and Renewal Strategies

Stage	Strategy	Product	Price	Promotion
Prelaunch	• Test market. • Speed development. • Build infrastructure.	• Prebrand product through clinical trials.	• Test price with physicians/payers.	• Capture opinion leaders, start publications. • Raise disease awareness.
Launch	• Build first mover advantage. • Fast rollout in key markets.	• Establish brand as gold standard. • Start Phase IV trials.	• Premium for breakthrough product.	• Induce trial via DTC, sampling. • Get top SOV in medical, mass media.
Early growth	• Lead category (data-driven). • Alliances to expand reach.	• Differentiate brand. • New indications.	• Price for profitability.	• Publicize megatrials. • Promote new uses.
Late growth	• Maximize share. • Raise customer switching costs. • Buy small players.	• New formulations. • Compliance programs.	• Price to deter competition.	• Stress brand benefits/new forms. • Monitor customer needs.
Maturity	• Deepen user base. • Focus on high-value segments.	• Combined product. • Compliance programs.	• Flexible pricing (bundling, managed care contracts).	• Segment-specific promotion. • Target loyal MDs, consumers.
Postpatent	• Change status (branded generic, OTC).	• Differentiate via formulations, line extensions.	• Higher than unbranded generics; premium within OTCs.	• Market to managed care; DTC, medical promotion.
Renewal	• Launch successor brand (new product, isomer, or metabolite).	• Set product as new gold standard.	• Discount versus original molecule.	• Aggressive conversion campaign.

Source: Françoise Simon/SDC Group, 2002.

SUMMARY POINTS

✓ *As biotechs mature* and expand into primary care, they need aggressive growth and renewal strategies.

✓ *Multiple renewal strategies should be used* at the franchise and brand levels, from product conversion to new indications and patent extensions.

✓ *Managing timelines* is critical; many strategies should start well before launch, and others, several years before patent expiry.

✓ While individual compounds have finite patent lives, their brand equity can be perpetuated through *successor products*.

✓ *Patent maximization strategies* (orphan drug status, pediatric trials) can extend brand lives, but late-stage litigation yields diminishing returns.

✓ *Change of status* to branded generic or OTC allows a life extension that is not time-limited but has a fairly low margin.

✓ *Evidence-based marketing* applies equally to building and sustaining biobrands; successful therapeutics retain their leadership through extensive clinical trials, which allow retention of key opinion leaders and support a dominant share of voice in medical publications.

PART THREE

MEETING
THE GLOBAL
CHALLENGE

BALANCING ACCESS
AND PRICE

We have heard quite clearly that the price of drugs matters—it matters to poor people, and it matters to poor countries.

Gro Harlem Brundtland, former director-general, World Health Organization[1]

Access and pricing have become front-page news in the United States, with headlines such as "Courting Trouble," and "Drug Prices—Why They Keep Soaring."[2] In Europe and Japan, aging populations and expensive new technology are intensifying cost containment—from price cuts to dereimbursement of entire drug classes.[3] In the United States, healthcare costs keep rising—although their dominant component is hospital care, not prescription drugs. However, the National Institute of Health Care Management reported a double-digit increase in retail spending on medicines. Significantly, the report ascribed 62 percent of the increase to only 50 drugs.[4] From the *New England Journal of Medicine* to the *Wall Street Journal,* media drew an instant connection between this and DTC advertising costs. At more than $100 million, the most heavily advertised drugs had a higher spend than some cola or beer brands.[5]

The media also focused on overall industry profits. A Fortune 500 survey rated it the most profitable in the United States on three counts: return on sales (18.5 percent), return on assets (16.3 percent), and return on equity (33.2 percent)—all indicators at three to eight times the medians for other industries. The next object of scrutiny was the gap between R&D and marketing expenditures. A Families United States report analyzed the SEC filings of nine leading companies and found that for eight, marketing/advertising/administration spend was at least double that of R&D. Industry association PhRMA retorted that, if administration was factored out, promotion amounted in 2001 to $15.7 billion (half on free samples) versus $25.7 billion on R&D.[6]

Another blow came from widespread coverage of record fines imposed by federal agencies on several manufacturers found guilty of pricing fraud. Given that the U.S. government spent more than $20 billion on drugs, it had a keen interest in investigating abuses. In 2001 alone, it garnered more than $1.2 billion in healthcare fraud settlements or judgments. The Department of Justice was casting a wide net and investigating about 20 companies.[7]

Employers were also increasing their activism. In a Kaiser Family Foundation survey of employer health benefit plans, 40 percent of the 2,000 respondents saw government price regulation as the most effective cost containment tool, 25 percent supported limits on DTC promotion, and 28 percent advocated cost-shifting via consumer copayments. Large employers were combining political action with pharmacoeconomic review and employee education. General Motors and other firms joined Blue Cross, the AFL–CIO, consumer groups, and governors of more than 10 states to petition Congress to reform legislation delaying generics. GM and Verizon also used extensive data mining to review drug utilization. GM launched an employee education program about the cost effectiveness of generics, and their utilization rose significantly among employees, thus generating substantial savings for GM.[8]

Given this incendiary context, an effective discussion of pricing strategies cannot take place in isolation. We first address in this chapter the cost effectiveness of biopharma therapies and analyze regulation dynamics in the major world markets. We then cover in the next chapter biopricing strategies in the context of these macroeconomic and regulatory forces. Emerging

FIGURE 8.1   Biopricing Strategy

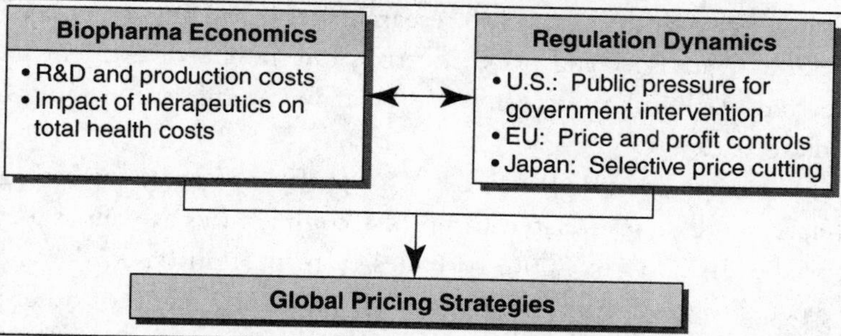

Source: Françoise Simon/SDC Group, 2002.

markets present a different challenge, centered on access to HIV drugs and therapies for region-specific diseases such as malaria. Most biotech firms rely on marketing partners and do not have direct exposure to developing economies. Therefore, we focus on Organisation for Economic Cooperation and Development (OECD) countries, which account for nearly 90 percent of the world market. Our approach is summarized in Figure 8.1.

BIOPHARMA ECONOMICS

Two fundamental debates concern the relationship between R&D costs and drug prices and also the impact of drug treatment on the overall cost of diseases.

R&D Costs

The latest study by the Tufts Center for the Study of Drug Development put the cost of a new therapy at $802 million, largely because of higher clinical trial costs. The costs of capital and research failures accounted for half of this total, given a 12-year average development time. Critics charged that this estimate did not take into account tax deductions and government subsidies of R&D, but a Boston Consulting Group study gave an even higher estimate of $880 million.[9]

In addition, U.S. firms are shouldering a disproportionate share of global innovation—two-fifths of the 130 research sites of leading drugmakers are in the United States. Drug price controls, low public investment in bioscience, and weak links between industry and academia are eroding European innovation.[10]

In addition to massive R&D costs, a significant hurdle for biologics is manufacturing expense related to process complexities as well as a capacity shortage. In 2002 to 2006, revenues from protein-based therapeutics are projected to grow 15 percent annually, versus 7 percent for other pharmaceuticals—yet the worldwide cell culture capacity of 450,000 liters is now almost fully utilized. Piper Jaffray estimates that more than 900,000 liters could be added in the next four to five years, but that would mostly come from a few firms (Amgen, Genentech, Biogen, and IDEC). Others turn to contract manufacturers such as Lonza or Boehringer Ingelheim, but these can command high payments.

The complexity of biologic production also leads to high indirect costs due to approval problems. In 2001, the FDA delayed approval for Genentech/Xoma's psoriasis drug Xanelim because of manufacturing modifications during late-stage trials. It also postponed approval for at least a year for Aviron/Wyeth's nasal spray vaccine Flumist, requesting more clinical and manufacturing data. Beyond approval, supply shortages cost Immunex more than $200 million in revenue for its arthritis drug Enbrel.[11]

While the public is highly sensitized to drug prices, it is not well informed of research and supply costs—and the industry's promotion approach, with its "miracle cures" theme, has not quantified these in mass media. This has led to persistent pricing problems for biotechs. As early as 1991, Genzyme's Ceredase (aglucerase) therapy for Gaucher's disease, priced at $50,000 to $200,000 or more per year (depending on dosage), generated widespread protests. Genzyme was able to maintain its launch price because Ceredase was the only therapy, it targeted a minuscule population (5,000 worldwide), and its production was difficult. It was approved in Europe in 1994, and global sales reached over $600 million by 2002—had it targeted a larger population, it would have met with much more opposition.[12]

Pharmaceutical Cost Effectiveness

While many medical and economic studies have demonstrated the cost effectiveness of biopharmaceuticals and the beneficial shift from surgery to drug treatment, the public remains underinformed.

Companies have at their disposal heavy ammunition from medical studies. A 43 percent decrease in inpatient hospital care for HIV sufferers was reported in the 16 months following the launch of antiretrovirals, according to the *New England Journal of Medicine*. The Department of Veterans Affairs reported that full access to new AIDS drugs for its patients saved $18 million in treatment costs in 1997.

The impact of some biologics is even more dramatic. For patients weakened by chemotherapy, treatment with a colony-stimulating factor was found to save an average $30,000 in hospitalization costs for bone-marrow transplants.[13] Economic studies have also demonstrated a cost migration from medical services to biopharmaceuticals. A Tufts University report showed that, in the 1990s, drug costs rose from 5.5 percent to 8.5 percent of overall healthcare spending, whereas hospital expenses declined from 37 percent to 33 percent.

For the drug cost debate to become more balanced, it would be critical to abandon the "silo thinking" compartmentalizing drug and nondrug costs and to focus on:

- The impact of biopharma therapy on *lifetime disease management.*
- The effect of Rx treatment on the *total societal cost of disease,* including lost productivity.

A major obstacle remains the managed care mindset in the United States. With a 20 percent annual member turnover rate and quarterly financial targets, managed care has few incentives to implement disease management. In one HMO study, diabetes patients in a managed setting used services such as glucose tests and eye exams at a higher rate than in other systems, thereby incurring higher costs. The long payback from drug use in chronic diseases is largely ignored by MCOs, as they tend to limit their cost management to drug utilization reviews. These stress short-term savings (use of lower-cost drugs) rather than systemwide economies (lower hospitalization rates be-cause of better compliance with newer drugs).[14] However, there is com-pelling evidence of the cost effectiveness of new therapies.

Because of their short-term orientation, drug utilization reviews do not distinguish between the different types of economic return yielded by

THERAPEUTIC AND ECONOMIC BENEFITS OF NEWER DRUGS

Economist Frank Lichtenberg tracked the links between the use of newer medicines and morbidity, mortality, and health spending, using data from the 1996 Medical Expenditure Panel Survey (MEPS)—a nationally representa-tive survey of healthcare use and spending by more than 23,000 people. The MEPS file held nearly 172,000 Rx events, including price, payment source, and national drug cost, from which the drug age was derived (number of years since FDA approval). More than 90 percent of prescriptions were linked to only one medical condition. Rx spending amounted to less than 14 per-cent of total health expenditure, compared with nearly 42 percent for hospital stays. Newer drugs (approved in the 1990s) accounted for only 17 percent of total prescriptions; more than half of all drugs used were ap-proved before 1980. Inevitably, the newer drugs had a price premium; the study found that replacing a 15-year-old drug with a 5.5-year-old therapy raised the prescription cost by about $18.

However, *the use of newer drugs was linked to better outcomes and lower nondrug costs.* Users of new drugs had significantly lower mortality rates and were less likely to suffer work-loss days than people using older drugs. They also had fewer hospital stays; because these accounted for a large share of total spending, the implied hospital cost reduction found by the study was $56. Newer drugs also reduced all types of nondrug expenses, yielding *a total cost reduction of $71—versus an added drug cost of only $18.* The study focused only on drug age; other quality indicators, such as innovativeness, should ideally be taken into account—in addition to determinants of drug access, comorbidities, and impact of one drug on several conditions.*

* Frank Lichtenberg, "Are the Benefits of Newer Drugs Worth Their Cost? Evidence from the 1996 MEPS," *Health Affairs* (September/October 2001), pp. 242–248.

biopharmaceuticals. These should prove useful in regulatory submissions and in negotiations with government payers. A systemic assessment weighing drug costs against increased productivity would also be compelling for employer purchasing groups. A recent study yielded a drug typology according to economic return:

	Fast Return	*Slow Return*	*Narrow Return*	*Mixed Return*
Impact	• Lower short-term health costs.	• Lower long-term health costs.	• Lower costs for a narrow population.	• Lower short-term costs/ higher long-term costs.
Examples	• Anticoagulants for stroke.	• Biphosphonates for osteoporosis.	• Congestive heart failure.	• Multiple sclerosis.

- The *fast return* category is well documented, including AIDS drugs that immediately save hospitalization costs and anticoagulant therapy costing about $1,000 a year, versus $100,000 in lifetime costs for a severe stroke.

- Preventative therapies yield *a slow return,* which explains why they often have low reimbursement levels. The osteoporosis drug Fosamax is reimbursed only after a fracture in several countries—whereas its cost effectiveness comes from its prevention use over many years: A single hip fracture costs more than $40,000, whereas drug treatment costs less than $1,000 annually.

- The *narrow return* class lowers costs for the small percentage of the target population with the severest symptoms. Therapies for congestive heart failure lower costs for severe cases by preventing hospitalizations or disability but raise them for the more prevalent, milder cases.

- The *mixed return* category lowers short-term costs but raises long-term spending. This includes high-cost biologics for conditions such as multiple sclerosis (Betaseron, Avonex, Rebif). These save hospitalization and disability costs, but increase spending in the long term.[15]

The dynamics of biopharmaceutical costs are, therefore, highly conflictual:

- R&D costs are escalating, but their estimation is subject to debate.
- Production costs are a burden for biologics, but this is not well-known.
- Cost migration is occurring from medical services to biopharmaceuticals, but the public, focused on drug prices, ignores benefits such as reduced hospitalizations.
- The cost effectiveness of biopharmaceuticals has been documented in medical and economic studies, but it relies on a systemic assessment (drug cost versus lifetime disease cost or total cost to society), which conflicts with the current short-term mindset.

In this context, pharmacoeconomics studies should target not only payers but also all other stakeholders, who may have more collective influence. For high-priced biologics in particular, outcomes studies will be increasingly important in submissions to the FDA and other regulators. As employers and states join in purchasing pools, they will be more receptive than payers to the long-term economics of drug therapies, including their impact on work productivity. Physicians are under increasing economic constraints, whether direct (MD budgets in Europe) or indirect (MCO formularies in the United States) and need to assess economic as well as therapeutic gains from new technology. Finally, consumers are burdened with increased cost-shifting and must be better informed of cost effectiveness. This is summarized in Figure 8.2.

At the international level, overall health spending shows both convergence and divergence. There is a degree of drug price convergence across OECD countries. However, divergence persists in the link between spending and performance.

SPENDING VERSUS PERFORMANCE

The 2001 World Health Organization (WHO) report listed the United States first in health spending, at 13 percent of GDP versus 7.5 percent in Japan and 10.5 percent in Germany. The summary indicator of population health used by the WHO was health-adjusted life expectancy (HALE), that is, the number of years in full health that a newborn could expect to live based on mortality and morbidity rates. By that measure, the United States came last among the top world markets. In addition, the

FIGURE 8.2   Biopricing—Stakeholders

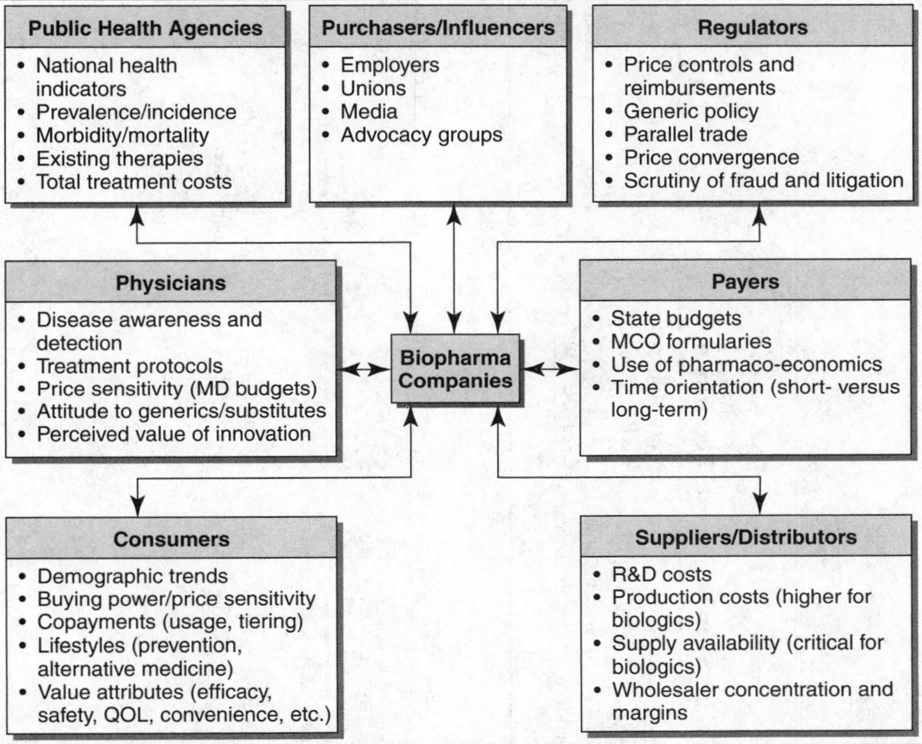

Public Health Agencies	Purchasers/Influencers	Regulators
• National health indicators • Prevalence/incidence • Morbidity/mortality • Existing therapies • Total treatment costs	• Employers • Unions • Media • Advocacy groups	• Price controls and reimbursements • Generic policy • Parallel trade • Price convergence • Scrutiny of fraud and litigation

Physicians		Payers
• Disease awareness and detection • Treatment protocols • Price sensitivity (MD budgets) • Attitude to generics/substitutes • Perceived value of innovation	**Biopharma Companies**	• State budgets • MCO formularies • Use of pharmaco-economics • Time orientation (short- versus long-term)

Consumers	Suppliers/Distributors
• Demographic trends • Buying power/price sensitivity • Copayments (usage, tiering) • Lifestyles (prevention, alternative medicine) • Value attributes (efficacy, safety, QOL, convenience, etc.)	• R&D costs • Production costs (higher for biologics) • Supply availability (critical for biologics) • Wholesaler concentration and margins

Source: Françoise Simon/SDC Group, 2002.

OECD tracked indicators of health prevention and access to technology. The United States lagged countries such as Finland and the United Kingdom on immunization rates. One proxy for new technologies was the availability of magnetic resonance imagers (MRIs); the United States ranked below Japan, Switzerland, and Finland in the number of MRIs per million persons.

In its 2000 report focusing on health system performance, the WHO had tracked responsiveness (based on criteria such as choice, promptness of medical care, confidentiality, and patient autonomy) as well as fairness (adequacy of services for people of all income levels). While the United States was ranked first on responsiveness, it was 54th on fairness in financial

TABLE 8.1 Health Spending versus Performance

	Total Spending on Health as % of GDP (1998)	Public Spending on Health as % of Total Health Spending (1998)	Per Capita Spending on Health (U.S. $, 1998)	Health-Adjusted Life Expectancy at Birth* (Years, 2000) Male	Female	Immunization Rate: DPT, Age 12 Months (%, 1998)	MRIs per million Population (1997)
France	9.4	76.1	2,297	68.5	72.9	84	2.5
Germany	10.5	75.8	2,697	67.4	71.5	NA	6.2
Japan	7.5	78.1	2,244	71.2	76.3	NA	18.8 (1996)
United Kingdom	6.7	83.3	1,628	68.3	71.4	92	3.4 (1995)
United States	13	44.8	4,055	65.7	68.8	84	7.6

*HALE indicator: Life expectancy at birth, adjusted for time spent in poor health (combining estimates from Global Burden of Disease 2000 study with WHO surveys).

Source: Compiled from *World Health Report 2001*, World Health Organization, Geneva, pp. 132, 138–143, 162–167; *OECD Health Data 2000*, Organization for Economic Cooperation and Development, Paris, 2000 (immunization rates and MRIs per million population).

contribution—largely due to the 44 million Americans who lacked health-care insurance.[16] These variations are summarized in Table 8.1.

While the United States stands out in its discrepancy between spending and performance, decades of cost containment have led to a degree of *convergence*—at least in drug prices—across developed economies. According to a study indexing Sweden's drug prices at 100, the price spread in Europe narrowed from 160/60 in 1986 to 120/90 in 1999 for Switzerland and France, the highest and lowest priced markets.[17]

Some health economists have questioned U.S. government studies such as one stating that U.S. drug prices were more than 70 percent higher than in Canada because this report overstated U.S. prices by relying on small samples of branded drugs. By contrast, a study covering both generics and branded products found that a U.S. consumer would have paid 30 percent less in France and 24 percent less in the United Kingdom—but 3 percent more in Canada and 27 percent more in Germany. The study could not factor in manufacturer discounts to government and MCO buyers, which would have lowered U.S. prices further.[18]

REGULATION DYNAMICS

In the same way as spending and performance show great variance across countries, the major OECD markets have fundamentally different regulation dynamics:

- The United States is driven by public pressure to increase government intervention and by leadership at the state level.
- Europe is using a full portfolio of cost containment measures.
- Japan is continuing price cuts and attempting to curb overprescribing.

UNITED STATES: FROM POLICY REFORM TO STATE ACTIVISM

Three main themes have come to the fore in the United States: legislative reform, Medicare drug benefit, and state activism.

The United States health market shows a growing antagonism between the public and the healthcare industry—including both payers and manufacturers. This stand-off can be summarized as follows:

Public Initiatives	Industry Response
• Litigation against MCOs.	• More choice ≠ cost shifting.
• Criticism of high profits.	• Ad campaigns (PhRMA, MCOs).
• Attack on drug prices.	• Drug discount card programs.
• Employer activism.	• Discounts to large purchasers.
• Demand for Medicare drug coverage.	• Support of coverage (privately led).
• State actions (parallel imports, discounts).	• PhRMA lawsuits against states.
• Public pressure for policy reform.	• Increased lobbying to protect patents.

Legislative reform focuses on proposals to reform the Hatch-Waxman Act—in particular, to eliminate multiple "30-month stays" gained by litigation against generic competition. Other reforms target last-minute filings of secondary patents to block generic entry and aim to reduce pricing fraud. Congress is also debating the reimportation of U.S.-made drugs from Canada, now done on a small-scale, mail-order basis—but opposed by the FDA because of safety concerns.

Medicare drug coverage is drawing attention away from a much larger national issue, the 44 million Americans without health insurance. A 2001 Medicare Rx plan by the federal government was met by a lawsuit from two national pharmacy associations, charging that there was no legal authority for the program—but in fact fearing an erosion of drugstore margins. A modified 2002 Medicare card plan proposed that discount card sponsors obtain manufacturer rebates and pass them through to pharmacies and consumers.

The main industry initiatives were *drug discount cards*. A study by the U.S. General Accounting Office (GAO) indicated that these could yield savings of up to 55 percent in retail purchases and 66 percent in mail-order deliveries—but critics charged that manufacturer discount cards applied to high-priced brands, for which savings would be limited. The proliferation of card programs with different channels, benefits, and eligibility criteria could also cause confusion among seniors. By spring 2002, in an effort to streamline programs, seven companies launched the Together Rx card offering discounts on more than 150 branded drugs to low-income Medicare enrollees with no Rx coverage.

However, the Generic Pharmaceutical Association stressed superior savings from generics—publicizing in 2002 a Brandeis study claiming that Medicare could save up to $250 billion over 10 years if it boosted its generic prescribing rate from its current 35 percent to the 51 percent achieved by the best private pharmacy programs.

Other initiatives relevant to biotech companies were individual drug programs. The most ambitious of these related to the oncology drug Gleevec, which cost as much as $24,000 a year in the United States. From January 2002, Novartis offered it at no cost to low-income patients and on a sliding scale to middle-income consumers. This was arguably the most innovative of the discounting programs because—unlike drug discount cards—it gave some relief to middle-class Americans, rather than the poorest segment alone.[19]

Given federal inaction, states had assumed leadership. A first purchasing coalition was formed in 2001 by Maine, New Hampshire, and Vermont to save 10 to 15 percent on their combined $387 million Medicaid drug bill. The Northeast Legislative Association on Prescription Drug Prices added to these three states Connecticut, Massachusetts, New York, Pennsylvania, and Rhode Island; this group planned to negotiate directly with drugmakers for deep discounts.[20]

State legislation was met with industry lawsuits. In May 2000, Maine passed an act mandating that the state negotiate rebates with drugmakers for state residents meeting preset criteria. Nonparticipating companies would be subjected to "prior authorization" for Medicaid prescriptions. PhRMA contested the constitutionality of the act, but a court upheld the Maine Rx program—which was followed by a PhRMA petition to the U.S. Supreme Court.

States such as California and Michigan enacted similar measures. Beyond these discounting efforts, a Florida initiative could be a model for a more comprehensive approach.

EUROPEAN UNION: FULL PORTFOLIO OF PRICING CONTROLS

As recently as 1990, Europe and the United States had roughly equal shares (about a third each) of the global pharmaceutical market. By 2002, Europe's share of the $430 billion total was down to 25 percent, while the United States had climbed to 51 percent. Annual sales in the United States grew

NEGOTIATED DISEASE MANAGEMENT IN FLORIDA

A Florida law mandates rebates in order for drugs to be "guaranteed" inclusion in the Medicaid formulary. An alternative is for drugmakers to fund disease management or education programs guaranteeing the state a minimum savings level. Two firms have pioneered collaborations. Pfizer signed in the summer of 2001 an agreement with the state of Florida, whereby it would fund a technology-based disease management program for four chronic conditions (congestive heart failure, diabetes, asthma, and hypertension). The two-year pilot program aimed to save the state more than $30 million and would ensure inclusion of Pfizer brands in the Medicaid formulary, without preauthorization. Bristol-Myers Squibb followed suit with two community education programs for minority Medicaid recipients with depression, AIDS, and certain cancer types, guaranteed to save the state more than $16 million. Another program would promote early detection of cardiovascular disease and depression. These programs could be win-win solutions, offering better health outcomes as well as cost savings.*

---

* Philip Lebowitz, "States Take Action," *Pharmaceutical Executive* (March 2002), pp. 76–80.

steadily over the past decade, boosted by free-market pricing. European drug prices showed a decline in the same period—although overall health spending continued to rise because of population aging and new technology.

Innovation Flight

While this trend was beneficial for payers and consumers, it also led to a decade-long shift in R&D investment, which included the relocation in 2002 of much of Novartis' research to a $250 million center in the Boston area. The United States now dominates biopharma innovation, accounting for two-thirds of the new drugs launched in the past five years.

Pricing policy is only part of the European innovation problem. Public funding, venture capital, and registration efficiency are all lagging the United States. The NIH annual budget dwarfs the EU research budget. Venture capital is underdeveloped, and European universities do not have legislation helping them commercialize their research (such as the Bayh-Dole Act in the United States).

The EU also lags the United States in biotechnology. Biologic registration is centralized through the European Medicines Evaluation Agency (EMEA); pharmaceuticals may use either this process or a country-by-country mutual recognition procedure. However, EU-wide legislation for biologic patents was formalized only in 2000 (16 years after the United States), and most members have yet to implement it.

Speed to market is also seriously compromised. After gaining market authorization, biopharma products still need to deal with national reimbursement authorities—leading to delays as long as four years. An EU directive called for a maximum review time of six months, but implementation has varied widely.

Pharma firms have voiced protests against these hurdles. Glaxo and AstraZeneca have warned that Europe will lose more innovation if research costs cannot be recovered, and Pfizer has proposed that the French government introduce a two-tier pricing system protecting innovative drugs and letting prices fall for older ones. This came after France announced in 2001 another round of price cuts.

From Parallel Traders to Cartels

Parallel trade in Europe stems from the conflict between EU principles and national pricing policies. The Treaty of Rome protects the free movement of goods, but member states price drugs individually. This has led to a brisk and growing parallel trade whereby specialized companies freely export products from low-priced to high-priced EU states and may repackage products, use trademarks, and rebrand drugs if necessary. Parallel imports' shares of national markets are as high as 13 percent in the United Kingdom and 15 percent in the Netherlands. Savings to consumers are low—for every $6 in lost revenue to pharma firms, $5 is the parallel trader's estimated operating margin and only $1 is saved by patients or payers. However, parallel imports are encouraged in most markets and actually mandated in Germany, where pharmacists were told in 2002 to ensure that at least 5.5 percent of their dispensed drugs are parallel imports—a share due to rise to 7 percent by 2003.[21]

In the same way as U.S. authorities are stepping up their scrutiny of biopharma firms, the European Commission (EC) is focusing its attention on cartels, for which it can levy fines of up to 10 percent of a company's turnover. In 2001 alone, the EC garnered €1.8 billion in fines—including a record €855 million from eight vitamin makers including Aventis, BASF, and Roche for fixing prices and setting sales quotas.[22] Roche subsequently divested its vitamins unit.

Beyond legal scrutiny, all major markets use a full portfolio of cost containment measures, from global budgets to generic substitution. (See Table 8.2.)

Direct price controls, whereby governments regulate product prices, are practiced by most EU states (Germany is a notable exception). The United Kingdom does not set prices but has imposed across-the-board price cuts and price freezes. France's low prices make it a reference market for many countries, and it has a full range of cost controls, including price cuts and direct negotiations with drugmakers. These include local performance requirements, whereby companies obtain preferential treatment if they produce locally, conduct R&D locally, or export from their local plants.

Indirect price controls are now universal, ranging from rebates to U.S. federal agencies to profit controls in Europe. France imposes price-volume linkages, whereby companies commit to volume targets for a new product; if these are exceeded, price cuts or rebates to the government are required. Global healthcare budgets are set by many governments, expecting the pharma sector to offset their cost overruns. In France, an "exceptional contribution" from pharma firms is levied to mitigate the health insurance deficit.

Profit controls are practiced in the United Kingdom via the Pharmaceutical Price Regulation Scheme, which imposes a 21 percent profit cap, measured as a return on average capital employed locally. Firms with no major capital investments in the United Kingdom can use a return on sales (ROS) measure. If profit limits are exceeded, companies must reduce prices or make a cash payback.

Physician budgets or prescribing guidelines are widely used. In the United Kingdom, drug expenditures are part of global budgets at the primary care group or hospital level. In Germany, MD budgets were introduced in 1998 but were met with opposition—including physician demonstrations and strikes. In January 2001, the new health minister reversed a previous decision to make all physicians within a region responsible for overprescription. The move led to a swift increase in drug spending.[23] Other constraints are limits on the number of products that can be prescribed in one consultation (Italy

TABLE 8.2   **Pricing Regulation–Key Markets**

	United States	Japan	Germany	France	United Kingdom
Direct price controls	No	Biannual price cuts.	No	Yes	No
Indirect price controls	Discounts to federal agencies.	Price cuts higher for older drugs.	MD budgets.	Excess sales repayment.	Profit control, MD budgets.
National reference pricing	No	No	Yes (includes biologics).	Yes	Equivalent
International reference pricing	No	Yes	No	Informal	No
Positive reimbursement list	MCO formularies.	Yes	Under development.	Yes	Yes
Negative reimbursement list	No	No	Yes	Yes (delisting).	No
Price negotiations	Discounts to federal agencies, large groups.	Yes	Yes	Negotiations with MOH.	Discounts to hospital purchasers.
Parallel imports	Under debate.	No	Required quota for pharmacists.	Allowed (within EU).	Allowed (within EU).
Use of generics	High	Negligible	Increasing	Substitution allowed.	High
Pharmaco-economics	Increasing (FDA filings).	Early stage at MHLW.	Yes	Yes	NICE assessments.
Consumer copayments	High (multi-tiered).	Yes	Yes	Yes	Yes

Source: Françoise Simon/SDC Group, 2002.

and Spain) and prescribing guidelines without quantitative limits (Germany, France, and the United Kingdom).

A widespread form of indirect price control is *reference pricing.* In internal reference pricing, national health authorities set a fixed reimbursement amount for a pharmaceutical, either by comparing it with another product or by including it in a cluster of drugs. Clusters may be narrow (same active ingredient) or broad (pharmacological equivalence or therapeutic area). Any amount above the maximum allowable cost is paid by patients or private insurance. Spain, Sweden, Denmark, and the Netherlands use this system.

In external reference pricing, countries use international price comparisons. Canada compares a proposed new product price to its average price in seven OECD countries. Sweden, Denmark, Italy, the Netherlands,

---

THE IMPACT OF REFERENCE PRICING IN GERMANY

Germany pioneered internal reference pricing, implementing it in three stages:

1989—Patented and generic products clustered by active ingredients.
1991—Cluster criteria expanded to pharmaceutical equivalence.
1992—Clusters included therapeutic equivalence (patented and off-patent drugs).

The immediate impact was a 4 percent reduction in total prescriptions in 1991 to 1995 and a decline in brand prices relative to generics, since most firms lowered their prices to the reference level. The system also decreased insurer expenditure by nearly 20 percent. However, critics charged that it forced some patients to switch medicines and adversely impacted compliance. After a court decision, new patented products were exempted from reference pricing in January 1996. Health spending, which had decreased as the system was implemented, rose again to reach nearly 11 percent by 2001. Even though prices had fallen for referenced drugs (i.e., off-patent products), prices and volumes for patented products increased— the system encouraged manufacturers to move away from branded generics and introduce new products for the same indication, which would be reimbursed at a higher level even if they were "me-too" drugs. Germany's system included biologics, and it was influential beyond its borders because it was referenced by Japan, Canada, Switzerland, and the Netherlands.*

---

* *Reference Pricing,* Datamonitor (October 2001), pp. 17–19, 42–44.

and Switzerland all use external references. Other countries that take international prices into account are Spain (country or origin plus lowest price in EU) and France (Spain, Portugal, Italy, and EU)—although France has no explicit formula. Across Europe, external reference pricing has shifted from matching the lowest EU price to reaching an average European price.[24]

Positive and negative reimbursement lists or their equivalents are now near universal. Positive lists of reimbursed products are used in France, Germany, and many other EU states, and the United States has an equivalent (managed care formularies). Negative lists of nonreimbursed products are used in Germany and Spain, and the United Kingdom has an equivalent (Selected List of 17 product categories not eligible for NHS reimbursement).

Several governments have engaged in massive *delisting*—that is, the removal of products or categories from reimbursement. In a recent review, France rated more than 800 reimbursable products as having an insufficient medical benefit, which made them targets for price cuts and later delisting.

Finally, *generics* have an uneven penetration in Europe but are increasingly encouraged. The United Kingdom has the highest generic prescription rate among leading markets. France allowed generic substitution in 1998 but remains underpenetrated because branded prices are low and physicians and consumers prefer branded products. Because of reference pricing, generics have a relatively high value share of more than 20 percent in Germany.[25]

JAPAN: DIRECT AND INDIRECT PRICE CONTROLS

With annual sales of nearly $50 billion, Japan is the second largest market worldwide—larger than Germany, France, and the United Kingdom combined—but it also presents several hurdles, from a specific epidemiology to different treatment protocols and a difficult approval and pricing process. Due to prevalence or cultural factors, therapeutic categories that are substantial in Western markets may be minor in Japan. Cardiovascular disease is less prevalent, for instance, and a culture of denial toward diseases such as depression has limited their therapies; as it was losing its patent in the United States, Prozac had still not been introduced in Japan. Approvals were historically a big hurdle because Japan required all trial phases to be redone on

Japanese patients—claiming a different physiology, but also protecting the domestic pharma industry from foreign competition. The Ministry of Health, Labor, and Welfare (MHLW), to harmonize its rules with international standards, recently allowed companies "bridging studies," whereby early-stage trials are redone with Japanese subjects, but if they show little variance from Western studies, bioequivalence is granted on the basis of Phase III clinicals in non-Japanese populations.[26] Prices are controlled by the government and set via reference to the United States, Germany, France, and the United Kingdom. Insurers reimburse at the National Health Insurance (NHI) price, but hospitals and physicians, who dispense most drugs, are entitled to the difference between the NHI level and their discounted purchase price from drugmakers.

In an effort to reduce this spread (which has historically led to over-prescribing), the government has adopted a two-prong approach: biannual price cuts since 1992 and an attempt to separate prescribing and dispensing. Because of price cuts (and despite the fact that generics are virtually non-existent), the Japanese drug market shrank from 22 percent of world sales to 13 percent in the past decade.

In 2002, price cuts averaged 6.3 percent, but a significant reform was a skewing of price cuts toward older drugs—which will be reduced by nearly 5 percent more than new medicines, while innovative therapies may command premiums. This demonstrated a policy shift from protecting the domestic industry to prioritizing the national budget. Many Japanese firms that prospered on high prices, market protection, and me-too products are now developing ex-Japan sales and signing deals with Western companies. Roche bought a 50.1 percent stake in Chugai, Abbott paid nearly $300 million to complete its acquisition of Hokuriku Seiyaku (for a remaining 33 percent share), and GlaxoSmithKline entered into an alliance with Shionogi to codevelop and market four therapies in the United States.[27]

SUMMARY POINTS

Drug access and price have become lighting rods of consumer criticism and government action and are a top strategic issue for the biopharma sector. This needs to be addressed by coordinating company strategies and industrywide policy initiatives. While there is some degree of global convergence on pricing and regulation, major world markets retain specific cost containment approaches and company policies must be adapted to each region and, to some extent, each national market.

At the industry level, more effort is needed to communicate biopharma economics to the public:

✓ *R&D costs* are escalating, but their estimation is subject to debate.
✓ *Production costs* are a growing burden for biologics, but this is not well-known.
✓ *Cost migration* is occurring from medical services to biopharmaceuticals, but the public, focused on drug prices, ignores benefits such as reduced hospitalizations.
✓ *The cost effectiveness of biopharmaceuticals* is well documented in medical and economic studies, but it relies on a systemic assessment (drug cost versus lifetime disease cost or total cost to society), which conflicts with the short-term orientation of managed care groups.

At the company level, pharmacoeconomic studies should go beyond payers to target other stakeholders who have a longer term mindset and more collective power:

✓ *Employers and states* that have formed purchasing pools can appreciate the long-term impact of drug therapies on work productivity.
✓ *Physicians* are under cost constraints and are increasingly relying on economic as well as clinical data for their prescribing decisions.
✓ *Consumers* are subjected to increased cost-shifting and must be better informed of the cost effectiveness of their therapies.

At the global level, balancing drug access and price must be done in the larger context of regulation dynamics and must be adapted to regional and national policy frameworks:

✓ In the United States, *states are assuming leadership* on Medicare drug coverage and the uninsured, and industry response has focused on discount care initiatives, but broader initiatives include tiered pricing and disease management programs.

✓ In Europe, governments use a full *portfolio of cost containment measures* including direct and indirect price controls; companies should prioritize breakthrough products because these are not subject to reference pricing, and they should also support them with pharmacoeconomic studies.

✓ In Japan, epidemiology, treatment protocols, approval, and pricing differ from those of other markets and require *a country-specific approach;* companies can benefit from recently allowed "bridging studies" that alleviate the requirement for local clinicals; breakthrough products should be privileged because price cuts are now more skewed toward older therapies.

BIOPRICING STRATEGIES

As a company and as an industry, we may not be doing enough. . . . So the challenge will be to ensure access to medicines, today and tomorrow. . . . We need to explain the balancing act between short-term cost savings and long-term access to medicines.

Henry McKinnell, chairman and CEO, Pfizer[1]

Given the escalating consequences of price decisions, companies are shifting from transaction tactics to comprehensive pricing strategies. In the context of the biosector's high public profile, the critical question is not "What is the highest price we can obtain for this product?" but rather "What pricing strategy will best meet our financial, social, and regulatory objectives?"

Given the growing emphasis on corporate accountability, pricing must, therefore, be integrated into an overall scientific and business plan as early as possible in a product's timeline—and all objectives need to be assessed equally. (See Figure 9.1.)

Trade-offs must be addressed at different levels:

- Shareholder interest versus stakeholder concerns.
- Maximized profit versus enhanced access and company image.

229

SOCIAL LEADERSHIP AND CORPORATE EQUITY

A survey of executives and analysts focused on *capitalized reputation*. It assessed 16 top biopharma firms on eight dimensions of business success—four of which were social (ethics, social responsibility, charitable support, and workforce/processes). Business factors were competitiveness (driven by innovation), marketing effectiveness, financial stability, and strategic alliances.

In terms of *overall reputation ranking,* the top five firms were J&J, Merck, Pfizer, Glaxo, and Genentech. Only J&J and Merck were top-rated on all dimensions. Genentech was number four on competitiveness, last on financial stability—but number one or number two on three social dimensions (workforce, charitable support, and social responsibility). When asked which company they would "pay a premium for" and "support in times of controversy," respondents ranked Genentech first on the former, and fourth on the latter (after J&J, Glaxo, and Merck)—demonstrating that company reputation is built, not only on financial and market performance, but also on social achievements.[*]

[*] Jeffrey Resnick, "A Matter of Reputation," *Pharmaceutical Executive* (June 2002), pp. 75–80; see also Shantanu Dutta et al., "Pricing as a Strategic Capability," *MIT Sloan Management Review* (Spring 2002).

- Return on investment versus reimbursement.
- High early payback versus market share acquisition.

Because, in most cases, an optimal return on investment will not be achieved without adequate reimbursement, the premium price that an innovative product may command needs to be supported by compelling pharmacoeconomic data. Differential pricing across borders, in theory maximizing profit, also needs to be weighed against a global price band supporting a worldwide positioning strategy.

ROI maximization varies according to a biobrand's competitive environment. Breakthrough products for critical therapeutic areas, with no substitutes and with high economic value, can command premium launch prices with relatively few reimbursement obstacles—however, price and

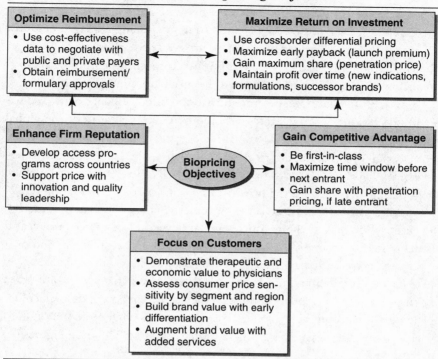

FIGURE 9.1   Biopricing Objectives

Optimize Reimbursement
- Use cost-effectiveness data to negotiate with public and private payers
- Obtain reimbursement/ formulary approvals

Maximize Return on Investment
- Use crossborder differential pricing
- Maximize early payback (launch premium)
- Gain maximum share (penetration price)
- Maintain profit over time (new indications, formulations, successor brands)

Enhance Firm Reputation
- Develop access pro- grams across countries
- Support price with innovation and quality leadership

Biopricing Objectives

Gain Competitive Advantage
- Be first-in-class
- Maximize time window before next entrant
- Gain share with penetration pricing, if late entrant

Focus on Customers
- Demonstrate therapeutic and economic value to physicians
- Assess consumer price sen- sitivity by segment and region
- Build brand value with early differentiation
- Augment brand value with added services

Source: Françoise Simon/SDC Group, 2002.

access still need to be balanced for lifesaving products. When launching its leukemia therapy Gleevec, Novartis tempered its high price with an innovative U.S. program ensuring access for low- and middle-income patients.

In the current environment, price maximization may be superseded by corporate reputation—as demonstrated by the Medicare discount cards launched by leading pharma firms in the United States. This is also what motivated their policy reversal in emerging markets: abandonment of their collective lawsuit against the South African government for violating patents on AIDS drugs and subsequent supply of these at cost or free of charge, together with public/private partnerships to support distribution.

For products that are not first in class, gaining share may be the main objective and can be achieved with *penetration pricing,* that is, a discount to the class leader.

Pricing objectives must be adapted to customer segments because price sensitivity and purchase attributes vary by region and customer group.

To be an effective part of corporate strategy, pricing management must be integrated into the development process at the earliest possible stage. Pharmacoeconomic analyses should be linked to clinical studies, and *dynamic pricing* should be used through the product's timeline.

Given regional differences in regulation, reimbursement policy, and social expectations, pricing strategy should be developed at both the global and national levels. Global decisions include the trade-off between differential pricing and a global price band, as well as the launch sequence between high-priced and low-priced countries. National strategies include negotiations with public and private payers and *price discrimination* to expand access (i.e., discounts to some customer segments, such as the elderly).

Pricing strategy at the product/segment level will be effective only if it is integrated over time (i.e., linked to R&D pre- and postlaunch) and over space (i.e., connecting national and global policies). The same principles apply here as in overall branding strategy; success comes from *evidence-based pricing*—that is, differentiation through therapeutic and economic value. Depending on the competitive context, launch options range from premium to parity and penetration pricing. These strategy steps are shown in Figure 9.2.

MANAGING THE PRICING TIMELINE

R&D portfolios are usually prioritized according to a product's revenue or market share potential, but price potential is also a key factor. The best scenario is a breakthrough product, which is the case for many biologics. Even late entrants can gain favorable reimbursement terms if they are well differentiated with a clinical and economic superiority. However, a top priority is to accelerate time to market for two reasons: A first-to-market status is a key pricing advantage (no comparator product and high unmet need); each additional month in development carries not only direct costs, but also the opportunity costs of lost sales. Speed to market can be accelerated through investment and coordination of clinicals—including electronic patient recruitment and simultaneous trials in key markets.

Portfolio management metrics should, therefore, reflect three types of criteria: scientific (innovativeness, safety, and efficacy), market (prevalence,

FIGURE 9.2   Key Pricing Steps

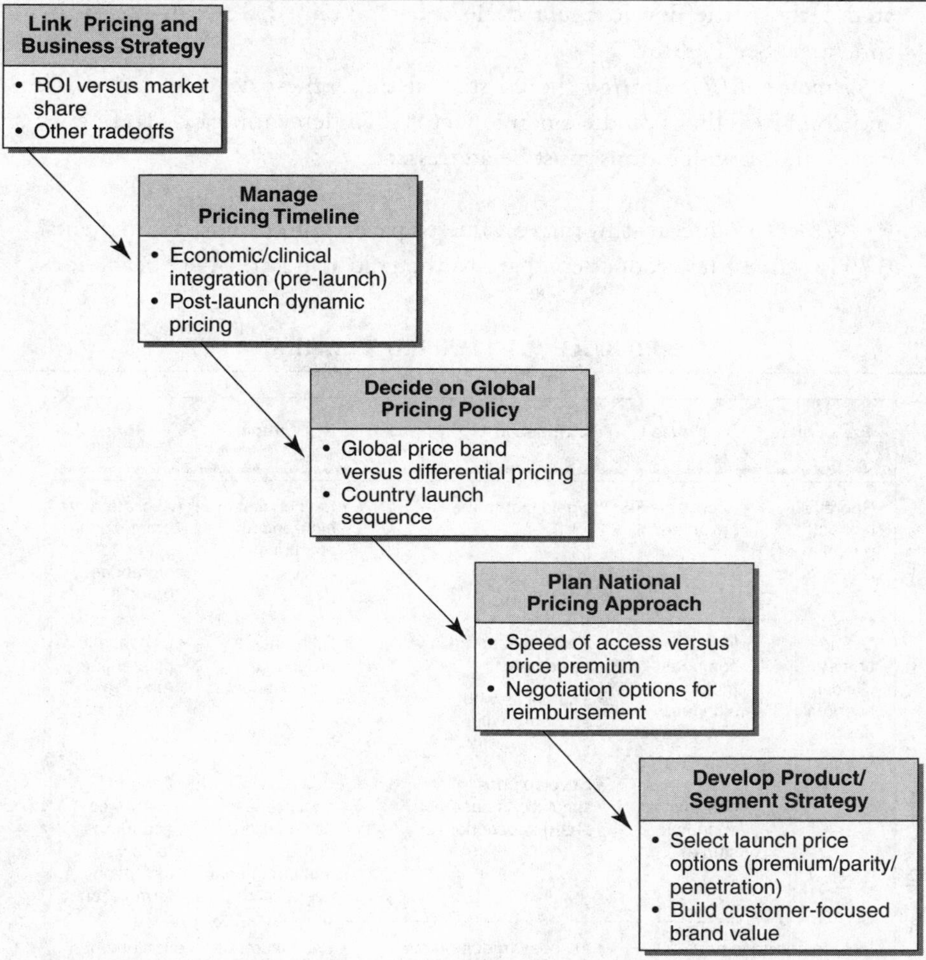

Link Pricing and Business Strategy
- ROI versus market share
- Other tradeoffs

Manage Pricing Timeline
- Economic/clinical integration (pre-launch)
- Post-launch dynamic pricing

Decide on Global Pricing Policy
- Global price band versus differential pricing
- Country launch sequence

Plan National Pricing Approach
- Speed of access versus price premium
- Negotiation options for reimbursement

Develop Product/ Segment Strategy
- Select launch price options (premium/parity/ penetration)
- Build customer-focused brand value

Source: Françoise Simon/SDC Group, 2002.

share potential, competitive advantage), and economic (price and reimbursement potential).

In addition, portfolios should be continually reviewed postlaunch, and resources should be concentrated on products that have met their reimbursement price targets because these can generate gross profits up to 30 percent higher than others.[2]

For each product, clinical and economic differentiation must be initiated early in the development cycle and maintained through the entire timeline. (See Figure 9.3.)

Product differentiation should start at the earliest development phase and combine clinical and economic factors. To determine a cost-effective price band, key questions must be addressed:

- Which product features have value to payers, physicians, and patients?
- How does the product compare to the gold standard (if applicable)?

FIGURE 9.3   Pricing Timeline

	Pre-clinical	Phase I	Phase II	Phase III	Launch	Phase IV
Portfolio	• Prioritize highest potential products	• Accelerate R&D to gain first-to-market advantage			• Launch first in high-priced countries	• Allocate more promotional spend to high-priced brands
Product	• Define unmet clinical, economic need	• Identify comparator (gold standard/ share leader)	• Head-to-head trials with comparator • End points with economic value		• Differentiate product on clinical and economic superiority	• Continue to differentiate (new indications)
Pharmacoeconomics		• Start pharmaco-economic studies	• Develop price simulations based on pharmacoeconomics		• Use cost effectiveness data in filings and reimbursement negotiations	• Expand pharmaco-economics to new indications, formulations
Pricing Strategy	• Include pricing in portfolio planning and market assessment		• Assess target markets' economic profile (reimbursement policy, price sensitivity by segment) • Create scenarios for revenues and profits at various price levels • Determine global price band		• Use differential pricing across countries • Premium pricing for breakthrough product • Penetration pricing for late entrant	• Implement dynamic pricing (review and adjustment)

Source: Françoise Simon/SDC Group, 2002; Partly adapted from *Reference Pricing,* Datamonitor (October 2001), p. 60.

- How can value be increased?
- Does the product's perceived value vary by application?[3]

The best information sources of a product's clinical value are the trial investigators, who can also most effectively "presell" it to the medical community. In addition, publications can communicate economic value and raise awareness with payers at an early stage. Further differentiation can be gained through product support and other added value services, such as support for patient networks. Prelaunch consumer research also helps define a product's potential value for patients, especially when the targeted condition is underdiagnosed and ill defined. For a new gastrointestinal therapy, Novartis conducted large-scale studies that uncovered segment-specific needs, depending on symptom severity, therapies already used, and lifestyle (i.e., alternative medicine versus mainstream orientation).

If a product is not first in class, it is critical to *choose the right comparator* at the preclinical phase and to conduct head-to-head trials to justify the product's position and pricing at launch. The comparator should be the existing gold standard, which usually commands a high price. Phase I studies can yield useful competitive comparisons, which can in turn influence the design and endpoints for Phases II and III trials. For instance, if the comparator has a narrow dosing range and high administration frequency, the new product can be monitored in Phase I to determine whether the dose range can be optimized; if so, this can be integrated into Phase II trials. The resulting advantage at launch could be once-daily versus twice-daily dosing.

During the development of Lipitor (atorvastatin), Warner-Lambert determined that it had a dosage advantage over class leader Zocor (simvastatin). Lipitor was as effective as Zocor at lower doses; in addition, it was consistently effective in a wide range of patients, whereas Zocor needed dose titration. Even though Lipitor was fifth to market and did not have the mortality and morbidity data of the established brands, Warner-Lambert was able to package its efficacy, dosage, and consistency advantages in a way that supported wide reimbursement in key markets.[4]

IMPACT OF PHARMACOECONOMICS

As they become standardized worldwide, pharmacoeconomic studies have the potential to be the key factor in setting prices, volumes, and global budgets. While their use now varies across OECD countries, these are exchanging health economic data and harmonizing their regulatory systems. EMEA has discussed a Medicines Information Network for Europe, which may include cost-effectiveness assessments. In the United States, FDA submissions are helped by economic data, and some insurers take into account economic assessments, including those by the U.K.'s National Institute of Clinical Excellence (NICE), which determines NHS reimbursement. Economic data are required for reimbursement in Australia, Portugal, the Netherlands, and Finland; they are needed for price negotiations in France and helpful for approval in Spain, Italy, and Germany. Canadian provinces rely on them for formulary decisions.[5]

Economic analyses should continue postlaunch, as part of postmarketing surveillance and utilization reviews for regulators and payers and to support new indications.

A Datamonitor report estimated that pharmacoeconomics studies entailed a 5 percent increase in R&D cost, which was outweighed by the resulting price advantage. With a conservative assumption of $600 million in average R&D costs, economic analyses would add $30 million; at an average annual revenue of $300 million, a product would need a 10 percent premium to cover the additional cost in its first year. Datamonitor estimated that this type of integrated R&D could yield a price premium of up to 20 percent.[6]

A full portfolio of pharmacoeconomic tools has been developed:

- *Cost-effectiveness analysis* evaluates the total costs of a given therapy—direct (drug and nondrug) and indirect (lost income and productivity).
- *Cost-benefit analysis* measures these in monetary terms.
- *Cost-utility analysis* tracks the quality-adjusted life years (QALYs) related to specific therapies.
- *Outcomes analysis* is derived from clinical trials, with endpoints ranging from efficacy and safety to morbidity/mortality and quality of life.

DYNAMIC PRICING STRATEGY

Supported by pharmacoeconomics, pricing strategy starts at the preclinical stage, includes market assessment and scenario development during clinicals, optimizes the launch sequence, and helps sustain biobrands after launch through price reviews.

GLAXO'S ADVAIR AND PHARMACOECONOMICS

One of GlaxoSmithKline's key franchises is its multibillion-dollar asthma business.

Leading brands Flovent (fluticonase) and Serevent (salmeterol) were threatened in 1998 by the leukotriene antagonist class, led by Merck's Singulair (montelukast). Whereas Serevent required twice-daily inhalation, the new class offered once-daily oral dosing—a significant advantage because inhaled products had low compliance rates.

To rejuvenate the franchise, Glaxo developed an inhaled combination of Serevent and Flovent. Branded as Advair in the United States, it was indicated for asthma and chronic obstructive pulmonary disease. Glaxo took a dual economic and clinical approach to identify the best indications for Advair. Drawing from the European Respiratory Health study, Glaxo identified moderate to severe asthma as the highest-potential indication. Focused trials were quickly done and showed that Advair could be used at a lower dose that reduced side effects.* Launched in Europe in 1998 and 1999 and in the United States in April 2001, Advair achieved more than $2 billion in global sales by 2002—outselling Merck's Singulair. Lessons from this case are threefold:

1. Combination products can significantly strengthen a maturing franchise.
2. Understanding disease economics helps pinpoint the most profitable indications.
3. Pharmacoeconomic studies can efficiently focus clinical trials.

---

* *Reference Pricing,* Datamonitor (October 2001), pp. 65–66.

Market assessment links medical, business, and economic dimensions, including:

- Medical data (disease prevalence and incidence, therapeutic need).
- Customer profiles (physician and patient demographics and price sensitivity).
- Competitive situation (class and share leadership, relative innovation, marketing strength, pricing strategy, and cost effectiveness of competitor products).

■ Regulatory/reimbursement factors (use of pharmacoeconomics, reference pricing, parallel trade, formulary rules).

Studies aiming to determine the price elasticity of demand across markets often attempt to identify a fixed trade-off between price and demand. In fact, the early development of customer-focused brand value and its enhancement over time can diminish price elasticity, thanks to customer-specific effects:

Effect	Customer Group
• *Unique value effect* (no substitutes, high unmet need).	• Regulators, MDs, payers, patients.
• *Total benefit effect* (efficacy, safety, tolerability, convenience, compliance).	• MDs, payers, patients.
• *Total expenditure effect* (reduction of nondrug costs, lost work days).	• Payers, employers.
• *Orphan drug effect* (small population).	• Payers.
• *Shared cost effect* (company discount to some buyers).	• Payers, patients.

The small population effect is particularly relevant for biologics, several of which are orphan drugs. While unit price matters to payers, total price (price × expected volume) is more important because an expensive therapy for a large population would consume a disproportionate share of a payer's budget. Conversely, payers would be less price-sensitive if the new therapy's high cost concerns a small population—especially if it decreases the total expenditure (i.e., reduces nondrug costs such as hospitalizations).

As U.S. employers form large purchasing groups, their buying decisions will have a large impact on sales. For them, a positive total expenditure effect (including higher productivity) may offset a premium price. The shared cost effect shifts demand positively if it entails company discounts to large buyers or segments such as the elderly. When it comes from cost-shifting to patients (in the form of copayments), it has the opposite effect, that is, it makes patients more price-sensitive and demand more elastic.

These effects are illustrated in Figure 9.4.

FIGURE 9.4   Biobrand Value and Price Elasticity

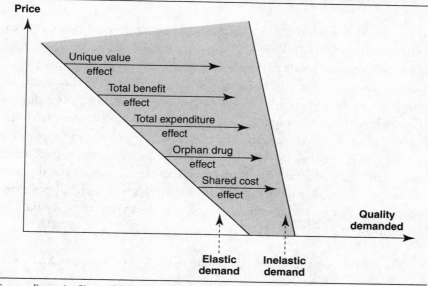

Source: Françoise Simon/SDC Group, 2002; partly adapted from Philip Kotler, *Marketing Management* (New York: Prentice-Hall, 2000), pp. 459–460, 462.

Postlaunch, pricing strategy needs to remain dynamic and market-responsive, answering questions such as:

- Have reimbursement price targets been reached?
- Do sales and market share meet forecasts?
- What are the reactions from competitors (if any)?
- Do some customer groups value the brand more highly and drive demand?
- Conversely, are any segments resistant and/or price sensitive? What added value would convert them?

Accurate answers to these questions require effective pricing information systems, including a standardized database about market, customer, and competitor profiles as well as internal costs and resources. The system must be able to create sales and share forecasts from scenarios developed at different price levels, and it should also have the capacity to adjust data through all stages of the product's timeline.[7]

DECIDING THE GLOBAL PRICING POLICY

In theory, differential pricing allows a maximization of profits across countries. In practice, it depends on the separability of markets, which is rapidly decreasing because of international reference pricing and parallel trade (allowed within the EU and growing in Asia). Parallel trade accounts for about 2 percent of total pharma sales in Europe, but it disproportionately affects premium-priced blockbusters because its profitability depends on a minimum 20 percent margin between high and low prices and high sales volume to offset the costs of relabeling and repackaging. Most companies adopt a global price band at launch, which has the dual advantage of minimizing parallel trade and supporting a global positioning strategy. For biologics especially, the price band is narrow for the following reasons:

- They are often breakthrough products with no substitutes and command price premiums.
- Parallel trade is not an issue for biologics because of production complexity (but it may be in the future as countries such as India develop biotech capabilities).

SETTING THE GLOBAL PRICE BAND

The global price band sets maximum and minimum prices for world markets. Within it, regional price bands may exist for the EU, the United States, and Asia. Because of external reference pricing, a European price band is relatively tight (average EU price plus or minus 30 percent) and likely to narrow further in the future. By contrast, the U.S. price band may expand as federal and state authorities, large purchasers, and segments such as Medicare enrollees demand ever-larger discounts. Asia has the broadest price band because of the different purchasing power of countries such as Japan and Vietnam and because of different national pricing policies.

Defining a global price band involves a four-step process:

1. Assessing the price potential in each key market, depending on reimbursement/price controls, price sensitivity of stakeholders, and product innovativeness/competitive position.

2. Aggregating the findings for key markets in each region and setting regional price bands; these vary according to the weight of each market (size and growth) and the perceived product homogeneity across countries.

3. Determining the width of the global price band, based on a combination of the regional bands.

4. Setting target prices for each market in the regional bands, giving priority to the countries used as benchmarks in international reference pricing.[8]

DECIDING THE LAUNCH ORDER

By launching first in high-priced countries that are benchmarked by others, companies can maximize revenues because the reference price of follower countries is likely to be set higher. In Europe, the optimal launch order would be Germany and the United Kingdom first, then France, and Spain and Italy last. France benchmarks the entire EU, but its price may be higher if it has only Germany and the United Kingdom to reference. Spain references the lowest EU price and that of the originator country, and Italy references four countries, two of which are price-controlled. However, there are several caveats to this strategy:

- It is most effective for products subject to reference pricing and less relevant for first-in-class compounds and biologics.
- The price premium gained may be outweighed by the sales volume lost from a delayed launch in several countries.
- Market and competitive factors may preclude launching in high-priced countries first (lower market growth, presence of a competitive product).[9]

Alternative options are to launch outside reimbursement at a high price or not to launch in countries where the price band floor cannot be reached. However, forsaking reimbursement is possible for life-enhancing drugs but not for life-saving therapies—a high-priced, breakthrough oncology product would not be viable without reimbursement. Similarly, excluding some markets because they do not meet price targets would entail lost sales and—more importantly—would not be ethically acceptable. These trade-offs are summarized in Table 9.1.

TABLE 9.1   Global Pricing Trade-Offs

Pricing Strategies	Biologics	Small Molecules
Differential pricing	Maximizes profits ≠ biologic prices vary little in OECD.	Maximizes profits ≠ facilitates parallel trade.
Global price band	Supports consistent global position ≠ limits gains in high-priced countries.	Minimizes parallel trade ≠ limits volume in price-sensitive markets.
Prioritize launch in high-priced countries	Maximizes early payback ≠ loses revenue from delays.	Raises reference price ≠ loses revenues from delays.
Set premium price outside of reference system	Applies to first-in-class products ≠ limits volume.	Applies to breakthrough products ≠ limits volume.
Obtain high reimbursement price via pharmacoeconomics	Feasible if alternatives are expensive ≠ lost revenues due to negotiation delays.	Applies to most products ≠ lost revenue due to negotiation delays.
Launch at high price outside of reimbursement	Unfeasible due to high price and unmet need of biologics.	Applies to lifestyle drugs ≠ volume limited by patients' willingness to pay.
Withhold from low-price countries	Unfeasible (central registration mandates EU-wide availability).	Minimizes parallel trade ≠ inadvisable for ethical and financial reasons.

Source: Françoise Simon/SDC Group, 2002.

DESIGNING A NATIONAL PRICING STRATEGY

In Europe, *optimal price versus speed of access* is a key trade-off that companies must address. The United Kingdom offers the fastest average time to market after product approval, but France, Spain, and Italy all entail protracted reimbursement negotiations. To recoup as fast as possible their development costs, manufacturers have tended to sacrifice optimal pricing for speed to market. Over the past decade, the European market penetration average was nearly two years for access to 60 percent of countries. This is accelerating: In 2000, several products accessed 60 percent of the market within nine months. Glaxo's HIV drug Ziagen (abacavir) had a record speed, reaching 60 percent of the market in six months and virtually all states within a year. In addition, Ziagen was able to achieve an average European price 10 percent above the U.S. average. In arthritis, biotech therapy Enbrel also was priced in Europe 5 percent higher than in the United States because of its innovativeness.

Speed versus price decisions need to be assessed by category and product type. The HIV category benefits from a very high level of patient activism, which influences both speed and reimbursement—this effect applies to life-saving therapies in general.

In addition, biologics do not face the speed/price trade-off that confronts small molecules. Because they are often first-in-class therapies with no substitutes and superior safety and efficacy, they can support a premium price across countries and bypass reference pricing—especially if their submission filings include compelling pharmacoeconomic data in addition to superior clinical endpoints.[10]

A key success factor in national pricing strategy is negotiation skill with government payers, which may include willingness to delay a launch to gain a better price, or conversely, pricing flexibility to ensure fast penetration.

An extreme option is the decision to launch outside of reimbursement. This is relevant for lifestyle drugs but has also been used in other categories when a country's price potential was below the target threshold. When it launched Viagra, Pfizer was facing either partial or no reimbursement, and it had to address these questions:

- Which markets were most likely to rate the drug as nonessential?
- What patient groups could drive demand due to higher unmet need and willingness to pay?
- What price and sales volume would be achievable under partial or no reimbursement?

Pfizer strove to build its brand's value through a comprehensive educational program; by helping change the condition's name from *impotence* to *erectile dysfunction,* it also wanted to reduce social stigma and resistance to seeking treatment. It successively targeted distinct segments such as older and younger men and specific ethnic and income groups and was able to achieve price premiums over existing therapies. By 2002, Viagra had reached

VIOXX VERSUS CELEBREX: EUROPEAN PRICE NEGOTIATIONS

The Cox-2 inhibitors, launched within six months of each other in the U.S. market (December 1998 for Pharmacia/Pfizer's Celebrex and May 1999 for Merck's Vioxx), entered a European arthritis market that was led by genericized nonsteroidal anti-inflammatory drugs (NSAIDs). Their clinical profile did not appear to justify their price premium; their efficacy was comparable to that of NSAIDs, but they claimed a tolerability advantage (less gastric irritation). Nevertheless, Merck and Pharmacia/Pfizer were positioning their brands as pioneers and attempting to set a new price point without reference to existing therapies. They convinced payers of their therapeutic superiority, and both brands were launched at prices 10 to 100 percent higher than those of the top NSAIDs. Both accessed the EU market faster than average, but they had different national strategies. *Pfizer prioritized speed*; reimbursement negotiations in France were only six months because Pfizer agreed to a price cut after three years, against an initial high price and a 65 percent reimbursement. By contrast, *Merck emphasized a price premium,* delaying launches to secure better terms. While reimbursement delays for Celebrex were six months or less in France, Italy, and Spain, Vioxx required from nine months to more than a year of negotiations in Southern Europe. Vioxx obtained a higher European price than that of Celebrex, but also lost sales from its delays.* By 2002, Celebrex was leading with more than $3 billion in global sales. Although the outcome of the Cox-2 battle was still unknown, some lessons could be learned:

- If speed is the key criterion, the most effective accelerator is an innovative concession such as Pfizer's price cut three years after launch.

- If a price premium is the primary objective, a company should be prepared to face longer negotiations—and this may be risky when a brand is not first to market.

---

* Andra Brichacek, "The European Pricing Game," *Pharmaceutical Executive* (July 2001), pp. 50, 54; *Reference Pricing,* Datamonitor (October 2001), p. 51.

more than $1.7 billion in global sales—an unprecedented achievement for a therapy with severe reimbursement restrictions.

Launching outside reimbursement may also apply in other cases. Approved in the United States at the end of 1996, Pfizer's and Eisai's Aricept (donepezil) did not gain reimbursement in Italy because of concerns about its efficacy. Aiming to offset low volume with a high price, Pfizer launched it in 1999 at a significant premium over its price level in high-priced Germany.

Surprisingly, Aricept generated Italian sales of $78 million in 1999 (second only to the United States) and had a 43 percent share of diagnosed Alzheimer's disease patients, versus 23 percent for Novartis' Exelon (rivastigmine), also unreimbursed. This low price sensitivity was due to unmet need and to a high level of private health insurance funding in Italy. In countries such as France where reimbursement drives market share, this approach would not have been advisable. By 2000, the Italian Health Ministry agreed to reimburse both Aricept and Exelon—but at a 30 percent discount.[11] In 2002, Aricept continued to lead its class among Alzheimer's disease medicines.

Success in Japan: Overcoming National Barriers

The world's second largest market, with more than $50 billion in 2002 sales, is also perceived as the most difficult. Success in Japan is dependent on a *localized approach,* based on partnerships and on a clear understanding of national peculiarities.

Regulation

The approval process traditionally required a full duplication of clinical trials on Japanese patients—officially justified by a difference in Japanese physiology but also indirectly protecting the domestic industry. However, foreign companies are now allowed *bridging studies,* that is, submission of Phase III trials in non-Japanese patients if early stage clinicals in Japan do not show significant differences between populations.

Launch Order

Japan's reference pricing system also needs to be taken into account. Because its external benchmarks include three higher priced countries (the United

States, the United Kingdom, and Germany), launch delays may have a positive price impact. AstraZeneca's antipsychotic Seroquel (quetiapine), approved in Japan in 2001, gained a reimbursement price four times that of the gold standard, J&J's Risperdal (risperidone), because Seroquel's price was compared to its U.S. and U.K. levels.[12]

Choice of Comparator

Japan's internal reference system is equally important, and most prices are set by the comparator method for nonbreakthrough products. As elsewhere, the best scenario is to have a first-in-class therapy, which can avoid reference pricing and command an innovation premium (although it is modest— typically, 5 percent). For other products, comparator choice is critical. If a company selects a gold standard with a low price, it will most likely be priced similarly, even if it is more innovative.

Epidemiology

There are significant differences between Japan and the West, including a lower incidence of cardiovascular disease but higher rates of stomach cancer. Many of these variations are due to environmental factors such as diet. However, there are unexpected successes, such as the strength of the statin category; despite a lower prevalence of heart disease, strong local partnerships led to high sales. Pravachol is the Japanese sales leader across categories with more than $1 billion in revenues, but it was discovered—and is marketed—by local firm Sankyo. Merck's Zocor is sold in Japan by local subsidiary Banyu. Pfizer's Lipitor passed a half-billion in dollar sales by 2001, and it is copromoted with Yamanouchi.

The Japanese market remains the most locally-dominated, with foreign companies accounting for only three of the top 15 firms (Pfizer, Merck/Banyu, and Novartis).

Differences in Culture and Medical Practice

Social stigma, high in Japan for mental illness and STDs, limits the size and growth of categories such as psychotropic drugs and HIV therapies—and causes delays as well. Among SSRIs, Paxil was launched in 2000—eight years after its U.S. launch. Oral contraceptives were only recently approved, and medical and consumer bias has kept total category sales at about $20 million, even though there are nine products on the market.

Importance of Education

For these reasons, extensive education programs are critical change agents. "Buy-in" from national and regional opinion leaders on new treatment concepts should be secured by sponsoring clinical studies and symposia. Although patients still have little general influence, they drive some categories such as the local tonics but can also act as barriers if a new therapy contravenes beliefs. Unbranded DTC can be effective if preceded by physician campaigns, and awareness can also be raised by screening programs at schools and offices.[13]

Key success criteria in Japan are sixfold:

1. Local subsidiary or copromotion partner.
2. Bridging studies to shorten clinical trials.
3. Launch order allowing reference to high-priced countries.
4. If applicable, choice of high-priced domestic comparator.
5. Understanding of epidemiology, culture, and treatment differences.
6. Education programs for physicians and patients.

DEVELOPING A PRODUCT/SEGMENT STRATEGY

After global and national policies have been developed, the product's value can be built and maintained with the same approach as overall branding, that is, through evidence-based pricing. Launch price levels need to be supported by tangible differentiation based on medical and economic value. In addition, brand value must reflect segment characteristics such as price sensitivity and need for added services.

Launch pricing options range from premium to parity and penetration pricing. Historically, innovation and high need could virtually guarantee both a premium price and wide reimbursement. However, some recent launches of life-saving products have balanced access and pricing and achieved a *market-adjusted premium*—that is, a high list price tempered by free or discounted supply to low- and middle-income patients with no reimbursement.

Parity pricing applies when innovation and other benefits are comparable to those of the competition or to gain advantage over a well-entrenched, older category.

Penetration pricing is used to gain share rapidly and is required when switches to successor brands have a short time window; this approach was used in the Prilosec/Nexium and Claritin/Clarinex conversions.

These launch options are shown in Figure 9.5.

Premium pricing is increasingly vulnerable to global and national scrutiny, not only by regulators and payers, but also by physicians and patient groups. In addition to reference pricing and information exchange by governments, Internet-enabled patients will drive more transparency in the coming years. A trend-setting project is taking place in Oregon, where the governor initiated a systematic effectiveness comparison for 25 drug classes. Early reports are followed by an electronic version on the state Web site.[14]

In this unforgiving context, achieving both a price premium and favorable reimbursement has stringent requisites. The winning combination is true innovation + unmet need + high economic value + strong patient demand. These conditions were met by the protease inhibitor class in the HIV

FIGURE 9.5   Launch Pricing Options

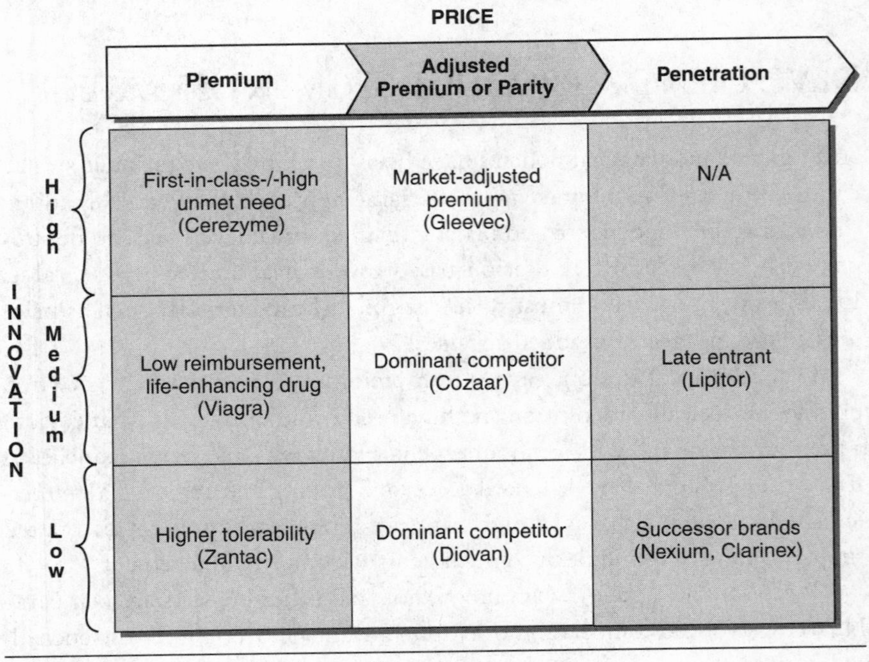

		PRICE		
		Premium	**Adjusted Premium or Parity**	**Penetration**
INNOVATION	**High**	First-in-class-/-high unmet need (Cerezyme)	Market-adjusted premium (Gleevec)	N/A
	Medium	Low reimbursement, life-enhancing drug (Viagra)	Dominant competitor (Cozaar)	Late entrant (Lipitor)
	Low	Higher tolerability (Zantac)	Dominant competitor (Diovan)	Successor brands (Nexium, Clarinex)

Source: Françoise Simon/SDC Group, 2002.

category. It was rushed to market because of global patient activism and commanded premium prices because it had no substitutes and high economic value. Within this new class, the first-mover advantage applied, even though the first three drugs were all launched within a few months of one another. Roche's Invirase (saquinavir) came first and achieved a premium over the others in countries such as Germany and France. External reference systems kept prices high for Invirase, Merck's Crixivan (indinavir), and

GLEEVEC: A PIONEERING ACCESS PROGRAM

Novartis aims to become a top-three oncology company by 2005, but it faces competition from established players such as Bristol-Myers Squibb, as well as biotechs such as Genentech.

As a molecular targeted therapy, Gleevec was a true innovation and *it was not optional*—it was a life-saving therapy for interferon-resistant, Philadelphia-positive chronic myeloid leukemia. It had orphan drug status because of its small target population. Its medical and economic value supported a high U.S. retail price of $24,000 to $30,000 per year—the only alternatives were interferon-alpha (at about $30,000 annually) and bone-marrow transplants, which could cost up to $200,000. To ensure access, Novartis rolled out a pricing system, which offered wide access and was well publicized. For patients with no drug coverage, Novartis would supply Gleevec free of charge to those earning less than $43,000 per year— and on a sliding scale to those earning between $43,000 and $100,000. The program generated value for Novartis in several ways:

- *It added value for physicians* because all their eligible patients could get the drug, which could lead to a preferred prescribing position for Novartis.
- It gave Novartis *a competitive advantage* because later entrants might follow its lead but would not get the same credit and publicity.
- Gleevec's high value and broad access would support the oncology franchise, facilitate forthcoming launches, and build significant *corporate equity* for Novartis as an innovator and social leader.★

★ Interviews by Françoise Simon with David Epstein, President, Novartis Oncology (March 22, 2001 and January 13, 2003); and Paula Boultbee, Global Brand Director, Gleevec, Novartis (September 19, 2001, July 25, 2002, and August 12, 2002); see also Jeffrey Dvorin, "Popular Prices," *In Vivo* (January 2002), pp. 20–24.

Abbott's Norvir (ritonavir) in most markets. In addition, Merck pioneered a pan-European price, helping prevent parallel trade.[15]

Parity pricing can be an effective launch strategy when the new bio-brand is facing a dominant and well-entrenched competition. When DuPont Merck launched Cozaar (losartan) in the United States in 1995, it pioneered a new class of antihypertensives, the angiotensin II inhibitors (AIIAs). It would compete against the ACE category, dominant in many markets and soon to become genericized with the first ACE patent due to lapse in 1996. The clinical profile of the AIIA class was not compelling. Its chief advantage was better tolerability, but the main ACE side effect was minor (persistent cough) and present in only about 10 percent of the patient population. DuPont Merck then took an aggressive course and priced Cozaar at the same level as the ACE blockers. It had a rapid sales uptake and now leads its class worldwide with more than $2 billion in 2002 revenues.[16]

Penetration pricing is an effective way to gain share rapidly and applies both to late entrants in a crowded market and to product conversions—especially when these must be done within a short time window. When converting Prilosec to its isomer Nexium, AstraZeneca had little time in the United States because Nexium was launched in February 2001 and the Prilosec patent was to expire by the following October (although generic entry was temporarily blocked by litigation). AstraZeneca launched Nexium at a 10 percent discount to Prilosec in the United States, similar discounts in Canada and the United Kingdom, and a much greater discount in Germany, where generic omeprazole was already marketed.[17]

BUILDING CUSTOMER-FOCUSED BRAND VALUE

Brand perception varies, not only across countries, but also across and within customer groups, according to differences in competitive environment, price sensitivity, and purchase drivers. These must be researched in key markets at the prelaunch stage, and a strategic compromise must be reached between standardization and localization of all branding components, including price.

GLOBAL POSITIONING VERSUS MARKET RESPONSIVENESS

At one end of the spectrum, building on commonalities is easiest for life-saving therapies targeting a small, highly specialized, and globally linked medical community with relatively little consumer influence on the decision process. This scenario fits many biologics such as Genentech's Rituxan (targeting hematologists/oncologists) as well as medicines in areas such as transplantation (Wyeth's Rapamune and Novartis' Neoral). Demand is the most inelastic for molecules concerning acute care because they are not subject to formularies, are reimbursed as part of hospital care, and have few or no substitutes.

At the other end of the spectrum, being responsive to market differences is essential in culturally sensitive, consumer-driven categories. In cough/cold, the top brand on the French market is a homeopathic compound with no comparable presence elsewhere. Demand is the most elastic in these categories.

Primary care presents substantial variations according to category. While cardiovascular disease is widespread through Western countries, treatment preferences vary greatly—in part because of differences in price sensitivity; the U.K. market is dominated by older, less expensive categories such as ACE blockers because of the impact of NHS guidelines on physician budgets. Other categories such as depression are culture-driven; botanical remedies such as St. John's Wort outsell Prozac by far in Germany, for instance.

Pricing drivers also vary by customer group. Regulators issue largely consistent science ratings, but vary in the relative weight they place on clinical and economic value. Among physicians, the global trend is toward more price sensitivity, but it is most acute in countries with MD budgets. Other variance factors include:

- *Direct purchasing* of oncology drugs and other in-office therapies (spread between purchase price and reimbursement).
- *Acute versus chronic illness* (higher price sensitivity for the latter).
- *First-line versus second-line therapy* (less price sensitivity for second-line therapy).
- *Patient reimbursement status* (higher sensitivity for patients under closed formularies or paying out-of-pocket).[18]

Consumers show the widest variations in price sensitivity, within and across countries. The least sensitive are in countries with low prices and wide reimbursement, such as France, and the most sensitive are in high-priced markets with limited reimbursement, such as the United States. Within countries, other factors affect price sensitivity:

- *Therapeutic area* (least sensitivity for critical illnesses).
- *Level of unmet need* (least sensitive if there are no alternative therapies).
- *Short versus long payback* (more sensitive for the latter; e.g., multiyear prevention therapy for osteoporosis).
- *Symptomatic versus asymptomatic disease* (more sensitive if asymptomatic).
- *Share of costs* (most sensitive if entirely out-of-pocket).

Pricing studies inevitably uncover contradictions between physician, payer, and patient preferences. For instance, a payer assesses asthma therapies primarily on cost-effectiveness, a physician rates them on efficacy and tolerability, but for a patient, convenience may outweigh other benefits and drive the choice of a tablet rather than a harder-to-use inhaled therapy. The value of time also matters for consumers and moves them to prefer once-daily formulations to twice-daily therapies. Quality of life, while taken into account by physicians, influences choice most directly among consumers.

DTC methods such as couponing may act as a double-edged sword for biobrands, just as they do in the consumer goods sector. Massive DTC campaigns such as the Prilosec-Nexium conversion in the United States, which add coupons for free seven-day doses to print ads, may move some consumers to ask their physicians to prescribe Nexium—but they may also in the long run create a switcher segment, which favors a competing brand as soon as it also offers coupons.

Finally, payers also need to be segmented and trade-offs must be addressed between profit maximization and the value of reimbursement. U.S. and ex-U.S. payers have a wide range of share-determining options, from reimbursement denial to copayments and prior authorizations. The following strategic steps are warranted:

- In the United States, managed care segmentation by *control level* and *ability to "move share."*

- Ex-U.S., payer segmentation by *relative influence and status* (public or private).
- Systematic comparison between the *value and the cost of formulary inclusion* or public reimbursement.
- *Negotiation process* to reconcile reimbursement and price objectives.

The two main dimensions of managed care segmentation are control level and influence on share. A high-control plan has a closed formulary and directly influences prescribing behavior. The current trend is toward lower control offset by increased cost-shifting to consumers—which

FIGURE 9.6   Customer-Focused Brand Value

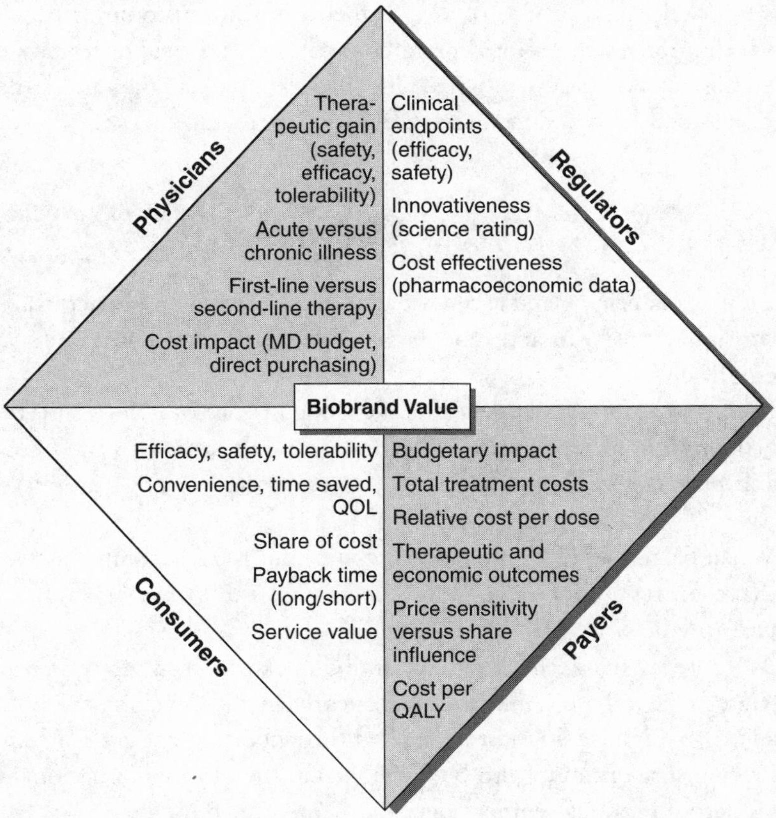

Source: Françoise Simon/SDC Group, 2002.

makes them more price-sensitive. Insurer influence on share depends on scope (national versus regional), size (number of members in plan), and growth rate.

To be effective, managed care contracting must move from discrete transactions to an umbrella reimbursement policy, which first sets overall price and volume objectives and then relates them to cost-benefit assessments with major accounts. These quantify the share potential of formulary inclusions or preferential positions (i.e., lower copayments). A recent study found that an insurer decision to impose a $20 copayment (versus no restrictions) would result in a 25 percent share loss—this needs to be weighed against the rebate required by the insurer to forego the copayment to determine a breakeven point as a basis for negotiations.[19]

The final step in pricing strategy at the product/segment level is to aggregate the demand profile of key segments within customer groups as a basis for regional and national price bands as well as to support marketing to the highest-potential segments. This process of evaluating and building customer-focused brand value is shown in Figure 9.6.

SUMMARY POINTS

✓ Biopharma pricing and access are drawing increasing payer activism and consumer criticism and must be addressed first at the corporate strategy level.

✓ Biopharma cost effectiveness is well documented in the medical and economic literature but remains undercommunicated to the public— and pharmacoeconomic data are still underused in negotiations with payers.

✓ When balancing price and access, companies must account for the fact that their reputation depends on social responsibility as well as business performance.

✓ As in overall marketing strategy, timing is a key success factor in pricing strategy; it must be linked to R&D early in the development process, and dynamic pricing must be applied throughout a product's timeline.

✓ Pricing strategy must also be developed at the global and national levels before product/segment decisions can be made.

✓ Key global decisions include setting global and regional price bands and determining the launch sequence among countries; national pricing strategies include varying degrees of localization.

✓ Strategic objectives such as price maximization versus rapid share gain determine the pricing options at launch (premium versus parity or penetration).

✓ Building customer-focused brand value depends on a thorough understanding of decision drivers in key customer groups and of their variations within and across countries.

LINKING ONLINE AND
OFFLINE STRATEGIES

> Genetic-based medicine, when it comes to pass, will drive all health care
> information into digital mode and usher in the era of information-based
> medicine.
>
> Caroline Kovac, vice president, IBM Life Sciences[1]

While information technology is transforming all stages of the bio-pharma value chain, many companies have yet to achieve a fully coherent approach that integrates online and offline activities from R&D to marketing and sales.

The industry is estimated to have spent about 1 percent of sales (close to $2 billion in the United States alone) in 2001 on all forms of e-technology, and an industry survey showed that its greatest impact was on marketing and sales (cited by 54 percent of respondents) and R&D (27 percent); supply chain management was a distant third area (13 percent). Some business-to-business structures have emerged, such as the Global Health Care Exchange, founded with a $150 million investment as a single purchasing source by five medical device companies.[2] However, most initiatives focus on the core biopharma value drivers, research and marketing/sales.

In R&D, postgenomic platforms use Web technologies for data mining, and virtual teams enhance the speed and consistency of research across countries. The most significant short-term improvements have come at the development stage, as clinical trials can be both shortened and optimized with electronic patient recruitment and data management.

In marketing, consumer websites have progressed from brochureware to interactivity and patient community building, but they are often not fully integrated with offline education and promotion, and they also show a "disconnect" between manufacturers and users. Surveys show that, across countries, consumers prefer medical and academic sources and have little trust in industry sites.

The medical market has a high potential for integrated e-solutions, from complementary online and offline detailing to videoconferencing and practice management. Aventis launched MyDocOnline to facilitate patient/physician connectivity; Pfizer, IBM, and Microsoft set up their Amicore joint venture to provide practice management solutions. Reaching full integration depends on resolving issues such as reimbursement and liability for e-consultations.

This chapter first explores the structure of e-health, then reviews global Internet trends, and analyzes the coordination of online and offline strategies. Figure 10.1 illustrates this integration process throughout the value chain.

STRUCTURE OF E-HEALTH

The biosector has a unique three-tier structure, from industry to the physician and consumer markets. This magnifies the need to tightly coordinate professional and patient communications because even consumer-driven brands such as Viagra depend on medical acceptance and recommendations.

The healthcare Web is not limited to business-to-business (B2B), business-to-physician (B2P), and business-to-consumer (B2C) communications. Other links originate from the medical community. Physician-to-physician (P2P) communications are becoming more formalized as they evolve from e-mail to interpractice networks. Physician-to-business (P2B) links are crucial at the research stage, as trial investigators and opinion leaders provide vital input for protocols, indications, and positioning.

FIGURE 10.1   Integrated Biopharma Value Chain

Research/ Development	Production/ Distribution	Marketing	Sales/ Customer Relationship Management
ONLINE			
• E-R&D platforms • Virtual teams • E-recruitment, e-trial management • E-submissions • Extranets (opinion leaders, investigators)	• E-procurement • E-contracting (outsourcing)	• Consumer websites (branded and unbranded) • Links to search engines • Patient communities	• E-detailing, e-sampling, conferencing • Physician/ patient connectivity (e-consultations, remote monitoring) • E-claims
OFFLINE			
• Global research infrastructure • Preclinical and clinical research	• Physical supply chain • Bio-manufacturing	• Consumer PR/promotion (multimedia) • Medical promotion	• Offline detailing • Patient education (multimedia) • Sample delivery

Source: Françoise Simon/SDC Group, 2002.

Physician-to-consumer (P2C) is still low but shows a high potential, from e-consultations to e-prescribing and remote patient monitoring; the latter would be especially helpful in diseases such as diabetes, which require frequent communication of glucose levels and drug response.

Finally, consumers are evolving from online information seekers to active global networkers, especially in life-threatening areas such as oncology and HIV. Consumer-to-business links (C2B) have played a crucial role in product approval and diffusion for drugs such as Gleevec and the HIV therapies. Consumer-to-physician communications (C2P) show a disconnect between patient demand and physician resistance; facilitating this connectivity is a high-potential area for biopharma companies. Consumer-to-consumer

TABLE 10.1   Structure of E-Health

	Business	*Physician*	*Consumer*
Business	B2B Vertical portals, exchanges, claims processing.	B2P Detailing, medical websites.	B2C Health websites.
Physician	P2B Research input, clinical trials.	P2P Interpractice networks.	P2C Provider websites, e-prescribing, remote monitoring.
Consumer	C2B Advocacy groups, interactive websites.	C2P E-mail, interactive physician websites.	C2C Advocacy groups, patient networks.

Source: Françoise Simon/SDC Group, 2002.

links (C2C) are steadily increasing and will become more influential as informal patient networks link with advocacy groups for political action—as they have done in areas such as HIV and breast cancer. Table 10.1 illustrates this triple-tier structure of e-health.

GLOBAL INTERNET TRENDS

While Internet use continues to spread worldwide, its rate of growth is slowing and its diffusion shows high regional variance in the medical as well as the consumer markets. According to IDC, Net users worldwide grew by 48 percent in 2000 and 27 percent in 2001, reaching more than 500 million people. Business-to-business e-commerce is rising more sharply, more than doubling in 2000 to 2001 to reach about $900 billion worldwide—although e-commerce still accounts for less than 2 percent of all trade.

Internet diffusion and delivery modes vary by region. Among major markets, penetration ranges from more than 50 percent in the United States to about 30 percent in France. Emerging markets such as Brazil have lower penetration but higher growth rates. While the United States leads in PC ownership (58 percent according to Datamonitor versus 41 percent in the United Kingdom and 29 percent in France), Europe has a commanding share of mobile phones, with 83 percent penetration in Sweden and 70 percent in

Germany, versus 58 percent in the United States. Personal digital assistants (PDAs) have a much lower penetration worldwide, from 11 percent in the United States and 10 percent in Sweden to 2 percent in France.[3] This has implications for point-of-care communications for physicians.

Across countries, a high proportion of Net users look for health care information. Japan leads with 90 percent of wired consumers seeking health information online, followed by Germany with 86 percent, the United States with 80 percent, and France with 69 percent. In the United States alone, online health seekers grew from 54 million in 1998 to 110 million by early 2002.[4]

Consumers are now at the center of biopharma e-strategies for several reasons:

- The Internet is the only way to reach consumers worldwide because direct-to-consumer (DTC) promotion of prescription drugs is prohibited except in the United States and New Zealand.
- Patients are increasingly proactive in managing their health and influencing prescribing decisions.
- Consumer-payer interactions are politicized, especially in the United States where protests have led to wider choice of physicians and therapies but higher copayments.

In e-health as in R&D, the biopharma sector is now at an inflection point; it can either take ownership of full relationship management with physicians and consumers or lose that position to third parties such as medical associations or infotech companies. Figure 10.2 illustrates how relationships between biopharma firms, consumers, physicians, and payers need to be reexamined in the e-health context.

We first review e-health consumer trends, then assess Internet usage and needs among physicians, and analyze their strategy implications through the value chain.

CONSUMER TRENDS: HIGH DEMAND, LOW SATISFACTION

While demand for e-health information and services is strong worldwide, it is also highly conflictual. Consumers want professional, disease-specific information but often use inadequate search techniques and find sources of variable quality. They want to reach their physicians online but face

FIGURE 10.2   E-Health Relationships

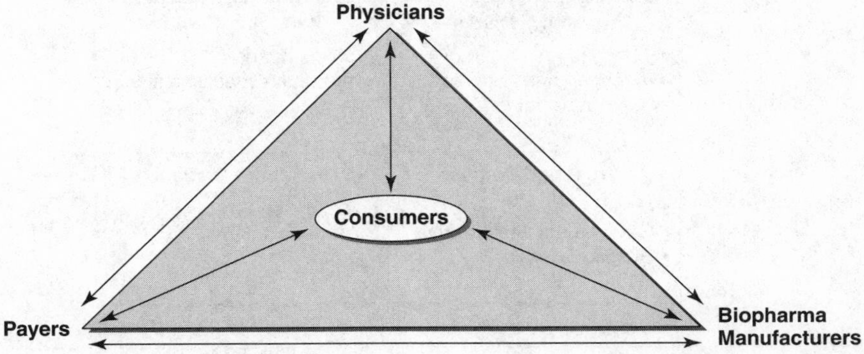

Source: Françoise Simon/SDC Group, 2002.

resistance because of reimbursement and liability issues. They are also very concerned about privacy and security—even more so in Europe than in the United States. Online health information seekers are younger, better educated, and more affluent than the general population. Harris Interactive data shows that they include in the United States 82 percent of people ages 18 to 29, 84 percent of those with postgraduate education, and 77 percent of those with household incomes over $75,000.[5] This profile explains their proactiveness and high information needs.

Inadequate Search Behavior

Despite their education level, consumers have been shown in both medical and marketing studies to search inefficiently for health care information. A 2002 Harris Interactive study found that 53 percent of online Americans started with a portal or search engine (versus only 26 percent with focused sites); a 2001 Boston Consulting Group (BCG) study in Europe found a similar pattern—with the same dissatisfaction because search engines such as Yahoo and AltaVista tend to generate long lists of sites with very little, if any, measure of credibility and generally broad and shallow data.

A behavior specific to healthcare seekers (by contrast to general online users) is that they do not browse. A 2001 BCG study in the United States found that 77 percent of health information seekers went online only when they had specific disease questions. This makes it more difficult for biopharma firms to attract patients online. Harris Interactive also found that more than three-quarters of users in the United States, France, and Germany

FIGURE 10.3   Consumer Healthcare Needs

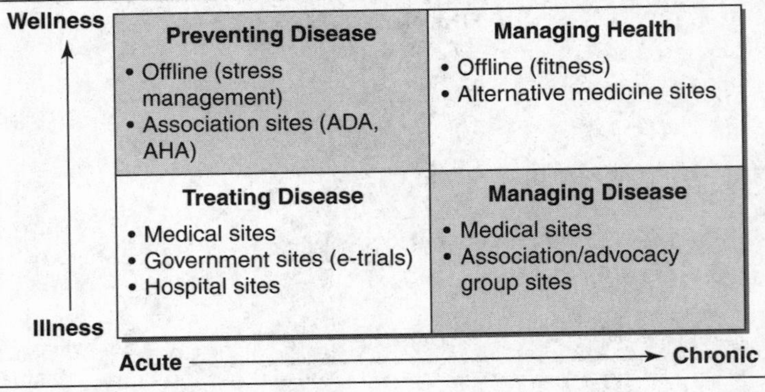

Wellness		
Preventing Disease • Offline (stress management) • Association sites (ADA, AHA)	**Managing Health** • Offline (fitness) • Alternative medicine sites
Treating Disease • Medical sites • Government sites (e-trials) • Hospital sites	**Managing Disease** • Medical sites • Association/advocacy group sites

Illness

Acute ————————————————————→ Chronic

Source: Françoise Simon/SDC Group, 2002.

went online for specific medical conditions—and so did 63 percent of Japanese Net users.[6]

Medical/Academic Sites Preferred

A disturbing pattern for biopharma firms is the global consumer preference for scientific sites and the universally low trust in industry sites.

Harris Interactive found that medical journals and societies as well as academic and advocacy group sites were among the top sources in the United States, Japan, France, and Germany. BCG found that, while three-quarters of European users favored university clinics or medical associations, only 25 percent used pharmaceutical sites; Harris reported a similar level in the United States.[7]

In addition, loyalty to specific health websites was reported to be low across countries (unlike the general online pattern of "stickiness" for successful sites).

There is, therefore, a disconnect between consumer needs and commercial offerings. Whereas consumers go online for specific disease information—especially when they have an acute illness, but also to manage a chronic disease—many consumer health sites offer broad and superficial wellness information that does not meet their needs. Figure 10.3 illustrates the links between online usage and disease status.

This has several implications for biopharma firms:

- A shift to deep, narrow sites with company-neutral data and links to medical and association sources could enhance consumer trust levels and contribute to branding the site and generating some degree of loyalty.
- A tighter integration of disease-specific online and offline programs could promote wellness better than a general website. Pfizer's consumer programs for Viagra coordinate offline DTC, online disease and product information, and event sponsorships including testing sites.

Online Consumer Segments

The online patient population subdivides, not only by disease state, but also by proactivity level. Across major markets, patients are shifting from passively accepting a physician's decisions to considering him or her as a partner and even taking over key decisions. BCG identified four distinct segments, based on disease state and physician role:

1. *Accepting (11 percent of online patient population):* Rely on physician, rarely use Internet for health information, generally not suffering from acute or severe illness.
2. *Informed (57 percent):* Rely on physician information but follow it up with Web verification of drugs and treatments for moderate to severe illness.
3. *Involved (23 percent):* Want a partnership with doctor and use Web before and after consultations for severe/acute illnesses.
4. *In control (9 percent):* Question and challenge medical decisions, use the Web to self-diagnose and/or determine the optimal treatment; often survivor or current sufferer from a severe illness. Despite this segment's small size, it represents a larger share of health care spend because its patients have more severe conditions and manage their care more actively.[8]

The suboptimal results of most consumer health care searches have several causes:

- They tend to start with search engines, which yield many irrelevant links and superficial data.
- Search engines and popular sites have few or no hyperlinks to scientifically accurate government and medical sites such as the National Library of Medicine (nlm.nih.gov) and Medline. Even Medline Plus (designed for consumer use), is not optimally accessible.

ONLINE CONSUMER SEARCHES:
A SORRY SIGHT

Several medical studies have evaluated both search quality and site quality. Search techniques were suboptimal for American and European consumers, and search engines and websites were also inadequate. In a 2000 study, a panel of 34 physicians assessed 14 popular search engines and 25 Web sites in English and Spanish for queries on four conditions (breast cancer, childhood asthma, depression, and obesity). Experts identified five to eight key clinical topics per condition and wrote consumer-oriented questions. For breast cancer detection, clinical elements were: Women over age 50 should be screened every one to two years, early detection improves outcomes, most cancers occur without a family history of the disease, and no consensus exists on screening for women in their 40s. Results were revealing:

- Among search engines ranging from Google to Yahoo, less than one-quarter of initial links led to relevant content (20 percent in English and only 12 percent in Spanish).
- On English-language Web sites ranging from general health (webMD) to condition-specific (MyAsthma), only 45 percent of the clinical elements were more than minimally covered and completely accurate; this dropped to 22 percent on Spanish sites.
- On English-language sites, 24 percent of the clinical elements were not covered at all—rising to 53 percent on Spanish sites. While the AMA and other groups have developed Web site evaluation criteria, these have not been systematically applied; their reliability is also an issue because many systems depend on voluntary self-assessments by Web site developers.★

★ Gretchen Berland, M. Elliott, L. Morales, et al., "Health Information on the Internet: Accessibility, Quality, and Readability in English and Spanish," *Journal of the American Medical Association,* vol. 285, no. 20 (May 23–30, 2001): 2612–2617; see also Gunther Eysenbach and C. Köhler, "How Do Consumers Search for and Appraise Health Information on the World Wide Web?" *British Medical Journal,* vol. 324 (March 9, 2002): 573–575.

Predictably, consumers are dissatisfied—and growing more so. A 2001 Harris study revealed a rising disenchantment when it asked 1,000 U.S. consumers whether the Internet had helped in four areas:[9]

	1999 (%)	2001 (%)	Change 1999–2001
Understanding own health problems	73	55	−18
Managing own health care	60	40	−20
Communicating with physician	51	31	−20
Complying with treatments	46	31	−15

In addition, privacy remains a strong concern. A 2000 Gallup survey found that 88 percent of U.S. consumers polled did not trust websites to keep personal health data secure; even among the "wired generation" of 15- to 26-year-olds, only 17 percent were found to trust the Internet.[10] This is paralleled by an equally dim view of offline DTC communications. In a U.S. telephone survey conducted by the FDA, fully 49 percent of respondents felt that prescription drug advertising did not give enough information about drug effects, and 58 percent agreed that ads "made the drugs seem better than they really were." In a survey by IMS Health, 63 percent of consumers polled also felt that DTC advertising increased health care costs.[11]

Suboptimal Links to Physicians and Payers

The vision of Web-enabled consumers freely communicating with their doctors and insurers falls far short of reality. Consumer demand for online links to physicians remains strong, largely because of a significant offline information gap. A survey of U.S. and European consumers conducted in 2000 and 2001 found that many had not received adequate information from their physicians or pharmacists:

- Risks of serious side effects were always conveyed to 56 percent of patients in the United States, 39 percent in France, and 40 percent in Germany.
- Contraindications were always given to 56 percent in the United States, 42 percent in France, and only 37 percent in Germany.
- Drug interactions were always indicated to 48 percent in the United States, 33 percent in France, and 34 percent in Germany.

Most consumers would like to fill that information gap with online queries (from 66 percent in Japan and 76 percent in the United States to 84 percent in Germany, according to Harris Interactive), but physician/patient connectivity remains limited by reimbursement and liability issues.[12]

Patient/payer communications are even worse. A Harris survey found in 2001 that more than three-quarters of online health information seekers said the Net made no difference in communicating with insurers, submitting claims, processing payments, or choosing health plans.[13] As could be expected, trust levels for insurer websites are also minimal. This leaves few options for payers—save their potential as "Net navigators" for patients, that is, steering them more effectively than search engines toward accurate, independent medical sources—while providing verifiable assurances of privacy and data security.

Business Impact of Online Consumer Use

Assessments of Web-driven consumer demand for medical consultations and prescriptions vary widely, but they all show an impact. In 2002, Harris Interactive found that a significant percentage had taken specific actions as a result of an Internet search:

	United States (%)	France (%)	Germany (%)	Japan (%)
Discussed information with doctor	38	13	19	9
Asked doctor for Rx medication	14	3	8	3
Started alternative treatment	9	2	8	7

While Net usage partly triggered discussions and some prescription requests, it was found to have little influence on compliance with prescribed treatments.[14]

Offline trends are similar. A 2001 study by health policy researchers in Canada and the United States found that patients exposed to DTC advertising requested prescriptions in 12 percent of surveyed visits; of those, 42 percent were for advertised brands. Physicians prescribed requested drugs to 9 percent of patients and requested/advertised drugs to 4 percent.[15] The low end result calls into question the return on investment (ROI) for DTC advertising—especially in view of the fact that advertising-driven prescriptions may be more than offset by the loss of goodwill among physicians, who have an increasingly negative view of DTC communications.

The low impact of online and offline promotion on compliance also suggests that companies need to rethink their strategies. Compliance has a much greater impact than new prescriptions in chronic, asymptomatic diseases such as hypertension, where more than 50 percent of patients may discontinue treatment after six months to a year. Achieving better compliance requires researching its root cause, which may range from side effects to drug interactions, delivery problems (injections or hard-to-use inhalers), and treatment costs—especially among U.S. seniors with no drug reimbursement.

Online consumer trends across major markets have strategic implications for biopharma companies:

- There is a disconnect between consumer needs and pharma websites on two levels: low trust and inadequate level of scientific information.
- Biopharma firms are now at an inflection point in their e-strategies with consumers; if they do not seize the opportunity to be leading health care information sources, others will take ownership of that position. Medical sources are well on their way to accomplish that.
- There is a significant opportunity in patient-physician connectivity because consumers want it and providers need legal and economic protections as well as technical tools to deliver it. Again, biopharma firms can enhance their customer relationship management by facilitating these linkages.

Physician Trends: Need for Integrated Solutions

Several trends are emerging in medical markets across countries:

- Internet use is high and driven by research needs.
- Unlike patients, physicians "stick" to a few preferred sites, but—like consumers—they universally favor scientific sources and rate pharma sites low.

- Online patient care varies by country, and its growth is hampered by unresolved reimbursement and liability issues.
- There is a high potential for e-solutions integrating medical education, patient care, and clinical and practice management tools; these are provided by fragmented players.

Internet Usage among Physicians

While PC use is quasi-universal and Net usage is high, practices such as electronic medical records (ERM) and provider websites still vary across countries. A European Union EuroBarometer 2001 study, combined with a Harris Interactive U.S. survey that same year, showed the following variance:[16]

	PC Use	PDA Use	Net Use	ERM	Practice Web Site
Netherlands	100	31	100	88	47
Germany	95	10	53	48	26
United Kingdom	95	18	87	58	27
France	89	11	80	6	11
EU average	80	11	61	29	13
United States	94	17	79	17	39

The fact that the United States significantly lags Europe for ERM is largely because of payer influence. In countries such as the United Kingdom, government payers may demand the adoption of ERM, but the U.S. system of fragmented private and public payers does not allow the same consistency.

Online use is dominated by knowledge acquisition and sharing; a 2001 BCG survey of 400 U.S. physicians showed that their top four activities were clinical information search (90 percent), journal articles (78 percent), consulting with colleagues (61 percent), and continuing medical education, or CME (45 percent). A parallel BCG survey of 250 European physicians that same year also showed research news, in-depth health care information, and expert advice as the top online activities.[17]

For biopharma companies, a worrisome trend is the low rating of pharma websites by both doctors and consumers. Datamonitor surveys in

2001 tracked the impact of online and offline activities on prescribing decisions in the United States and Europe (where 0 = No impact and 5 = Greatest impact):[18]

	United States	Europe
Peer-reviewed journal article	4.2	4.1
Information from other physicians	3.9	3.5
Information at a conference	3.8	3.5
Peer-reviewed online journal	3.7	3.7
Availability of free samples	3.7	2.2
Objective medical information website	3.6	3.3
Physician organization website	3.5	3.2
Patient request of a particular drug	3.2	2.8
Physician detailing visit	2.8	2.1
Pharmaceutical company website	2.3	1.7
Advertising banner	1.4	1.0

Predictably, U.S. and European physicians were similar in their preference for objective scientific information, but Europeans appeared less subject to patient or sales rep influence. Pharma websites had strikingly low rankings in both regions. A U.S. survey of primary care practitioners found that pharma sites ranked first in unaided awareness were those of Pfizer, Merck, GlaxoSmithKline, and Novartis—but awareness level was low (from 36 percent to 18 percent).[19]

For biopharma companies, the best way to enhance the perceived value of their websites is to greatly increase their "company-neutral" content through links to scientific sources and medical associations. MerckMedicus is an example of these offerings; this online portal can be used to research medical information and obtain CME credit, and it is promoted through the Merck salesforce.

Physician/Patient Connectivity: Low and Risky

Online patient care ranges from e-consultations to ERM, e-prescribing, and remote monitoring, but it still faces legal and economic issues. Harris Interactive U.S. surveys show that patient/physician e-mail has stagnated at 13 percent to 14 percent of respondents in recent years. The top five barriers cited were lack of uniform standards, liability, privacy/security, lack of system expertise, and setup costs. The BCG European study also showed security of patient data and setup costs (in learning time and system expenditures) as top barriers.[20]

Several initiatives are addressing these issues. Large employers such as General Motors are promoting the use of electronic prescribing tools and medical records. A more comprehensive solution was pioneered by Healinx, in collaboration with self-insured Silicon Valley employers including Adobe, Oracle, and Cisco. The Healinx system includes structured e-consultations that meet malpractice insurers' guidelines and are reimbursed at a flat fee.[21]

While e-consultations may improve patient knowledge and compliance, e-prescribing presents a substantial risk. It has a high potential for reducing medical errors and improving outcomes, but it is still hampered by a lack of standards. RxHub, a joint venture of pharmacy benefit managers, aims to develop compatible standards for providers, payers, and pharmacies. A negative factor for biopharma companies is that physicians using e-prescribing (still a small minority) report that it increases their compliance with managed care formularies—thereby potentially shifting prescriptions from premium therapies to generic drugs.

Remote monitoring (RM) is the least prevalent of clinical tools but has a high market potential for diseases such as diabetes, where outcomes may be improved by constant tracking of glucose levels via Web-connected monitors.

Strategic Implications

Although biopharma companies now devote about 1 percent of their medical marketing spend to the Internet, it may yield a high return if it focuses on connectivity gaps and provides integrated e-solutions. Focused, market-driven actions include:

- Optimizing medical content of websites through links to scientific sources.
- Facilitating patient/physician connections with tools such as Aventis' MyDocOnline, promoted through the salesforce.

- Providing point-of-care clinical information on dosages, product questions, treatment guidelines, and key trial results through PDA-based programs such as those of ePocrates with Lilly, AstraZeneca, and J&J.
- Offering a suite of practice management tools such as those of Amicore.
- Minimizing setup costs by demonstrating products through the salesforce, providing training, and documenting efficiency gains and security.
- Focusing efforts on e-health opinion leaders and targeting high-potential segments such as endocrinologists with large diabetic patient populations who stand to gain from electronic diaries and remote monitoring tools.

INTEGRATED VALUE CHAIN STRATEGIES

Information technology has already led to substantial efficacy improvements at both ends of the biopharma value chain, from R&D to marketing and sales.

WEB-ENABLED DEVELOPMENT: E-CLINICALS

While the Internet has already optimized all phases of research, from worldwide virtual teams to *in silico* drug design, the greatest impact on cost and cycle time can be achieved at the clinical trial stage. Phases I to III now consume 40 percent of the time and two-thirds of the cost of development and have become more burdensome in recent years:

- In the past two decades, the average number of patients per trial rose from 1,700 to 4,000.
- Clinical trial time grew from 4.4 years to 6.7 years.
- Regulatory filings now require more than 90,000 pages, if submitted on paper.
- New technologies to support efficient trials require a $70 to $130 million investment.[22]

This process has a high potential for optimization, in part through Web enablement.

The Tufts Center for the Study of Drug Development calculated that reducing development and regulatory review times by 25 percent would lower total drug development costs by $129 million. Boosting clinical success rates from the current one-in-five to one-in-three would significantly lower the average drug development cost, and cutting one year from Phase III trials would deduct more than $71 million from the $802 million cost of a new drug.[23]

Optimizing the Clinical Process

Trial planning starts with the *design of a protocol* defining patient eligibility criteria, study endpoints, treatment, and monitoring guidelines. To be fully effective, this initial stage should be planned by an integrated development and marketing team because the "branding" of the trial through choice of investigators, conference presentations, and publications is a key factor of early adoption.

Site selection is important because the trial investigators' reputation, patient base, and track record influence outcomes and diffusion in the medical community. Patient recruitment is critical because problems at this stage account for 25 percent of trial delays and nearly 75 percent of missed Phase III deadlines. Recruiting often takes up to a year and requires a DTC campaign with potentially high costs, depending on disease prevalence, exclusion criteria, and need for invasive procedures such as endoscopies.

According to Datamonitor, the cost of patient recruiting can be reduced from $1,200 to $300 by use of the Internet. For an average Phase III trial of 3,000 patients, this is a direct cost savings of $2.7 million. Web enablement can also shorten the one-year recruiting period by two months or more.[24]

Beyond recruitment, *electronic data capture* and *scrubbing* can improve trial effectiveness. While third-party transcriptions of paper-based data carry a high risk of error, computer programs can capture and scrub data at the same time.

Final reporting can also be optimized with e-submissions to regulators. Under the Prescription Drug User Fee Act, the FDA agreed to establish a paperless system for new drug applications (NDAs), and more than 120 companies have provided e-submissions.[25] Beyond NDAs, Web enablement can optimize trial databases. *Data mining* combines multiple sources and may be used for forecasting and market intelligence; it also yields proprietary databases of trial patients and physicians—the latter with performance tracking for patient enrollment and retention success.[26] The clinical trial process is illustrated in Figure 10.4.

Web-enabled trials have numerous potential advantages beyond cost and cycle time:

- Broader geographic reach of investigators and patients.
- More diverse demographics via e-recruitment.
- Better patient education and monitoring.
- Reduction in data entry errors and efficiency improvement.
- Better outcomes, as online access to data allows investigators to identify in mid-trial whether a subset of participants needs more attention or whether protocols and endpoints need midcourse corrections.
- Potential to build long-term e-relationships with trial participants and investigators—the strategic "ownership" of a patient and physician population in a low-prevalence disease can create a substantial competitive advantage.

According to Forrester Research, Web-enabled trial starts were 4 percent of total starts in 2001, but more than one-third of trials are expected

FIGURE 10.4   Clinical Trials: Key Stages

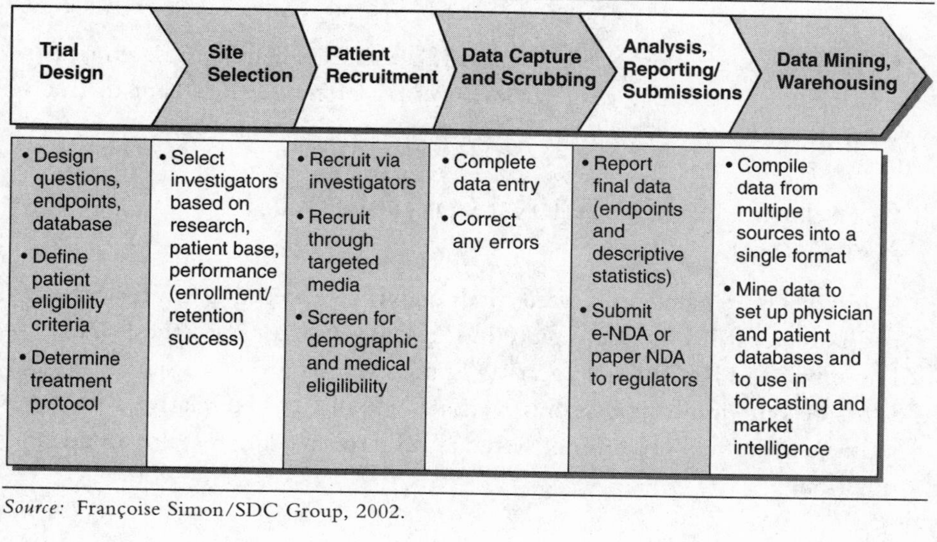

Trial Design	Site Selection	Patient Recruitment	Data Capture and Scrubbing	Analysis, Reporting/ Submissions	Data Mining, Warehousing
• Design questions, endpoints, database • Define patient eligibility criteria • Determine treatment protocol	• Select investigators based on research, patient base, performance (enrollment/ retention success)	• Recruit via investigators • Recruit through targeted media • Screen for demographic and medical eligilibility	• Complete data entry • Correct any errors	• Report final data (endpoints and descriptive statistics) • Submit e-NDA or paper NDA to regulators	• Compile data from multiple sources into a single format • Mine data to set up physician and patient databases and to use in forecasting and market intelligence

Source: Françoise Simon/SDC Group, 2002.

to be e-enabled by 2006. Forrester calculated that, after accounting for Net-related costs such as site access, data entry compensation, and license and usage fees, net operational savings for a Phase III trial were nearly $800,000 (out of total trial costs of $10.7 million for 200 sites of 10 patients each). However, the value of accelerated time to market was vastly greater, amounting to more than $65 million from the additional sales period gained. Launch delays can cost from $800,000 a day in lost sales for niche products to more than $5 million daily for a blockbuster.[27]

Strategic Actions

Beyond optimizing trials with Web enablement, biopharma firms can enhance their competitive advantage through internal and external initiatives:

- Trial success depends on early functional integration, as marketers can research consumer behavior and design and monitor recruitment campaigns.
- Trial managers should also be accountable for recruitment metrics (i.e., adequacy of patient numbers and recruitment speed).
- Segmenting physicians is critical, according to their status on several dimensions:
  —Size of patient base and fit of patients to study protocol.
  —Adequacy of staff to manage trial protocols.
  —Trial performance (percentage of patients successfully screened and completing the trial).
- Researching patient needs also optimizes recruitment because motivations to enroll may range from access to effective treatment to free medical care.[28]

CONSUMER COMMUNICATIONS: CONTROVERSIAL, NOT GLOBAL

While DTC remains prohibited in all countries except the United States and New Zealand, it rose rapidly in the United States since the FDA allowed branded Rx advertising in 1997; however, its growth is slowing and it has become increasingly controversial. In addition, the relative ROI of online and offline media is not systematically tracked and remains an open question.

DTC Spending Trends

In the United States, companies spent $2.8 billion on DTC advertising in 2001—almost triple their $1 billion expenditure in 1997, but with a slowing growth rate (12 percent in 2000 to 2001, versus 30 percent-plus growth in preceding years). Top DTC spenders were GlaxoSmithKline with nearly $500 million, followed by Pfizer with almost $350 million and Merck with about $300 million.

For the second consecutive year, the top-promoted brand was Merck's Vioxx, with a DTC spend of $131 million—on a par with the budgets of major soft drinks or beer brands and yet still number two in its class ($2.6 billion in worldwide 2001 sales, versus $3.1 billion for category leader Celebrex).[29]

An emerging trend is the spread of DTC from mass market, primary-care drugs to biopharmaceuticals targeting niche markets. The most promoted of these was J&J/Amgen's anemia drug Procrit, with a 2001 DTC spend of nearly $61 million.

To support the 2002 launch of Neulasta (pegfilgrastim), Neupogen's successor molecule treating chemotherapy-induced infections, Amgen coordinated medical and consumer marketing to promote proactive use. Only 10 percent of patients receive proactive protection from infection because physicians generally treat chemotherapy-related infections as they occur. A multimedia patient education program combines print and television ads with disease information (brochure and video) via a toll-free number and website.

Because the use of DTC for biologics is recent, it is too early to assess the appropriateness and effectiveness of mass media for low-prevalence conditions.[30]

Table 10.2 shows the 20 brands with the highest DTC adspend for 2000 and 2001.

Media Mix: TV Overuse, Net and Public Relations Underuse

The global marketing spend of biopharma companies remains dominated by physician detailing, which accounts for 75 percent of total—compared with 6 percent for DTC. While Internet marketing accounts for only 1 percent of total spending, it has reached 5 percent of total DTC expenditures.[31]

TABLE 10.2   Top 20 Brands by DTC Spend

Brand	Adspend ($ thousand) 2001	2000	Indication	Company
Vioxx	130,476	143,366	Osteoarthritis	Merck
Celebrex	129,221	82,216	Osteoarthritis	Pharmacia and Pfizer
Nexium	126,104	0	Gastric reflux	AstraZeneca
Viagra	88,431	88,201	Erectile dysfunction	Pfizer
Allegra	88,189	66,530	Allergic rhinitis	Aventis
Zocor	80,731	83,021	Hyperlipidemia	Merck
Claritin	80,457	97,019	Allergic rhinitis	Schering-Plough
Imitrex	71,999	37,563	Migraine	GlaxoSmithKline
Flonase	70,733	76,608	Allergic rhinitis	GlaxoSmithKline
Paxil	65,547	91,591	Depression, anxiety	GlaxoSmithKline
Zyrtec	65,513	57,629	Allergic rhinitis	Pfizer
Singulair	63,404	60,164	Asthma	Merck
Procrit	60,565	25,201	Anemia	Johnson & Johnson
Valtrex	56,158	42,611	Herpes	GlaxoSmithKline
Advair Diskus	55,057	0	Asthma	GlaxoSmithKline
Ortho Tri-Cyclen	54,354	45,228	Contraception, acne	Johnson & Johnson
Zoloft	53,377	0	Depression	Pfizer
Avandia	52,897	26,176	Type 2 diabetes	GlaxoSmithKline/BMS
Lipitor	47,619	58,426	Hyperlipidemia	Pfizer
Actonel	46,595	3,765	Osteoporosis	Aventis/P&G

Source: Company Reports; "Direct-to-Consumer Spending by Brand," Med Ad News (June 2002), p. 44.

Media mix trends show a sharp increase in television's share, at the detriment of medical journal advertising:[32]

	1997	1998	1999	2000
DTC Spend ($M)				
Television	310	664	1,127	1,574
Print/other	759	652	721	893
Total	1,069	1,316	1,848	2,467
Medical Promotion ($M)				
Detailing (office plus hospital)	3,364	4,057	4,320	4,803
Journal ads	510	498	470	484
Samples	6,047	6,602	7,230	7,954
Total	9,922	11,157	12,020	13,241
Total Marketing Spend	10,991	12,473	13,868	15,708

While TV allocation could top 70 percent of DTC spend for top-advertised brands, its relative effectiveness does not justify its dominance.

Two underused media with a higher potential ROI are public relations (PR) and the Internet. Both are most effective when integrated with a multimedia campaign including links to advocacy groups and medical societies. After the 1996 launch of Aricept (donepezil) in the United States, Eisai and

---

THE ALLERGY WARS: DUBIOUS ROI OF MASS MEDIA

PERQ/HCI Research studied the ROI from major ad campaigns for the top five allergy drugs in 1996 to 2000 and concluded that their media mix was suboptimal.

A sample of nearly 4,000 was polled, taken from the 45 million adult allergy sufferers in the United States. For a TV spend of $20 million to $50 million, the average brand name recall was only 1 to 6 percent. Recall was higher (6 to 13 percent) for a magazine spend of $25 million or less. Correct message association was achieved by 9 percent for print, 8 percent for TV, and 17 percent for print and TV combined—a disappointing result for a high-prevalence, symptomatic condition.

Claritin led with a 33 percent share of voice and a DTC spend peaking at $97 million in 2000 (versus $67 million for Allegra, $78 million for Flonase, and $58 million for Zyrtec). By 2001, Claritin was still the category leader—but it had benefited from unusual market conditions. When Schering-Plough started large-scale DTC ads including TV, rival brands Hismanal and Seldane were being withdrawn because of side effects.

Claritin's media exposure had a downside; a managed care group petitioned the FDA to switch it to OTC status, arguing that intensive marketing to consumers implied that they could self-treat. After some resistance, Schering-Plough caved in, hoping that its successor molecule Clarinex could maintain margins—but the switch threatened the entire category. In addition, Claritin's DTC ads triggered a first-ever lawsuit for deceptive advertising leading to inflated prices by the consumer safety group Prescription Access Litigation.*

---

* Milton Liebman, "Return on TV Advertising Isn't a Clear Picture," *Medical Marketing and Media* (November 2001); Sue Woodman, "The Battle over Drug Ads," *My Generation* (AARP, January/February 2002).

its partner Pfizer conducted consumer research that showed the burdens placed on caregivers by Alzheimer's disease. Eisai then formed an advisory council recruited from groups as diverse as the AARP, the Alzheimer's Association, and the National Alliance for Caregiving. Over three years, the council developed and field-tested a comprehensive caregiver training manual, distributed since 2001 free of charge to qualified nonprofits and also available online. For setting a new standard in caregiver training, Eisai and its council partners received the American Society on Aging's award for Best Practices in Human Resources and Aging.

PR programs are most effective when they target both physicians and patients. In partnership with Impact Health, the Wyeth salesforce invited medical practices to participate in bone mineral density screenings that positioned physicians as expert resources—and program planning and follow-up allowed Wyeth reps to increase their face-to-face time with these physicians.[33]

While PR is difficult to measure except in highly controlled situations, it has been found to correlate positively with corporate reputation. A recent study showed that the top 200 companies on *Fortune's* Most Admired list invested more than twice as much in PR as other firms. Assessing the value of PR should be derived from both *output measures* (people reached, information requests, media impressions, website hits) and *outcome measures* (product sales and trial, market share, as well as change in audience knowledge, attitude, and behavior).[34]

Need for Better DTC Metrics

While Internet marketing is more cost-effective than offline media, it often lacks appropriate metrics. Biopharma companies can develop a full-feature brand site for about $600,000, according to eMarketer—whereas the cost of a single 30-second prime-time TV spot is $130,000. Cyber Dialogue found that, to drive a single prescription request, online marketing needs a $171 investment, whereas print requires $728 and television absorbs $474.

In addition, the Internet can offer much more in-depth content than television—and this is what patients want. Of the respondents polled by the FDA in 2000, 73 percent said they would read the small print in a DTC ad if it covered an area in which they were especially interested.[35]

However, most biopharma websites still have insufficient company-neutral content and links to scientific sources—although biotech sites tend to perform better in this area than pharma sites. Genentech's Herceptin site has sections for patients, caregivers, and professionals and includes extensive disease information as well as a clinical efficacy section with trial summaries.

Internet marketing also often stops at website development instead of adopting a fully integrated approach that reflects consumer needs and behavior. Because most consumer queries start with search engines, companies should track their brands' relative exposure on systems such as Google and Yahoo. A survey of the leading 15 search engines assigned a numerical value to their top 30 rankings. While J&J's Procrit had the second-best ranking (after Prozac/Sarafem), the same biologic, branded as Epogen by its original marketer Amgen, did not have direct visibility on these search engines.[36] This may be due to the fact that Procrit has more extensive DTC marketing than Epogen.

According to Datamonitor, 63 percent of pharmaceutical companies do not have established metrics for e-business activities. E-business objectives are often hard to quantify because they are multifunctional (improved efficiency, time savings, reduced costs), qualitative (improved company image), or contaminated by other factors (increased sales).[37] Areas such as customer service improvement, however, lend themselves to effective monitoring.

Global Challenges for DTC Marketing

DTC marketing now faces two major challenges: a potential consumer, payer, physician, and regulator backlash in the United States; and continued resistance in Europe and Japan.

In the United States, a well-publicized study by the National Institute for Health Care Management (a nonprofit founded by BlueCross BlueShield) found that the top 20 brands by DTC spend accounted for half of the $21 billion rise in prescription drug sales in 2000. In addition, the top 50 most heavily advertised drugs had combined sales of more than $41 billion in 2000—that is, more than 31 percent of retail prescription drug sales.[38]

Heavy DTC marketing also risks alienating physicians, especially if consumer campaigns are not supported by medical programs that include patient education materials. Medical journals in the United States and Europe are publishing a steady stream of studies stressing the inaccurate or misleading nature of DTC ads, and a 2001 Harris Interactive survey of 300 U.S. physicians showed negative trends:[39]

- Only 47 percent agreed that DTC ads helped educate the public (versus 64 percent in 2000).

- 51 percent wrote more prescriptions for advertised drugs (versus 55 percent in 2000).
- Only 30 percent felt that DTC marketing increased patient compliance (versus 40 percent in 2000).
- 70 percent believed that DTC ads encouraged people to have unnecessary treatment (versus 58 percent in 2000).

In Europe, DTC advertising is not allowed for ethical drugs and a European Commission proposal to relax the ban in three underdiagnosed areas (asthma, HIV, and diabetes) was turned down by the European Parliament. However, the use of U.S. websites by European consumers partly negates the EU ban.

Like the EU, Japan bans DTC advertising of prescription drugs, and it has much less patient activism. Some firms have linked unbranded disease awareness campaigns with screenings at worksites or schools. The maker of a new growth hormone therapy persuaded school health administrators to add a screening test to students' physical exams, thereby facilitating nationwide detection.[40] Given the power of physicians in Japan, a key success factor is a medical detailing program preceding the consumer initiative, enlisting opinion leaders as national and regional speakers, and providing other physicians with patient education materials.

STRATEGIC IMPLICATIONS

To increase the effectiveness of DTC marketing, companies can take a number of steps. They should rethink the media mix and integrate online and offline activities as well as consumer and physician programs. Figure 10.5 shows this integration at each stage of treatment decisions.

Rethinking the Media Mix

The direct application of a consumer-goods approach to healthcare marketing, with its emphasis on television and emotional appeals, is at best a double-edged sword. It may have driven some categories such as antihistamines, but its very scale and visibility have also angered physicians, payers, and regulators. Given a negative industry image, shifting the mix toward lower profile, content-rich media and increasing social activities would seem advisable.

FIGURE 10.5   Integrated Communication Strategies

Decision Stages	Consumer Communications	Physician Communications
Disease awareness	• Unbranded DTC promotion/PR • Company-neutral site, links to medical sources	• Clinical trials, publications, conference presentations • Opinion leader extranet
Medical consultation	• Online self-test, script for medical consultation	• Detailing/e-detailing • Point-of-care PDA messaging, FAQ, treatment guidelines
Diagnosis	• Campaign with associations and advocacy groups • Sponsorship of testing sites	• Co-publications with medical societies • Online expert forum
Networking	• Offline/online patient communities • Access to online medical expert forums	• Symposia, speakers' bureaus • Videoconferencing
Treatment selection	• Branded DTC campaign • Branded websites	• Detailing/e-detailing • Point-of-care patient information
Trial	• Free trial vouchers • Online feedback (personalized site)	• Sampling • Direct-from-consumer feedback
Compliance	• Online/offline research on compliance barriers • Online support groups/e-diaries	• Sampling • Online/offline research on compliance patterns
Data collection	• Loyalty program membership	• Salesforce feedback • Tracking of prescription response to online and offline promotion

Source: Françoise Simon/SDC Group, 2002.

Increasing Educational Content

Many articles in medical journals from *JAMA* to *The Lancet* have criticized pharma ad content. These, together with an onslaught of ill-informed patients demanding possibly inappropriate drugs, will continue to fuel physician resistance unless ad content is substantially modified.

Among others, a quantitative study of print ad content had the following findings:

- 67 percent used emotional appeals.
- 87 percent conveyed the drug benefit with vague, qualitative terms rather than with data, such as "Take clear control. Take Claritin."

- Even when the benefit was explicit, only 13 percent provided evidence to support claims, but many presented only relative risk reductions without specifying the base rate—a format that exaggerates the benefit.
- By contrast, due to the FDA's "fair balance" requirement, half the ads used data to describe side effects.[41]

Other studies showed that the inclusion of both promotional and risk-related information in the same ad negatively affected consumers' ability to understand each type of information.[42] In addition, DTC advertising rarely mentions lifestyle changes, which are as important as pharmaceuticals in areas such as glucose control and cholesterol reduction.

Public pressure may eventually lead the FDA to consider what the medical community recommends, that is, a standardized presentation of benefits and side effects (similar to the nutrition facts list required of food manufacturers); this would include absolute event rates for both treatment and control groups, clinical endpoints, and side effects prioritized by seriousness.[43]

Because it does not have the time and space limitations of mass media, the Web lends itself to a content-rich approach. This could include diagnostic questionnaires, drug and nondrug treatment options, access to company-neutral expert panels and patient forums, reimbursement status, and links to scientific sources and advocacy groups.

Building virtual communities is a capability that many websites overlook. To support its multiple-sclerosis (MS) therapy Avonex (interferon beta–1a), Biogen commissioned an online survey of nearly 200 patients. It found that 76 percent wanted to access research and clinical trial information, 70 percent wanted disease management tools, and 68 percent needed to learn about therapy options. To reach the more than 300,000 MS sufferers in the United States, as well as their counterparts worldwide, Biogen developed an unbranded site, MSActiveSource.com, along with its Avonex.com branded site. This created a virtual community of more than 30,000 people accessing information about local educational programs and clinical trials.

Biogen also tightly coordinates online and offline media. Patient queries to the company call center are directed online for more information, and "Ask the Expert" questions from online visitors lead to print brochures available in neurology offices.[44]

SALESFORCE STRATEGY: FROM DETAILING TO CUSTOMER RELATIONSHIPS

While companies have greatly increased their salesforces in recent years, the number of physicians has remained largely static—leading to diminishing returns.

From 1995 to 2001, the number of reps in the United States doubled to 80,000. In addition, "mirrored" or overlapping salesforces call on the same physicians with different lead drugs, thus multiplying the demand on their time.

As a result, almost 40 percent of practices now restrict the number of detail visits, and some opinion leaders and high prescribers have become "no-call" physicians. Only 20 percent of U.S. reps visiting an office actually get "face time" with the physician, and 87 percent of those calls last less than two minutes—with many of them reduced to a 30-second sound bite while standing at the sample closet. Given these conditions, its not surprising that, according to McKinsey studies, physicians recall only 4 percent of all sales details attempted.[45]

Detailing costs have also escalated. In North America, the fully allocated cost of a single sales rep is now nearly $200,000 a year, and in Western Europe, about $150,000 a year. This translates into a cost per detail of up to $70 a minute. The hiring process takes four months and a year is needed to move from training to breakeven—but the average tenure of a drug company rep is less than four years.[46]

In addition, salesforce practices are severely restricted in Europe and have also come under scrutiny in the United States. In September 2002, the inspector general of the Health and Human Services Department issued a draft guidance to the pharma industry, suggesting that companies set up compliance programs to prevent abuses, including paying bonuses to physicians to switch drugs; offering entertainment, trips, or consulting fees to influence prescriptions; and disguising drug price data to government reimbursers. While these standards are voluntary, they may become mandatory in the coming years.[47]

These economic and political trends send clear signals that companies should rethink their sales strategies and shift from a "one-size-fits-all" approach centered on physical details to a more customer-centric, multichannel model.

Offline Strategy: Segmenting Doctors, Managing Markets

Unlike DTC advertising, detailing has a long track record of effectiveness in driving sales, as the statin category demonstrates. When launching the first statin, Mevacor, in 1987, Merck emphasized detailing, averaging 228,000 physician contacts a year—an intensive schedule at the time. Five years later, Merck's objective of switching prescribers to its successor brand Zocor also relied heavily on detailing, supported by a comarketing alliance with SmithKline Beecham. By 1997, Warner-Lambert and its partner Pfizer launched Lipitor as the fifth statin, but with a clear performance advantage. Again, the marketing strategy focused on physician contact; the joint sales-force out-detailed the competition with 860,000 contacts in 1997 and more than 1 million by 1999. After one year on the market, Lipitor generated sales of $583 million.[48] By 1991, Zocor and Lipitor were the two category leaders, with $6.7 billion and $6.5 billion, respectively, in worldwide sales. There was no DTC advertising during Lipitor's launch. In 2001, Lipitor had a relatively modest DTC adspend of $48 million (versus $80 million for Zocor), and it outsold Zocor by 2002.

Leveraging salesforce power requires a targeted approach to physicians and a deeper knowledge of their needs and market influences.

Whereas most companies still segment physicians by prescribing volume and adoption status, they would benefit from more comprehensive segmentation bases:

- The *lifetime value* of a physician is more important than prescription volume, because it allows companies to focus on young physicians not yet besieged by armies of sales reps and to develop long-term relationships with them with proactive services such as practice management counseling and tools.
- *Attitudes toward disease and therapies* are under-researched and are key to effective resource allocation. For an emerging disease such as inflammatory bowel syndrome (IBS), gastroenterologists with a large base of symptomatic and frustrated patients will be more receptive to new therapies than primary-care practitioners, who may favor diet and lifestyle changes. Knowing these attitudes would allow a pharmaco to assign reps to receptive specialists and educate low-interest physicians with online detailing.

- *Technographics* are also underutilized, yet critical to identify which physicians would be more receptive to e-detailing and online conferencing and with what patterns (daytime or evening hours, PC-based or PDA-based, etc.).
- *Customer insights* are also critical to differentiate a sales strategy; reps should research not only a physician's medical needs and attitudes, but also his or her market influences, such as patient demographics and managed care power.

Online Detailing: High Potential, Regional Variance

E-detailing is attractive for pharmacos as well as physicians because it is cost- and time-effective. A major draw for physicians is round-the-clock availability. Surveys by RxCentric and Medix found that more than 80 percent of U.S. and U.K. physicians planned to try the service. For companies, e-detailing yields a superior ROI.

A Novartis e-detailing program using the iPhysicianNet system allowed reps to complete 13 calls per day compared with 8 calls for field detailers. Online calls also lasted 9 minutes, compared with 3 minutes for physical details. The cost per virtual visit was $14 per minute versus $58 for a field visit. Return on investment for virtual detailing was 20 percent more than that of field detailing. Forrester Research studies confirmed this comparison, with data showing that e-detailing is 25 percent to 90 percent less expensive than physical visits.[49]

While physicians show interest worldwide, countries vary in their e-detailing maturity:

- Internet penetration of professionals is higher in the United States than in Germany.
- Cultural readiness (comfort level with technology) is highest in the United States, medium in Germany, and low in France.
- Regulation is more favorable in the United States and the United Kingdom than in France, which is very restrictive (telephone detailing banned, free samples restricted).

E-detailing subdivides into different technology levels, and their diffusion also varies by country:

- *Personalized messaging* is the most straightforward. Sony's unit SOnet signed up about 10 pharmacos by 2002 and is projecting a user base of more than 30,000 Japanese physicians by 2008; key success factors are incentives and 24/7 availability.
- *Virtual detailing* presents products with video streaming and interactive queries.
- *Videoconferencing* involves one-on-one sessions with a live rep; incentives are significant—equipment (PC, camera, ISDN link) is provided free of charge for a three-year contract involving about 10 details per month. Given equipment costs, this approach is not scalable and should be used for the highest-potential physicians.
- *Web-based conferencing* is the most complex virtual approach, with an opinion leader presenting a new therapy to a group of invited physicians. Attendees are provided with honoraria and the presenter gets a speaking fee.[50]

These three modes of interaction, from *push* (company messaging physician) to *pull* (physician requesting an e-detail) and to *facilitation* (company enabling physician-to-physician links) are most effective when integrated with offline communications.

E-detailing is ideally suited to biologics and niche products with highly wired, globally linked, small specialist audiences. For all brands, virtual detailing helps raise awareness and increases launch speed. Later in a product lifecycle, it can complement offline media to communicate new indications and successor molecules.

Physician segmentation also matters. E-detailing can be equally useful to reach high prescribers restricting physical visits and low prescribers for whom field calls are not cost-effective. For new categories and complex product/disease areas such as oncology, e-detailing is also vastly superior to field calls in its potential depth of scientific content.

Key success factors include:

- Adequate product selection (therapeutic area, lifecycle stage).
- Appropriate physician segmentation (technographics, prescribing volume).
- Aggressive retention strategy (technology training for physician and staff, incentives, equipment loan, CME credits, access to opinion leaders).

■ Strong partners for content and services such as e-prescriptions, e-claims processing, and remote patient monitoring.

From Detailing to Customer Relationship Management

Customer relationship management (CRM) will be the key competitive advantage for biopharma companies that want to build long-term partnerships with influential physicians. CRM begins with a 360-degree customer view, first collecting a deep knowledge of a physician's context (patients, payers, and other influencers) and then integrating a full range of interactions, from office and Web visits to trial investigations, and publication support. While pharma CRM budgets ranged from $500,000 to $25 million in 2001, CRM spend tends to come out of the IT budget. This has historically skewed CRM toward operational objectives (productivity improvement and reduction of fulfillment and customer response errors). To be fully effective and competitive, CRM objectives need to become more analytical (customer insights research, customer acquisition and retention, physician segmentation, and long-term partnership building).[51]

The evolution of the sales representative role, from transactional detailer to long-term strategic partner, is shown in Figure 10.6.

FIGURE 10.6   Evolving Salesforce Roles

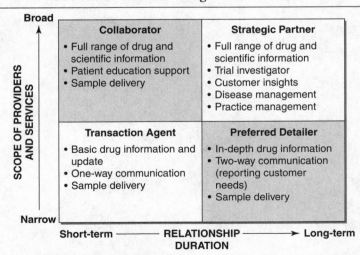

Source: Françoise Simon/SDC Group, 2002.

SUMMARY POINTS

✓ E-health trends are fairly similar worldwide and show a disconnect between the industry and its target audience.

—Consumers have deep information needs, which are not met by biopharma online and offline communications.

—Physicians are Net users and receptive to e-communications but, like consumers, favor scientific sources and have low trust for biopharma offerings.

✓ The Internet has the highest impact at both ends of the biopharma value chain.

—E-clinicals are clearly reducing development costs and cycle time.

—DTC communications can be improved by a shift of resources from mass-media to content-rich, educational online/offline material.

—Detailing remains the key driver of prescriptions, but offline salesforces are outnumbering physician capacity and need to be supplemented by e-detailing.

—An integrative approach is needed to combine detailing and DTC into customer relationship management, building long-term strategic partnerships with physicians, their patients, and payers.

CONCLUSION

The biotechnology revolution presents unique opportunities for companies to set up cross-industry innovation networks, create new fields such as bioinformatics, and leverage the power of new technologies and consumer demand to build and sustain global biobrands. Our analysis and case studies yield key findings for companies rethinking their business structures, marketing models, and global strategies.

NAVIGATING THE NEW BIO MARKETPLACE

- Biotechnology is the innovation driver for many sectors, but these vary widely in their business appeal; while biopharmaceuticals and biomaterials hold high promise, hybrid fields such as medical foods may be better suited to consumer goods players than biopharma companies.
- The biosector is facing three transforming forces—the twin technologies of informatics and systems biology and the grassroots trend of consumerism. Success will depend on integrating these key forces into company strategies.
- Informatics leads to both sustaining and disruptive innovations because it offers high-end and low-end solutions to infotech and biopharma firms.
- As consumerism combines with technology to accelerate disruption, companies must evolve from pill sellers to health partners by offering a full range of products, services, and information. Consumer ambivalence about biotechnology needs to be addressed through a more consistent legal framework and an industrywide public education effort. The high-tech/high-touch paradox of consumer demand for sophisticated medicine and alternative care offers opportunities to broaden product lines.
- Postgenomic technologies may increase R&D costs in the next three to five years but reduce costs and time to market in the long term. As bioscience creates an alternative paradigm (targeted therapy with a dominant

share of a global niche), companies must be prepared to develop dual business systems.

- M&As and alliances have turned into a high-stakes game, as merger scale has skyrocketed and alliance partners are assuming more development risk. Building network equity is a key component of competitiveness; it is achieved through a systematic process, which includes benchmarking performance, selecting the right partner, developing alliance metrics, and structuring a stepwise alliance management process.

LEVERAGING THE POWER OF BIOBRANDS

- The biosector is at an inflection point that entails a rethinking of disease, therapies, and branding models. Biobrands have an exceptionally broad scope and require a hybrid strategic approach, combining *experience-based and evidence-based marketing.*
- Biomarketers need to address this complexity with a triple prelaunch strategy of shaping the product, the market, and the company; this includes targeting new segments and creating new market space through a broader range of partners, customers, and product lines.
- Biobranding success depends on a combination of experience- and evidence-based marketing, a focus on new segments such as genotypes and technographics, and a dual branding model for mass-market and targeted therapies. Effective global reach can be achieved by balancing centralized strategy and local execution.
- Biobrands can be grown optimally at the portfolio, franchise, and product levels by managing timelines and starting value protection strategies at the development stage. Product scope can be extended with new formulations, indications, and a deeper customer base.
- Companies can manage beyond the lifecycle by using multiple renewal strategies ranging from product conversion to patent maximization and change in legal status.

MEETING THE GLOBAL CHALLENGE

- Drug access and price have become lightning rods of consumer and legislator criticism and are a top strategic issue for the biosector.

- At the industry level, biopharma economics must be better communicated to the public, focusing on the cost effectiveness of biobrands.
- At the company level, pharmacoeconomic studies should go beyond payers and target other stakeholders such as employer groups, who have a longer-term mindset and increasing collective power.
- At the global level, balancing drug access and price must be done in the larger context of regulation dynamics and must be adapted to regional and national policy frameworks.
- As in overall strategy, timing is a key success factor in biopricing. Dynamic pricing must be linked to R&D early in the development process and must be adjusted through the product's timeline.
- Pricing strategy must also integrate global and national approaches. Key global decisions include setting global and regional price bands and determining the launch sequence. Building customer-focused brand value depends on a deep understanding of decision drivers in key customer groups and of their variance across countries.
- Finally, global communications depend on an understanding of the structure of e-health and its impact on the biopharma value chain.
- Global Internet trends show a slowing penetration rate for consumers but a rise in Net use among physicians; however, dysfunctions exist between patients and physicians and between manufacturers and their customers, as medical and government sites are preferred to biopharma sources.
- Integrating online and online strategies has maximum impact at the development stage (e-clinicals) and in marketing and sales (DTC communications and customer relationship management for physicians).

NOTES

Chapter 1 The New Bio Marketspace

1. Freeman Dyson, *Imagined Worlds* (Cambridge, MA: Harvard University Press, 1997).
2. This view was expressed most prominently in Jeremy Rifkin, *The Biotech Century* (New York: Penguin Putnam, 1998); see also Mae-Wan Ho, *Genetic Engineering-Dream or Nightmare?* (New York: Continuum International Publishing, 2000); and Francis Fukuyama, *Our Posthuman Future* (New York: Farrar, Straus & Giroux, 2002).
3. *Genomics and World Health* (Geneva, Switzerland: World Health Organization, 2002), p. 67; X. Ye, S. Al-Babili, A. Kloti, J. Zhang, P. Lucca, P. Beyer, and I. Potrykus, "Engineering the Provitamin A (beta carotene) Biosynthetic Pathway into (carotenoid-free) Rice Endosperm," *Science,* vol. 287 (January 14, 2000): 303–305.
4. "LifeShirt for Clinical Trial Data," *R&D Directions* (July/August 2002), p. 32.
5. "Something to Watch over You," *The Economist* (August 17, 2002), p. 61; "E-Health's Long-Term Prognosis," *BusinessWeek* (April 9, 2001), p. 6; "Gold Award," *BusinessWeek* (July 8, 2002), p. 88.
6. *Biotech 2001* (San Francisco: Burrill & Company, 2001), p. 139; Faith Keenan, "Will Chips Make Pills and Shots Obsolete?" *BusinessWeek* (June 24, 2002), p. 81; Burrill & Company, *Biotech 2002—Life Sciences: Systems Biology* (2002), pp. 181–183.
7. See note 6, *Biotech 2002,* pp. 169, 172.
8. Richard Oliver, *The Coming Biotech Age* (New York: McGraw-Hill, 2000), p. 20.
9. Howard Gleckman, "Welcome to the Health Care Economy," *BusinessWeek* (August 26, 2002), p. 152.
10. Eldridge and Gould, cited in *Evolution—Ernst & Young's Seventh Annual European Life Sciences Report* (April 2000), p. 9; David Champion, "Mastering the Value Chain," *Harvard Business Review* (June 2001), p. 111.
11. Kerry Capell, Catherine Arnst, and Arlene Weintraub, "At Risk: A Golden Opportunity in Biotech," *BusinessWeek* (September 10, 2001), p. 85.
12. Paul Griffiths, "Xenotransplantation: One Trotter Forward, One Claw Back," *Lancet* (September 23, 2000): 1049–1050.
13. Arlene Weintraub and Faith Keenan, "The Clone Wars," *BusinessWeek* (March 25, 2002), pp. 94–96.
14. *IMS World Review 2002* (London, 2002), p. 2; see note 6, *Biotech 2002,* pp. 6–8.

15. Hermann Mucke, "State of the Industry: Genomics," *Spectrum* (December 10, 2001), p. 17-1.

16. Melanie Senior, "Can France Stay in the Game?" *Start-Up* (September 2001), pp. 9, 27, 32.

17. See note 6, *Biotech 2002,* p. 222; Ernst & Young, *Beyond Borders: The Global Biotechnology Report* (2002), pp. 82–83.

18. "Amgen Secures Neupogen," *Med Ad News* (July 2002), p. 5; Melanie Senior, "Biotech's Euro-Marketing Gambit," *In Vivo* (April 2002), p. 39.

19. See note 6, *Biotech 2002,* pp. 245–246; see note 17, *Beyond Borders,* pp. 131–133.

20. See note 17, *Beyond Borders,* pp. 125–126.

21. "India's Fermentation Queen," *The Economist* (September 1, 2001), p. 58; see note 17, *Beyond Borders,* pp. 127, 129.

22. Andrew Pollack, "A Bright Shining Industry," *New York Times* (October 21, 2001), sec. 3, pp. 1, 10, 11; Christiane Truelove, "In the Right Place at the Right Time," *Med Ad News* (December 2001), p. 44.

23. Richard Oliver, *The Coming Biotech Age* (New York: McGraw-Hill, 1999), p. 103.

24. Otis Port and Roger Crockett, "The Tech Outlook," *BusinessWeek 50* (Spring 2002), p. 184.

25. *Physician's Desk Reference,* 52nd ed. (Montvale, NJ: Medical Economics, 1998), pp. 1984–1988.

26. "Fragrance Helps You Live Longer," *The Economist* (October 23, 1993), p. 86.

27. Burrill & Company, *Biotech 2000* (2000), p. 94; see note 6, *Biotech 2002,* pp. 124–127, 136–137.

28. See note 6, *Biotech 2002,* pp. 142, 147, 149.

29. M. J. Friedrich, "Genetically Enhanced Rice to Help Fight Malnutrition," *Journal of the American Medical Association* (October 27, 1999): 1508.

30. "What Will Europe Do Now That the EU Has Deemed GM Foods Safe?" *Wall Street Journal—Europe* (October 16, 2001), p. 10; see also M. Gasson and D. Burke, "Scientific Perspectives on Regulating the Safety of Genetically Modified Foods," *Nature Reviews Genetics,* vol. 2 (2001): 217–222.

CHAPTER 2   Transforming Forces in the Biosector

1. Louis Gerstner, "What New Economy?" Interview, *Technology Review* (January/February 2001), pp. 45–50.

2. Freeman Dyson, *The Origins of Life* (Cambridge, MA: Cambridge University Press, 1985), p. 6; cited in Jeremy Rifkin, *The Biotech Century* (Newark, NJ: Penguin Putnam, 1998), p. 188.

3. Frost & Sullivan, *Custom Report for IBM* (2001); cited by Verna G. Hamman, IBM Life Sciences, Global Health Care Conference presentation, ESOMAR, Miami, FL (February 18, 2002).

4. Burrill & Company, *Biotech 2002—Life Sciences: Systems Biology* (2002), p. 25.

5. This section draws on private presentations and communications to F. Simon by Mike Svinte, Vice President of Marketing, and Ajay Royyuru, Manager/Structural Biology, IBM Life Sciences (April 2002).

6. See note 4, *Biotech 2002,* pp. 24, 29.

7. Margaret Farr, "Genomics Dealmaking," *Spectrum* (May 18, 2001), p. 3-21.

8. Ernst & Young, *Focus on Fundamentals: The Biotechnology Report* (2001), p. 58.

9. Cynthia Robbins-Roth, *From Alchemy to IPO* (Reading, MA: Perseus, 2000), pp. 74, 76; R. Sachidanandam, D. Weissman, S. Schmidt, et al., "A Map of Human Genome Sequence Variations Containing 1.42 Million Single Nucleotide Polymorphisms," *Nature,* vol. 409 (2001): 928–933.

10. See note 4, *Biotech 2002,* pp. 32, 35; Mark Ratner, "Motorola: Paging Diagnostics," *In Vivo* (March 2001), pp. 47–51.

11. Darnell Little and Ira Sager, "Who Needs Supercomputers?" *BusinessWeek* (June 3, 2002), pp. 82–83.

12. Deborah Erickson, "IBM Dives into the Life Sciences," *In Vivo* (July/August 2001), pp. 27–28.

13. Clayton Christensen, R. Bohmer, and J. Kenagy, "Will Disruptive Innovations Cure Health Care?" *Harvard Business Review* (September/October 2000), pp. 104–106; see also Clayton Christensen, *The Innovator's Dilemma: When New Technologies Cause Great Firms to Fail* (Boston: Harvard Business School Press, 1997).

14. Martin Dewhurst, V. Hunt, and S. Wilson, "Leveraging Patient Segmentation to Shape Winning Products," *Achieving World-Class Performance in Pharmaceutical Product Launches* (McKinsey, April 2002), pp. 20–21.

15. M. Richmond, N. Mattison, and P. Williams, *Human Genomics* (London: Pharmaceutical Partners for Better Health Care, 1999); cited in *Genomics and World Health* (Geneva, Switzerland: World Health Organization, 2002), pp. 177–179.

16. Peter Neumann, J. Hammitt, C. Mueller, et al., "Public Attitudes about Genetic Testing for Alzheimer's Disease," *Health Affairs,* vol. 20 (September/October 2001): 252–253.

17. Robert Blendon et al., "Physician's Views on Quality of Care: A Five-Country Comparison," *Health Affairs,* vol. 20 (May/June 2001): 233–244; and "The Public versus the World Health Organization on Health System Performance," *Health Affairs* (May/June 2001), pp. 10–21; Harris Interactive Survey, May 2002, cited in "Random Sampling," *Marketing News* (September 2, 2002), p. 4.

18. David Eisenberg et al., "Trends in Alternative Medicine Use in the United States, 1990–1997," *Journal of the American Medical Association* (November 11, 1998): 1569–1575; and "Unconventional Medicine in the United States," *New England Journal of Medicine,* vol. 328 (1993): 246–252.

19. Harris Interactive Survey of 1,013 adults, May 15–21, 2002, cited in "DNA Disclosure," *BusinessWeek* (July 15, 2002), p. 12; "DNA: Handle with Care," Interview with Lori Andrews, *Harvard Business Review* (April 2001), p. 2; see also Lori Andrews, *Future Perfect: Confronting Decisions about Genetics* (New York: Columbia University Press, 2001).

20. Kevin Gopal, "Genetic Test Results Off Limits—for Now," *Pharmaceutical Executive* (December 2001), p. 28; *Genomics and World Health,* pp. 158–159; see note 15.

21. See note 20, *Genomics and World Health,* p. 154; J. Gulcher and K. Stefansson, "The Icelandic Healthcare Database and Informed Consent," *New England Journal of Medicine,* vol. 342 (2002): 1827–1830.

22. See note 20, *Genomics and World Health,* pp. 7, 121, 164, 170; see also J. Robertson, "Human Embryonic Stem Cell Research: Ethical and Legal Issues," *Nature Reviews Genetics,* vol. 2 (2001): 74–77; E. Parens, ed., *Enhancing Human Traits: Ethical and Social Implications* (Washington, DC: Georgetown University Press, 1998).

23. Katharine Bach, L. Donato, et al., "When the Consumer Drives Demand," *Achieving World Class Performance in Pharmaceutical Product Launches* (McKinsey, April 2002), pp. 42–51.

24. For the drafting of the genome: see E. Lander, L. Linton, et al., "Initial Sequencing and Analysis of the Human Genome," *Nature,* vol. 409 (2001): 860–921; J. C. Venter, M. Adams, et al., "The Sequence of the Human Genome," *Science,* vol. 291 (February 16, 2001): 1304–1349; for proteomics, see Lance Liotta, E. Kohn, and E. Petricoin, "Clinical Proteomics," *Journal of the American Medical Association,* vol. 286 (November 14, 2001): 2211–2215; and Rosamonde Banks, M. Dunn, et al., "Proteomics: New Perspectives, New Biomedical Opportunities," *Lancet,* vol. 356 (November 18, 2000): 1740–1743.

25. *The Fruits of Genomics,* vol. 2 (Lehman Brothers, January 30, 2001), pp. 6–7, 20, 34, 42.

26. "Vertex and Novartis: The Kinase Collaboration," presentation by Alexander Wood, Executive Director, Novartis Institute for Biomedical Research, Windhover Conference on Strategic Alliances (New York, October 1, 2001).

27. Karen Berstein, "Old versus New Biotech," *BioCentury* (September 25, 2000), pp. 1–17.

28. See note 25, *The Fruits of Genomics,* p. 37.

29. For the clinical impact of pharmacogenomics: see John Weinstein, "Pharmacogenomics—Teaching Old Drugs New Tricks," *New England Journal of Medicine,* vol. 343, no. 19 (November 9, 2000): 1408–1409; and Allen Roses, "Pharmacogenetics and the Practice of Medicine," *Nature,* vol. 405 (2000): 857–865; see also G. Subramanian, Mark Adams, Craig Venter, and Samuel Broder, "Implications of the Human Genome for Understanding Human Biology and Medicine," *Journal of the American Medical Association,* vol. 286 (November 14, 2001): 2296–2307.

30. See note 4, *Biotech 2002,* p. 96.

31. *A Revolution in R&D,* pp. 6–7.

CHAPTER 3   Innovating with Bionetworks

1. William Haseltine, "Biotech-Pharma Relationships Enter New Era," *Focus on Fundamentals: The Biotechnology Report* (Ernst & Young, 2001), p. 66.

2. Burrill & Company, *Biotech 2002—Life Sciences: Systems Biology* (2002), pp. 57, 77; Gabby Ashton, "Growing Pains for Pharmaceuticals," *Nature Biotechnology,* vol. 19 (April 2001): 307; "New Medicines," *Med Ad News* (February 2003), p. 1.

3. *The Fruits of Genomics,* vol. 2 (Lehman Brothers, January 30, 2001): 7; Roger Longman, "The Search for Certainty," *In Vivo* (October 2001), pp. 22–23.

4. Murray Aitken, S. Baskaran, et al., "A License to Cure," *McKinsey Quarterly,* vol. 1 (2000): 83.

5. "BioWorld Database," cited in Ernst & Young, *Beyond Borders: The Global Biotechnology Report* (2002), p. 72.

6. Walter Powell, "Learning from Collaboration: Knowledge and Networks in the Biotechnology and Pharmaceutical Industry," *California Management Review,* vol. 403 (Spring 1998): 232–233.

7. "IMS World Review 2002," *IMS Health,* pp. 2, 34.

8. Recombinant Capital database, cited in Ernst & Young, *Beyond Borders: The Global Biotechnology Report* (2002), p. 71.

9. Andrew Humphreys, "Merging to Be Free," *Med Ad News* (July 2002), pp. 1, 32.

10. Roger Longman, "Dealmaking Roundup 2001," *In Vivo* (February 2002), pp. 24–25.

11. See note 2, *Biotech 2002,* p. 258; see note 9, p. 34.

12. Personal communication to Françoise Simon by Lothar Krinke, former Vice President, Business Development, Celera (September 22, 2002).

13. See note 8, *Beyond Borders,* p. 71.

14. See note 2, *Biotech 2002,* pp. 252–254.

15. Amy Barrett, "Time for a Miracle Drug," *BusinessWeek* (July 22, 2002), p. 44.

16. "BusinessWeek 50," *BusinessWeek* (Spring 2002), p. 38.

17. "Spin-off," *R&D Directions* (February 2002), p. 16; "The World This Week," *The Economist* (September 7, 2002), p. 9.

18. Amy Barrett and K. Capell, "Big Pharma: Getting Too Big for its Own Good?" *BusinessWeek* (July 29, 2002), p. 74.

19. Philip Haspeslagh and D. Jemison, *Managing Acquisitions* (New York: Free Press, 1991), pp. 145–149, 190, 210, 223.

20. See note 16.

21. Roger Longman, "Pfizer's Balancing Act," *In Vivo* (July/August 2002), pp. 21–22.

22. Robert Frank and T. Burton, "Side Effects: Cross Border Mergers Results in Headaches for a Drug Company," *Wall Street Journal* (February 4, 1997); cited in Rosabeth Moss Kanter, "Troubled Marriages," Harvard Business School case (December 13, 1999), pp. 7–10.

23. See note 5; "Trends in First Tier Biotech In-Licensing," *In Vivo* (June 2002), p. 10; see note 2, *Biotech 2002,* p. 263; "Late-Stage Upfront Payments Hit New Highs," *In Vivo* (July/August 2002), p. 12.

24. See note 2, *Biotech 2002,* pp. 278–279.

25. Kenneth Klee, "Biotech Alliances 2001: Feeding and Riding the Tiger," *Spectrum* (May 22, 2002), pp. 4–6; see note 2, *Biotech 2002,* pp. 278–279.

26. Mark Ratner, "Motorola: Paging Diagnostics," *In Vivo* (March 2001), pp. 47–51.

27. This section draws on personal communications to Françoise Simon from Mike Svinte, vice president of marketing, and Ajay Royyuru, manager, computational biology, IBM Life Sciences (April 2002).

28. This section draws on interviews by Françoise Simon with Dr. George Milne, former President, Worldwide Strategic Operations & Management, Pfizer (June 25, 2001); Dr. Allen Roses, Senior Vice President, Genetics Research, GlaxoSmithKline (June 18, 2001); and Dr. Bennett Shapiro, Executive Vice President, Worldwide Licensing & External Research, Merck (June 20, 2001; June 22, 2001).

29. Roger Longman, "The Foundations of High-Value Discovery Deals," *In Vivo* (May 2002), p. 32.

30. See note 21, pp. 24–26.

31. Amgen Annual Report (2001); L. Sellers, "Amgen's New Dream Team," *Pharmaceutical Executive* (July 2001), p. 41; "Amgen Wins Arbitration," Amgen press release (October 18, 2002). This section also draws from a personal communication to Françoise Simon by George Morrow, Executive Vice President, Worldwide Sales & Marketing, Amgen (December 26, 2002).

32. This section draws from interviews by Françoise Simon with Hans-Peter Hasler, EVP, Commercial Operations (February 6, 2003) and John Palmer, SVP, Corp. Development, Biogen (January 28, 2003); see also Biogen SEC Form 10-K (2001), pp. 5-6, 28; and Sibyl Shalo, "Biogen's Big Picture," *Pharmaceutical Executive* (January 2003), pp. 34–42.

33. This section draws from interviews by Françoise Simon with Kenneth Conway, former CEO, Millennium Predictive Medicine, May 1, 4, 24, 2001; see also David Champion, "Mastering the Value Chain," interview with Mark Levin, *Harvard Business Review* (June 2001), p. 113.

34. Personal communication to Françoise Simon by Lothar Krinke, former Vice President, Business Development, Celera (September 22, 2002).

35. PricewaterhouseCoopers, *High-Performing Strategic Alliances* (August 1999) and *Global Pharmaceutical Company Partnering Capabilities Survey* (September 2000). See also Joel Bleeke and David Ernst, *Collaborating to Compete* (New York: Wiley, 1993); John Harbison and Peter Pekar, *Smart Alliances* (San Francisco: Jossey-Bass, 1998); Yves Doz and Gary Hamel, *Alliance Advantage* (Boston: Harvard Business School Press, 1998); Jordan Lewis, *Trusted Partners* (New York: Free Press, 2000); Robert Mockler, *Multinational Strategic Alliances* (New York: Wiley, 2001); and Alice Sapienza and Diana Stork, *Leading Biotechnology Alliances* (New York: Wiley-Liss, 2001).

36. See note 35, *High-Performing Strategic Alliances.*

37. K. Troy, *Change Management: Strategic Alliances,* The Conference Board (New York, 1994); see note 35, *Smart Alliances;* see note 35, *Global Pharmaceutical Survey.*

38. See note 35, *Global Pharmaceutical Survey.*

39. Hari Krishnan and S. Hehner, "Enhance Value through Effective Partner Selection," *Achieving World-Class Performance in Pharmaceutical Product Launches* (McKinsey, April 2002), pp. 72–80.

40. James Bamford and David Ernst, "Managing an Alliance Portfolio," *McKinsey Quarterly,* vol. 3 (2002), pp. 29–31; see also Jeffrey Dyer, P. Kale, and H. Singh, "How to Make Strategic Alliances Work," *Sloan Management Review,* vol. 42, no. 4 (Summer 2001): 37–43.

41. See note 40, "Managing an Alliance Portfolio," pp. 30–36.

42. Tom Finn and D. McCamey, "P&G's Guide to Successful Partnerships," *Pharmaceutical Executive* (January 2002), pp. 56–60.

43. PricewaterhouseCoopers, *High-Performing Strategic Alliances* (August 1999), p. 27.

CHAPTER 4   Formulating Biomarketing

1. Kevin Clancy and Jack Trout, "Brand Confusion," *Harvard Business Review* (March 2002), p. 22.

2. This chapter draws from interviews by Françoise Simon with the following executives: at Wyeth, Bernard Poussot, President (September 26, 2002); Cavan Redmond, Senior Vice President, Global Strategic Marketing (September 26, 2002); Leanne Wagner, Vice President, Strategic Planning (September 23, 2002). At Novartis: Andrew Kay, Head of Global Marketing & Sales (March 26, 2001); Martin Cross, Head of Global Marketing Capabilities (December 10, 2001); Kurt Graves, Vice President, U.S. Commercial Operations (September 27, 2001); Deborah Dunsire, Senior Vice President, Oncology (August 27, 2002).

3. "R&D Costs Are Staggering," *Med Ad News* (February 2002), p. 15.

4. Consulting Resources projections, cited in "Biotech Investment Will Triple in the Next Decade," *Med Ad News* (March 2002), p. 26; see also consultingresources.net.

5. Katherine Bach, L. Donato, et al., "When the Consumer Drives Demand," *Achieving World-Class Performance in Pharmaceutical Product Launches* (McKinsey, April 2002), pp. 42–51.

6. "Prescriptions of Weight-Loss Drugs Are on the Rise," *Med Ad News* (January 2000), p. 72.

7. *The Future of Pharmaceutical Branding,* Datamonitor (October 2001), pp. 27, 31.

8. "Vitamin-Enriched Profits," *BusinessWeek* (September 10, 2001), p. 16.

9. For an overview of nutraceuticals, see Hugo Ehrenreich, "Nutraceuticals," *Brand Medicine,* eds. Tom Blackett and R. Robbins (New York: Palgrave, 2001), pp. 255–273.

10. Cited in "Who's Wearing the Trousers?" *The Economist* (September 8, 2001), pp. 25–27; see Naomi Klein, *No Logo: Taking Aim at the Branding Bullies* (Picador, 2000); Jonathan Bond and Richard Kirschenbaum, *Under the Radar: Talking to Today's Cynical Customer* (New York: Wiley, 1997); François Dufour and José Bové, *The World Is Not for Sale* (Versos Books, 2001); Eric Schlosser, *Fast Food Nation*

(Boston: Houghton Mifflin, 2001); Robert Frank, *Luxury Fever* (Princeton, NJ: Princeton University Press, 1999).

11. "The 100 Top Brands," *BusinessWeek* (August 6, 2001), pp. 60–64; Kevin Clancy and Jack Trout, "Brand Confusion," *Harvard Business Review* (March 2002), p. 22; see also www.copernicusmarketing.com/about/docs/brandtables.htm.

12. Patrick Kelly, President, Pfizer U.S. Pharmaceuticals, interview, *Med Ad News* (March 2001), p. 65.

13. Andrew Kay, personal communication to Françoise Simon (March 26, 2001); Andrew Kay, "World Class Marketing Plans," *Pharmaceutical Executive Supplement* (May 2001), p. 44.

14. *Global Cyberchondriac Study* (Rochester, NY: Harris Interactive, January 2002), p. 11.

15. Neil Holtzman and T. Marteau, "Will Genetics Revolutionize Medicine?" *New England Journal of Medicine,* vol. 343 (July 13, 2000): 141–144.

16. Personal communications to Françoise Simon by Kenneth Conway, former CEO, Millennium Predictive Medicine (May 1–4, 2001). This section also draws from communications to Françoise Simon by Dr. Allen Roses, Senior Vice President, Genetics Research, GlaxoSmithKline (June 18, 2001); Dr. Gualberto Ruaño, CEO, Genaissance (May 16–17, 2001); Taylor Crouch, former President and CEO, Variagenics (May 14, 2001); and Dr. Conrad Gilliam, co-Director, Human Genome Center, Columbia College of Physicians and Surgeons (May 9, 2001); as well as Dr. George Milne, former President, Worldwide Strategic Operations & Management, Pfizer (June 25, 2001); and Dr. Bennett Shapiro, Executive Vice President, Worldwide Licensing and External Research, Merck (June 20, 2001; June 22, 2001).

17. Jason Lazarou, B. Pomeranz, and P. Corey, "Incidence of Adverse Drug Reactions in Hospitalized Patients: A Meta-Analysis of Prospective Studies," *Journal of the American Medical Association,* vol. 279 (April 15, 1998): 1200–1205; see also David Bates, "Drugs and Adverse Reactions: How Worried Should We Be?" *Journal of the American Medical Association,* vol. 279 (1998): 1216–1217; and Kenneth Fremont-Smith et al., "To the Editor," *Journal of the American Medical Association* (November 25, 1998): 1741.

18. Allen Roses, "Pharmacogenetics and the Practice of Medicine," *Nature,* vol. 405 (June 15, 2000): 857–865.

19. John Weinstein, "Pharmacogenomics—Teaching Old Drugs New Tricks," *New England Journal of Medicine,* vol. 343, no. 19 (November 9, 2000): 1408–1409.

20. Raymond Hill, B. Frankel, and D. Kurdikar, "Modeling Pharmacogenomics' Impact," *In Vivo* (November 2001), pp. 77–78.

21. Jeffrey Dvorin, "Large Molecules: Too Late for Big Pharma?" *In Vivo* (December 2001), pp. 53, 57.

22. "Big Diagnostics Companies See the Genomic Light," *In Vivo* (September 2001), pp. 4–6.

23. Lynda Applegate, "Medtronic-Vision 2010," Harvard Business School case (March 29, 2000), p. 34.

24. See note 18, pp. 854, 864.
25. Urs Meyer, "Pharmacogenetics and Adverse Drug Reactions," *Lancet,* vol. 356 (November 11, 2000): 1667–1671.
26. Vivian Hunt and Sarah Wilson, "Leveraging Patient Segmentation to Shape Winning Products," *Achieving World-Class Performance* (McKinsey, April 2002), pp. 20–22.
27. David Eisenberg et al., "Trends in Alternative Medicine Use in the United States, 1990–1997," *Journal of the American Medical Association,* vol. 280 (November 11, 1998): 1569–1575; see also J. A. Austin, "Why Patients Use Alternative Medicine: Results of a National Study," *Journal of the American Medical Association,* vol. 279 (1998): 1548–1553.
28. Patricia Tan, "Complementary and Alternative Medicines," *Brand Medicine,* eds. Tom Blackett and R. Robbins (New York: Palgrave, 2001), pp. 274–295.

CHAPTER 5   Building Biobrands

1. Niall Fitzgerald, cited in "Who's Wearing the Trousers?" *The Economist* (September 8, 2001), p. 27.
2. Pfizer Annual Report (2001), p. 58; Al Branch, "Claritin Hits Store Shelves," *Pharmaceutical Executive* (January 2003), p. 24.
3. "The 100 Top Brands," *BusinessWeek* (August 6, 2001), pp. 60–64.
4. James Gregory and L. J. Sellers, "Building Corporate Brands," *Pharmaceutical Executive* (January 2002), pp. 38–44.
5. *Pharmaceutical Branding Strategies,* Datamonitor (October 2001), pp. 25–28.
6. Gilles des Gachons, "Best-in-Class Marketing Practices: Marketing Therapeutics for Growth," *Spectrum* (December 14, 2001), pp. 20–22.
7. M. E. Reff, "Depletion of B Cells in Vivo by a Chimeric Mouse Human Monoclonal Antibody to CD20," *Blood,* vol. 83, no. 2 (1994): 435–445; D. Maloney et al., "Phase I Clinical Trial Using Escalating Single-Dose Infusion of Chimeric Anti-CD20 Monoclonal Antibody in Patient with Recurrent B-cell Lymphoma," *Blood,* vol. 84, no. 8 (1994): 2457–2466.
8. *Clinical Success Factors in Market Launch,* Datamonitor (November 2001), pp. 71–72; Genentech corporate documentation (Rituxan sales).
9. Genentech, Annual Report and Proxy Statement (2001), pp. C-4, C-5.
10. This section draws from interviews by Françoise Simon with David Epstein, President, Novartis Worldwide Oncology (March 22, 2001 and January 13, 2003); Deborah Dunsire, Senior Vice President (September 3, 2002); and Paula Boultbee, Global Marketing Director (September 19, 2001; August 26, 2002). See also Novartis Annual Report (2001).
11. M. Deininger et al., "The Tyrosine Kinase Inhibitor CGP57148B Selectively Inhibits the Growth of Bcr-Abl-Positive Cells," *Blood,* vol. 90 (1997): 3691–3698; and P. Le Coutre et al., "In Vivo Eradication of Human Bcr-Abl-Positive Leukemia Cells with an Abl Kinase Inhibitor," *Journal of the National Cancer Institute,* vol. 91 (1999): 163–168.

12. Pfizer Annual Report (2001).

13. See note 9, "Critical Success Factors in Market Launch," pp. 39–44.

14. Mary Hallahan, "The Most Valuable Player in the Statin League," *Pharmaceutical Executive* (October 1999), pp. 118–120.

15. Anthony Wild, "The Lipitor Story," presentation at Marketing Pharmaceutical Innovation, Windhover Conference, Philadelphia (November 7–9, 2001).

16. Catherine Arnst and A. Weintraub, "Biotech," *Business Week 50* (Spring 2002), pp. 195–196.

17. Christopher Bogan and D. Wang, "Launching a Blockbuster," *Pharmaceutical Executive* (August 2000), p. 100.

18. Amgen Securities and Exchange Commission Form 10K (2001); Genentech Annual Report and Proxy Statement (2001).

19. Deborah Erickson, "Branding Goes Global," *In Vivo* (May 2001), p. 63.

CHAPTER 6   Sustaining Global Biobrands

1. Thomas Ebeling, personal communication to Françoise Simon (March 22, 2001).

2. Jean-Pierre Garnier, cited in Amy Barrett, "No Quick Cure," *Business Week* (May 6, 2002), p. 30.

3. FDA Orange Book, cited in Karl Schroff, "The Power of First," *Pharmaceutical Executive* (April 2002), p. 114.

4. Merck Securities and Exchange Commission Form 10-K (2001), p. 7.

5. Bernard Wysocki, "Sensing an Opening, Firms Will Urge Congress to Allow Approval of Knockoff Medicines," *Wall Street Journal* (August 6, 2002), p. A4.

6. "Biogenerics: When Will They Become a Reality?", Datamonitor (October 8, 2002 news release).

7. Thomson data, cited in Eric Pierce, "Earnings Lull?" *BioCentury* (April 8, 2002), p. A5.

8. "Genentech on the Verge of Something Big," *Med Ad News* (May 2002), pp. 38–39.

9. "Glaxo's Licensing Binge Continues," *In Vivo* (April 2002), p. 79.

10. Susan Berfield, "A CEO and His Son," *Business Week* (May 27, 2002), pp. 79–80.

11. *Countdown to Patent Expiry,* Datamonitor (July 2000), pp. 62–63.

12. See note 11, p. 18.

13. Schering-Plough Annual Report (2001), pp. 5, 7; corporate documentation, 2003.

14. Eli Lilly Annual Report (2001), pp. 5, 18, 20, 31; corporate documentation, 2003.

15. See note 14, pp. 2, 3, 18, 22, 26.

16. See note 11, pp. 55–57.

17. See note 11, p. 61; Novartis Annual Report (2001), pp. 16–17.

18. Sarah Venis, "Huge Increase in Patients Eligible for Lipid-Lowering Drugs," *Lancet,* vol. 359 (January 19, 2002): 234; see also *Circulation,* vol. 105 (2002): 152–156.

19. Merck Annual Report (2001), p. 29; Schering-Plough Annual Report (2001), p. 11.

20. See note 11, p. 65.

21. Novartis corporate documentation (2002).

22. Genentech news release (January 23, 2002).

23. Medline publication search; Amgen Annual Reports (1993 to 2001).

24. Medline, embase; Merck Annual Report (2001); Merck corporate documentation, 2003.

25. Medline; SmithKline Beecham Annual Report (1993); GSK, Pfizer, & Lilly corporate documentation, 2003.

26. Pfizer Annual Report (2001), p. 21; Frank Scussa, "On Its Way to $10 Billion," *Med Ad News* (May 2002), pp. 62–63.

27. This section draws from interviews by Françoise Simon with Dr. Sidney Mazel, then Vice President/Osteoporosis, Merck (April 15, 2002) and with Jennifer Taubert, Executive Director, Osteoporosis, Merck (February 3, 2003); and from Françoise Simon, *Global Brand Building at Merck* (A) and (B), Columbia Business School Case (2002).

28. Cited in Mark Vanelli, S. Adler, and J. Vermilyea, "Moving beyond Market Share," *In Vivo* (March 2002), pp. 69–70.

29. Françoise Simon, *Global Brand Building at Merck* (A) and (B), Columbia Business School Case (2002), p. 5.

30. See note 28, "Moving beyond Market Share," pp. 70–74.

31. See note 28, "Moving beyond Market Share," p. 74.

32. This section draws from interviews by Françoise Simon with Marion Morton, Brand Director, Cardiovascular/Metabolism Group, Novartis (April 5 and 8, 2002).

33. J. N. Cohn and G. Tognoni, "A Randomized Trial of the Angiotensin Receptor Blocker Valsartan in Chronic Heart Failure," *New England Journal of Medicine,* vol. 345, no. 23 (December 6, 2001): 1667–1675.

34. Medline publication search (May 26, 2001).

CHAPTER 7   Renewing Biobrands

1. Joseph Riccardo, cited in Roger Longman, "Pharma Future: Is the Glass Half-Empty or Half-Full?" *In Vivo* (April 2002), p. 25.

2. Astra AB, Corporate documentation, 1995; "AstraZeneca's Sarah Harrison," *Pharmaceutical Executive* (April 2002), p. 41.

3. "Major Disappointments," *R&D Directions* (May 2002), p. 58.

4. *Countdown to Patent Expiry,* Datamonitor (July 2000), pp. 129–130, 136.

5. Peter Howard, "Purple Reign," *Med Ad News* (March 2002), pp. 35–36; "Holding on to Prilosec," *Med Ad News* (January 2003), p. 6.

6. P. Kahrilas, G. Falk, and D. Johnson, "Esomeprazole Improves Healing and Symptom Resolution as Compared with Omeprazole in Reflux Esophagitis Patients: A Randomized Controlled Trial," *Aliment Pharmacol. Ther.,* vol. 14 (2000): 1249–1258; J. Richter, P. Kahrilas, J. Johanson, et al., "Efficacy and Safety of Esomeprazole Compared with Omeprazole in GERD Patients with Erosive Esophagitis: A Randomized Controlled Trial," *American Journal of Gastroenterology,* vol. 96 (2001): 656–665; AstraZeneca Medical Resources, "A Randomized Eight-Week Comparative Efficacy

and Safety Study of Esomeprazole 20 mg and Omeprazole 20mg in Subjects with Erosive Esophagitis," Study 174 (2002).

7. Jill Wechsler, "FTC Justice Examine Patent Protection and Abuse," *Pharmaceutical Executive* (March 2002), p. 24.

8. *Countdown to Patent Expiry,* Datamonitor (July 2000), pp. 128–132.

9. See note 8, pp. 43–47; "Unexpected Rival," *Med Ad News* (June 2002), pp. 3, 62.

10. See note 8, p. 38.

11. See note 8, pp. 17, 50; Kevin Gopal, "The Children's Hour," *Pharmaceutical Executive* (April 2002), p. 36; Jill Wechsler, "Prices, Privacy, Pediatrics," *Pharmaceutical Executive* (May 2002), p. 42; Thomas Parker and Amy Manning, "Buying Time," *Pharmaceutical Executive* (July 2002), pp. 68–72.

12. Maiken Engsby, M. Kwan, and D. Allen, "Patent Extension Strategies—Augmentin," STRATX-INSEAD Case (2001), Part I, p. 2 and Part II, pp. 2–3; Peter Howard, "GSK Braces for Patent-Ruling Aftermath," *Med Ad News* (July 2002), p. 4.

13. "Protection Racket," *The Economist* (May 19, 2001), p. 58; see also www.ftc.gov. /opa/2000/10/genericdrug.htm; Martin Arnold and Christopher Bowe, "Aventis and Andrx Settle," *Financial Times* (January 28, 2003), p. 20.

14. Bristol-Myers Squibb Annual Report (2001), p. 44; Frank Scussa, "Trying to Look Past 2002," *Med Ad News* (March 2002), p. 54; "Generic Taxol Approval Reversed," Leydig, Voit & Mayer, Report (January 2002), p. 3; "Courting Trouble," *The Economist* (June 8, 2002), p. 58.

15. Wyeth Annual Report (2001), p. 20; "Conjugated Estrogens: A Question of Composition," Wyeth corporate documentation (2001).

16. See note 14, "Courting Trouble."

17. See note 12, "Patent Extension Strategies—Augmentin," p. 4.

18. "Countering Delays in Introduction of Generic Drugs," *Lancet,* vol. 359 (January 19, 2002): 181.

19. Novartis Annual Report (2001), pp. 26–27, 87, 103.

20. Wendy Diller, "Andrx's New Style," *In Vivo* (September 2000), pp. 51–54.

21. *OTC Facts and Figures,* Consumer Health Care Products Association (2001), www.chpa-info.org/otc_facts_and_figures.asp; A. Carlsten, M. Wennberg, and L. Bergental, "The Influence of Rx-to-OTC Changes in Drug Sales: Experiences from Sweden 1980–1994," *Journal of Clinical Pharm. Ther.,* vol. 21 (1996): 423–430; cited in Eric Brass, "Changing the Status of Drugs from Prescription to Over-the-Counter Availability," *New England Journal of Medicine,* vol. 345, no. 11 (September 13, 2001): 812–813.

22. See note 21, "Changing the Status of Drugs from Prescription to Over-the-Counter Availability"; see also National Council on Patient Information and Education, OTC Survey (January 2002), www.bemedwise.org.

23. Neil Grubert, "The Impact of Rx-to-OTC Switching on the Pharmaceutical Market," Decision Resources, *Spectrum* (June 27, 2001), p. 7-6.

CHAPTER 8   Balancing Access and Price

1. Gro Harlem Brundtland, cited in "A Matter of Life and Death: The Role of Patents in Access to Essential Medicines," Médecins Sans Frontières Report (November 2001), p. 1.

2. "Courting Trouble," *The Economist* (June 8, 2002), p. 58; Ann Zimmerman and D. Armstrong, "Drug Prices—Why They Keep Soaring," *Wall Street Journal* (May 1, 2002).

3. This chapter draws from interviews by Françoise Simon with Jillian Clare Cohen, World Bank, Human Development Department (December 7, 2001); Rachel Cohen, U.S. Advocacy Liaison, Médecins Sans Frontières (April 29, 2002); Sharon Cohen, Public Policy Department, BIO (April 29, 2002); Linda Distlerath, Vice President, Merck & Company (January 21, 2002); and Peg Willingham, Vice President, PhRMA (December 7, 2001).

4. "Hospitals Boost Costs," *Pharmaceutical Executive* (November 2001), p. 28; "Another Year of Escalating Costs," report by the National Institute of Health Care Management (2001); cited in Jill Wechsler, "Pharma Expenditures Keep Rising," *Pharmaceutical Executive* (May 2002), p. 19; "Drug Spending on the Rise," *Marketing Health Sciences* (Summer 2002), p. 1.

5. Robert Steinbrook, "The Prescription Drug Problem," *New England Journal of Medicine,* vol. 346, no. 11 (March 14, 2002): 790; "Direct-to-Consumer Spending by Brand," *Med Ad News* (June 2002), p. 44.

6. "New Scramble over Drugs," *AARP Bulletin* (June 2002), p. 9; Ron Pollack, "In Defense of Accuracy," *Pharmaceutical Executive* (October 2001), p. 130; Alan Holmer, "Check the Numbers," *Pharmaceutical Executive* (October 2001), p. 18.

7. Brent Saunders, A. Farino, and J. Kellerman, "Caught in the Crosshairs," *Pharmaceutical Executive* (April 2002), p. 52; Milton Liebman, "Beyond Ethics," *Medical Marketing & Media* (February 2002); see also the OIG website at www.oig.hhs .gov/publications/docs/workplan/2002/cms.pdf.

8. Jill Wechsler, "Pharma Takes the Blame," *Pharmaceutical Executive* (October 2001), p. 26; Paul Raeburn and Amy Barrett, "Employers Are Seeking a Second Opinion," *BusinessWeek* (May 27, 2002), p. 67.

9. Tufts Center for the Study of Drug Development, report cited in Jill Wechsler, "Drug Development Costs Skyrocket," *Pharmaceutical Executive* (January 2002), p. 20.

10. "Just a Placebo," *The Economist* (May 11, 2002), p. 59.

11. Ameet Mallik, Gary Pinkus, and Scott Sheffer, "Biopharma's Capacity Crunch," *McKinsey Quarterly,* Special Edition (2002): 10; "Biotech," *BusinessWeek 50* (Spring 2002), pp. 195–196.

12. Barrie James, "Pricing Innovative Drugs," *Spectrum* (April 1, 1996), pp. 121-9, 121-11, 121-12.

13. Samuel Bozzette, "Providing Antiretroviral Therapy for HIV Infection," *New England Journal of Medicine,* vol. 344, no. 11 (March 11, 2001); Abid Rahman et al., "Inversion of Inpatient/Outpatient HIV Service Utilization: Impact of Improved Therapies, Clinician Education and Case Management in the U.S. Department of Veteran Affairs," International Conference on AIDS (July 1998); W. P. Peters, "Comparative Effects of G-MCSF and G-CSF on Priming Peripheral Blood Progenitor Cells," *Blood,* vol. 81, no. 7 (April 1, 1993): 1709–1719; see also *The Value of Medicines* (Washington, DC: PhRMA, 2001).

14. J. D. Kleinke, "The Price of Progress: Prescription Drugs in the Health Care Market," *Health Affairs,* vol. 20, no. 5 (September/October 2001): 48–51.

15. See note 14, pp. 53–55.

16. *World Health Report 2000 and 2001* (Geneva, Switzerland: World Health Organization); *OECD Health Data 2000* (Paris); see also Gerard Anderson and P. Hussey, "Comparing Health Systems Performance in OECD Countries," *Health Affairs* (May/June 2001), pp. 220–229; and "The Health of Nations," *The Economist* (June 24, 2000), p. 93.

17. Apoteket AB survey, cited in Klaus Hilleke, "The Impact of Parallel Importing on the European Pharmaceutical Market," *Spectrum* (October 31, 2001), p. 13-9.

18. Patricia Danzon, "Making Sense of Drug Prices," *Regulation,* vol. 23, no. 1 (2000): 56–57.

19. Charles Boersig, "Shuffling the Cards," *Med Ad News* (May 2002), p. 44; Jill Wechsler, "How Much Money Do Generics Save?" *Pharmaceutical Executive* (March 2002), p. 29; "The Top Managers," *BusinessWeek* (January 14, 2002), p. 58.

20. See note 19, "Shuffling the Cards"; Patricia Barry, "New Scramble over Drugs," *AARP Bulletin* (June 2002), p. 6.

21. Klaus Hilleke, "The Impact of Parallel Importing on the European Pharmaceutical Market," *Spectrum* (October 31, 2001), pp. 13-3 to 13-5; Edwin Bailey, "Parallel Trade: A Bigger Problem in a Bigger EU?" *In Vivo Europe Rx* (2002), pp. 12–13.

22. "Fixing for a Fight," *The Economist* (April 20, 2002), pp. 63–64.

23. *Reference Pricing,* Datamonitor (October 2001), pp. 82–87; *Health System Reform Principles* (Washington, DC: PhRMA, September 2001), pp. 27–33, 38–39; "Misprescribing for Health Care," *The Economist* (April 14, 2001), p. 49.

24. *Health System Reform Principles,* pp. 31, 39–40; see note 23, "Reference Pricing," pp. 19–20.

25. See note 24, *Health System Reform Principles,* p. 23; see also "Germany's Generic-Drug Law Concerns Doctors," *Lancet,* vol. 359 (April 27, 2002): 1498.

26. Michael Devlin et al., "Successful Product Launches in Japan," *In Vivo* (May 2002), p. 71.

27. Naoko Nakame and D. Pilling, "Japan Introduces New Drug-Pricing Regime," *Financial Times* (April 1, 2002), p. 20; "Japan Looks Good," *Pharmaceutical Executive* (June 2002), p. 26.

Chapter 9   Biopricing Strategies

1. Henry McKinnell, cited in Wayne Koberstein, "Pfizer on the Front Line," *Pharmaceutical Executive* (February 2002), p. 54.
2. "Reference Pricing," Datamonitor (October 2001), p. 5.
3. Susan Neale, "Successful Pricing Strategies," *Spectrum* (December 5, 2001), p. 15-2.
4. See note 2, pp. 63–64.
5. "The Economic Evaluation of Medicines," *Health System Reform Principles* (Washington, DC: PhRMA, September 2001), p. 6.
6. See note 2, pp. 58, 64.
7. See note 3, p. 15-13.
8. See note 3, p. 15-5; Klaus Hilleke, "The Impact of Parallel Importing on the European Plarmaceutical Market," *Spectrum* (October 31, 2001), pp. 13-7, 13-8.
9. See note 2, pp. 16, 69–70.
10. Andra Brichacek, "The European Pricing Game," *Pharmaceutical Executive* (July 2001), pp. 52–54.
11. *Pharmaceutical Branding Strategies,* Datamonitor (October 2001), pp. 74–75.
12. See note 2, p. 7.
13. Michael Devlin et al., "Successful Product Launches in Japan," *In Vivo* (May 2002), pp. 70–75.
14. Carol Marie Cropper, "Getting the Best Care from Your Health Plan," *BusinessWeek* (May 6, 2002), p. 104 (see also www.ohppr.state.or.us).
15. See note 2, pp. 48–50.
16. Barrie James, "Pricing Innovative Drugs," *Spectrum* (April 1, 1996), p. 121-10.
17. See note 3, p. 15-13.
18. Andrew Parece, P. Rankin, et al., "Optimal Pricing Strategies," *Pharmaceutical Executive* (June 2002), pp. 88–90.
19. See note 18, pp. 92–93.

Chapter 10   Linking Online and Offline Strategies

1. Caroline Kovac, personal communication to Françoise Simon (April 12, 2001). This chapter draws from interviews by Françoise Simon with Humphrey Taylor, Chairman, Harris Interactive (March 18, 2002); Julie Rubinstein, Director and Team Leader/E-business, Pfizer (October 14, 2002); David McGettigan, Director, E-business, Wyeth (September 2002); and Matthew Timms, Chief Web Officer, Novartis (May 24, 2001).
2. Cap Gemini Ernst & Young survey, cited in Milton Friedman, "E-Impact on the Pharmaceutical Industry," *Medical Marketing & Media* (October 2001), pp. 42–50.
3. IDC study (Net users) cited in Robert Hof and S. Hamm, "How Ebiz Rose, Fell and Will Rise Anew," *BusinessWeek* (May 13, 2002), p. 67; Gartner Group (B-to-B e-commerce report) and Datamonitor study (PC, cell phone and PDA ownership) cited in "International Media Survey," *Marketing News* (July 8, 2002), pp. 16–22.

4. Harris Interactive poll, January 2002, cited in "The Online World," *Marketing Health Services* (Fall 2002), p. 8.
5. Telephone survey of 707 U.S. online adults, March 2002, reported in *Health Care News* (Rochester, NY: Harris Interactive, May 8, 2002).
6. Boston Consulting Group, "Vital Signs Update: The E-Health Patient Paradox" (May 2001), pp. 1–2; Harris Interactive, "Four-Nation Online Survey," March 2002 (sample base: 309 online health information seekers in the U.S., 327 in France, 407 in Germany, and 275 in Japan), reported in *Health Care News* (May 28, 2002).
7. See note 6, "Four-Nation Online Survey"; Andreas Poensgen and S. Larsson, "Patients, Physicians and the Internet: Myth, Reality and Implications," telephone interviews of 1,000 European consumers including 700 Net users (Boston Consulting Group, January 2001).
8. Deborah Lovich, M. Silverstein, and R. Lesser, "Vital Signs: Online Patient Behavior" (Boston Consulting Group, February 2001), pp. 13–14.
9. "Strategic Health Perspectives," Harris Interactive telephone survey of 1000 U.S. consumers seeking online health information (May–June 2001).
10. Gallup survey of U.S. consumers, cited in "Survey Finds Americans Distrust Net to Transmit Health Care Info," *Pharmaceutical Executive* (December 2000), p. 80; "Generation Rx.com: How Young People Use the Internet for Health Information," Kaiser Family Foundation/ICR survey of 1,209 respondents ages 15–24 (September/October 2001), pp. 2–3.
11. "The Attitudinal and Behavioral Effects of Direct to Consumer Advertising," national FDA telephone survey, 1999; IMS Health Survey and FDA survey cited in Kathleen Blankenhorn, N. Duckwitz, and M. Sheer, "Power to the People," *Medical Marketing & Media* (August 2001).
12. Prevention's *International Survey on Wellness and Consumer Reaction to DTC Advertising of Rx Drugs,* Rodale, 2000–2001 (sample base: 1,222 in U.S. and 4,006 in Europe), cited in Neil Grubert, "Pharmaceutical Marketing in Europe: The Challenge of Reaching Consumers," *Spectrum* (November 15, 2001), pp. 15-2 to 15-9; Harris Interactive, "Global Cyberchondriacs Study," January 2002, cited in *Health Care News* (June 20, 2002).
13. See note 9.
14. Harris Interactive, "Four-Nation Survey" (January 2002).
15. Barbara Mintzes, M. Barer, R. Kravitz, et al., "Influence of Direct to Consumer Pharmaceutical Advertising and Patients' Requests on Prescribing Decisions: Two site cross-sectional survey," *British Medical Journal* (February 2, 2002): 278–280.
16. European Union EuroBarometer, June/July 2001 (numbers repercentaged by Harris on the base of all GPs) and Harris Interactive U.S. Surveys, June 2001 and January/February 2001, reported in *Health Care News* (August 8, 2002).
17. "Vital Signs Update: Doctors Say E-Health Delivers," Boston Consulting Group (September 2001); see note 7.
18. *Physician Insight Surveys,* Datamonitor (April and August 2001).

19. "The Internet and the Future Practice of Medicine," Ziment/Web-Survey MD.com (2000).

20. See note 9; see note 7.

21. Personal communication to Françoise Simon by Dr. Giovanni Colella, CEO, Healinx (April 2001); see also Ann Carrns, "Employers Urge Doctors to Make 'Visits' by E-Mail," *Wall Street Journal* (March 23, 2001).

22. Lehman Brothers estimate of new technology cost, cited in Ian Lazarus, "CROs Cross over Now," *Pharmaceutical Executive* (July 2001), pp. 68, 72.

23. Tufts Center for the Study of Drug Development, study cited in "Real Savings," *R&D Directions* (September 2002), p. 102.

24. Bonnie Brescia, "Better Budgeting for Patient Recruitment," *Pharmaceutical Executive* (May 2002), pp. 82–90; Datamonitor study cited in Joseph Brown, "The Online Territory Ahead," *Med Ad News* (December 2001), p. 46.

25. Styli Engel, "The Paper Phaseout," *R&D Directions* (May 2002), p. 6.

26. Ian Lazarus, "E-Rasing Obstacles," *Pharmaceutical Executive Supplement* (September 2001), p. 20.

27. Forrester Research study, cited in "Time for the Internet," *R&D Directions* (November/December 2001), p. 42; Janice Cruz Rowe, M. Elling, et al., "A Cure for Clinical Trials," *McKinsey Quarterly,* vol. 2 (2002): 136.

28. See note 27, "A Cure for Clinical Trials," pp. 138–140.

29. Meredith Rosenthal, E. Berndt, et al., "Promotion of Prescription Drugs to Consumers," *New England Journal of Medicine,* vol. 346, no. 7 (February 14, 2002): 498–500; Frank Scussa, "Consumer Ads Reach Peak," *Med Ad News* (June 2002), pp. 1, 42.

30. "Chemotherapy-Induced Infection Out in the Open," *Med Ad News* (June 2002), p. 12.

31. *DTC Marketing 2001,* Datamonitor (March 2001), p. 29; Andra Brichacek and L. J. Sellers, "Flexing Their Budgets," *Pharmaceutical Executive* (September 2001), p. 86.

32. Data from IMS Health and Competitive Media Reporting, cited in Meredith Rosenthal, E. Berndt, et al., "Promotion of Prescription Drugs to Consumers," *New England Journal of Medicine,* vol. 346, no. 7 (February 14, 2002): 500.

33. Teri Cox, "Forging Alliances," *Pharmaceutical Executive Supplement* (September 2002), pp. 13, 16.

34. Joy Scott, "Burden of Proof," *Pharmaceutical Executive Supplement* (September 2002), pp. 24–25.

35. David Reim, "Online Behavior: A Brand Builder's Best Friend," *Pharmaceutical Executive* (April 2002), p. 108; FDA/DDMAC, "Attitudinal and Behavioral Effects of Direct-to-Consumer Promotion of Prescription Drugs," cited in "Market Pulse," *Pharmaceutical Executive* (April 2000), p. 128; see note 31, "Flexing Their Budgets."

36. Survey by Peter Sonnenreich, Kikaku American International, reported in "Web Search Engine Exposure Index," *Pharmaceutical Executive* (January 2002), p. 66.

37. *ROI Metrics for Health,* Datamonitor (April 2002), p. 12.

38. "Study of Rising Health-Care Costs: Consumer Ads Are Cause," *Med Ad News* (May 2002), p. 11.

39. Sidney Wolfe, "DTC Advertising—Education or Emotion Promotion?" *New England Journal of Medicine,* vol. 346, no. 7 (February 14, 2002): 525–526; Harris Interactive survey of 300 U.S. physicians, May–June 2001.

40. Roger Longman, "Successful Product Launches in Japan," *In Vivo* (May 2002), pp. 74–75.

41. Steven Woloshin, Lisa Schwartz, et al., "Direct-to-Consumer Advertisements for Prescription Drugs: What Are Americans Being Sold?" *Lancet,* vol. 358 (October 6, 2001): 1141–1146; see also Lisa Schwartz and S. Woloshin, "Marketing Medicine to the Public: A Reader's Guide," *Journal of the American Medical Association,* vol. 287, no. 6 (February 13, 2002): 775.

42. Michael Wilkes, R. Bell, and R. Kravitz, "DTC Prescription Drug Advertising: Trends, Impact and Implications," *Health Affairs* (March 4, 2000), p. 117.

43. See note 41, "Direct-to-Consumer Advertisements for Prescription Drugs," pp. 1145–1146.

44. "Virtual Community Generates ROI," *Pharmaceutical Executive* (March 2002), p. 118.

45. Martin Elling, H. Fogle, et al., "Winning the Commercial Arms Race," *In Vivo* (October 2001), p. 75; see also Martin Elling, H. Fogle, et al., "Making More of Pharma's Sales Force," *McKinsey Quarterly,* vol. 3 (2002): 88–89.

46. Barrie James, *The Little Black Book of Pharmaceutical Marketing,* Quiller Management (2002), p. 76.

47. "Message to Big Pharma: Behave," *BusinessWeek* (October 14, 2002), p. 56.

48. Milton Liebman, "DTC's Role in the Statin Bonanza," *Medical Marketing and Media* (November 2001), pp. 89–90.

49. RxCentric/Medix study cited in Peter Howard, "Physicians Receptive to E-Detailing," *Med Ad News* (July 2002), p. 68; Novartis data cited in Joseph Brown, "The Online Territory Ahead," *Med Ad News* (December 2001), p. 46.

50. Silke Birlenbach, G. André, et al., "E-Detailing in Europe: Now or Never?" *In Vivo* (December 2001), pp. 70–72.

51. *CRM in the Pharmaceutical Industry: Strategies for Increasing Lifetime Customer Value through Technology,* Datamonitor (May 2002), pp. 2–3.

GLOSSARY

Adjuvant   Compound that nonspecifically enhances an immune response; increases the formation and persistence of antibodies when injected with an antigen.

Allele   Any of several alternative forms of a gene.

Amino Acid   Building block of proteins. There are 20 common amino acids: alanine, arginine, aspargine, aspartic acid, cysteine, glutamic acid, glutamine, glycine, histidine, isoleucine, leucine, lysine, methionine, phenylalanine, proline, serine, threonine, tryptophan, tyrosine, and valine.

Amplification   The process of increasing the number of copies of a particular gene or chromosomal sequence.

Antibody   Protein produced by the B cells of the immune system in response to the presence of a specific antigen.

Antigen   A molecule (often a protein) that, when introduced into the body, induces an immune response by a specific antibody.

Antisense   A piece of DNA producing a mirror image (antisense) messenger RNA that is opposite in sequence to one directing protein syntheses. Antisense technology is used to selectively turn off production of certain proteins.

Apolipoprotein E (Apo E)   Certain alleles of the gene that encodes the protein Apolipoprotein-E are linked to the development of heart disease and Alzheimer's disease.

Apoptosis   Programmed cell death.

Autoimmune disease   A disease in which the body's lymphocytes attack its own normal cells and tissues.

Autosome   Any chromosome other than a sex chromosome.

Bacteriophage   Virus that infects and kills bacteria. Also called phage.

Bacterium   Microscopic organism with a very simple cell structure.

Base   On the DNA molecule, one of the four chemical units that represent the different amino acids. The four bases are adenine (A), cytosine (C), guanine (G), and thymine (T). In RNA, uracil (U) substitutes for thymine.

Base pair   Two nucleotide bases on different strands of the nucleic acid molecule that bond together. The bases can pair in only one way: adenine with thymine (DNA) or uracil (RNA) and guanine with cytosine.

B cell   A class of lymphocyte (white blood cell) released from the bone marrow that secretes antibodies in response to a foreign antigen.

Biochip   An electronic device that uses organic molecules to form a semiconductor.

Bioinformatics   The science of informatics as applied to biological research.

Biologic response modifier   A substance that alters the growth of functioning of a cell. Includes hormones and compounds that affect the nervous and immune systems.

Biomaterials   Biological molecules, such as proteins and complex sugars, used to make medical devices, including structural elements used in reconstructive surgery.

Bioremediation   The use of microorganisms and plants (phytoremediation) to convert pollutants and hazardous wastes to nontoxic elements.

Cell   The smallest structural unit of living organisms that is able to grow and reproduce independently.

Cell line   Cells that grow and replicate continuously outside the living organism.

Chimera   A recombinant DNA molecule or organism produced by grafting an embryonic part of one species onto an embryo of either the same or a different species.

Chromosome   Threadlike component in the cell that contains DNA, RNA, and protein. Genes are carried on the chromosomes, which are contained in the nuclei of eukaryotic cells.

Clinical studies   Human studies that are designed to measure the efficacy of a new drug or biologic. Phase I tests safety in healthy volunteers, and Phases II and III assess efficacy and safety in larger groups of patients.

Clone   Gene, cell, or organism that is derived from—and genetically identical to—a single common ancestor gene, cell, or organism, respectively.

Codon   A sequence of three nucleotide bases that specifies an amino acid or represents a signal to stop or start a function.

Colony-stimulating factors (CSFs)   A group of lymphokines that induces the maturation and proliferation of white blood cells in the primitive cell types present in bone marrow.

Complementarity   The relationship of the nucleotide bases on two different strands of DNA or RNA. When the bases are paired properly (adenine with thymine [DNA] or uracil [RNA]; guanine with cytosine), the strands are complementary.

Complementary DNA (cDNA)   DNA synthesized from messenger RNA rather than from a DNA template. This type of DNA is used for cloning or as a DNA probe for locating specific genes in DNA hybridization studies.

Cytochrome   Hemoprotein whose main function is electron and/or hydrogen transport.

Cytogenetics   Study of the cell and its heredity-related components, especially chromosomes.

Cytokine   Protein regulating immune response and mediating cell-cell communication; cytokines include interferons, interleukins, lymphokines, colony-stimulating factors, and tumor necrosis factors.

Cytoplasm   Cellular material that is within the cell membrane and surrounds the nucleus.

Cytotoxic   Able to cause cell death.

Deoxyribonucleic acid (DNA)   Molecule that carries the genetic information for most living systems. The DNA molecule consists of four bases (adenine, cytosine, guanine, and thymine) and a sugar-phosphate backbone, arranged in two connected strands to form a double helix.

Diagnostic   Assay used to detect a disease, pathogen, or DNA mutation. Molecular diagnostics include monoclonal antibodies and DNA probes.

Differentiation   The process of biochemical and structural changes by which cells become specialized in form and function.

Diploid   A cell with two complete sets of chromosomes. Chromosomes of each pair are termed homologous.

DNA fingerprinting   The use of restriction enzymes to measure the genetic variation of individuals (often used as a forensic tool to identify blood and tissue samples).

DNA probe   A small piece of nucleic acid labeled with a radioactive isotope, dye, or enzyme to locate a nucleotide sequence or gene on a DNA molecule.

DNA sequence   The order of nucleotide bases in the DNA molecule.

Drug delivery   The process by which a drug is administered to the patient. Traditional routes have been oral or intravenous perfusion. New methods include transdermal patches and nasal sprays.

Electrophoresis   A technique for separating different types of molecules based on their patterns of movement in an electrical field.

Enzyme   A protein catalyst that facilitates chemical or metabolic reactions necessary for cell growth and reproduction.

Erythropoietin (EPO)   A protein that boosts production of red blood cells. It is used in treating certain types of anemias.

Escherichia coli (E. coli)   A bacterium that inhabits the intestinal tract of most vertebrates. Much of the work using recombinant DNA techniques has been carried out with this organism because it has been genetically well characterized.

Eukaryote   A cell or organism containing a membrane-bound nucleus. All organisms except bacteria, viruses, and blue-green algae are eukaryotic.

Exon   In eukaryotic cells, that part of the gene that is transcribed into messenger RNA and encodes a protein.

Expression   In genetics, manifestation of a characteristic that is specified by a gene. In industrial settings, production of a protein by a gene inserted into a new host organism.

Fermentation   The process of growing cells or microorganisms for the production of chemical or pharmaceutical compounds. These are cultured in the presence of nutrients in large tanks called bioreactors.

Fusion   Joining of the membrane of two cells, thus creating a daughter cell that contains some of the properties of each parent cell. Used in making hybridomas.

Gene A segment of chromosome that encodes information for a protein or RNA product. Some genes direct the syntheses of proteins, while others have regulatory functions.

Gene cloning (splicing) Insertion of DNA into a vector and transfer of the recombinant molecule into a host for duplication.

Gene mapping Determination of the relative locations of genes on a chromosome.

Gene sequencer A specialized computer determining the sequence of nucleotide bases in a strand of DNA.

Gene therapy The replacement of a defective gene in an organism suffering from a genetic disease. Recombinant DNA techniques isolate the functioning gene and insert it into cells.

Genetic code The mechanism by which genetic information is stored in living organisms. It includes 3 stop codons and 64 triplet codons that encode the 20 amino acids that, in turn, constitute proteins.

Genetic screening The use of a biological test to screen for inherited diseases or medical conditions. Testing can be conducted prenatally to check for metabolic defects or congenital disorders in the developing fetus as well as postnatally to screen for carriers of heritable diseases.

Genome The total hereditary material of a cell, comprising the entire chromosomal set found in each nucleus of a given species.

Genomics The study of genes and their functions to understand the molecular mechanisms of disease, including the interplay of genetic and environmental factors.

Genotype Genetic makeup, that is, the two alleles carried by an individual at a given gene locus.

Germ cell Reproductive cell (sperm or egg). Also called gamete or sex cell.

Glycoprotein A protein conjugated with a carbohydrate group.

Granulocyte One of three types of white blood cells. Granulocytes digest bacteria and other parasites.

Granulocyte-macrophage colony stimulating factor (GMCSF) A natural hormone that stimulates white blood cell production, particularly that of granulocytes and monocytes (the precursors of macrophages).

Growth hormone   Also called somatotropin, a protein produced by the pituitary gland that is involved in cell growth.

Haploid   A cell with half the usual number of chromosomes, or only one chromosome set. Sex cells are haploid.

Heterozygous   Having different alleles of a gene at a given locus on homologous chromosomes.

Homeobox   Family of genes that regulates activities of other genes (turns genes on and off). A homeotic gene controls a major developmental pathway.

Homozygous   Having two identical alleles of a gene at a given locus on homologous chromosomes.

Hormone   A chemical or protein that acts as a messenger or stimulatory signal, relaying instructions to stop or start certain physiological activities.

Host   A cell or organism used for growth of a virus, plasmid, or other form of foreign DNA or for the production of cloned substances.

Hybridization   Production of offspring, or hybrids, from genetically dissimilar parents. The process can be used to produce hybrid plants (by cross-breeding two different varieties) or hybridomas.

Hybridoma   The cell produced by fusing two cells of different origin. In monoclonal antibody technology, hybridomas are formed by fusing an immortal cell (lymphocyte tumor cell) and an antibody-producing B lymphocyte.

Immune response   Recognition and attack of foreign substances or organisms by the host immune system.

Immune system   The aggregation of cells, biological substances (such as antibodies), and cellular activities that work together to provide resistance to disease.

Immunoassay   Technique for identifying antigens (proteins or glycoproteins) by using antibodies specific to these antigens.

Immunodiagnostics   The use of specific antibodies to measure a substance. This is used in diagnosing infectious diseases and the presence of foreign substances in human and animal fluids.

Immunogen   Any substance that can elicit an immune response.

Immunology   Study of all phenomena related to the body's response to antigenic challenge (i.e., immunity, sensitivity, and allergy).

Immunomodulators   A class of proteins that boost the immune system. Many are cell growth factors that accelerate the production of cells important to the immune response.

Immunotoxins   Monoclonal antibodies that have a protein toxin molecule attached. The antibody targets a tumor cell, and the toxin is designed to kill that cell when the antibody binds to it.

Insulin   Hormone secreted by pancreatic B cells to regulate glucose metabolism.

Interferon   A class of lymphokine proteins important in the immune response. There are three major types of interferon: alpha (leukocyte), beta (fibroblast), and gamma (immune). Interferons inhibit viral infections and may have anticancer properties.

Interleukin   A type of lymphokine that regulates the growth and development of white blood cells. Twelve interleukins (IL-1 through IL-12) have been identified to date.

Intron   In eukaryotic cells, a sequence of DNA that is contained in the gene but does not encode for protein.

Investigational new drug application (IND)   An application to begin studies of a new drug or biologic on humans. The IND contains formulation, manufacturing, and animal test results information.

In vitro   Literally, "in glass." Performed in a test tube or other apparatus.

In vivo   In the living organism.

Isomerism   Chemical compound in two or more forms, identical in percentage composition but different as to the positions of one or more atoms within the molecules.

Karyotype   Complete set of chromosomes from a somatic cell.

Leukocyte   A colorless cell in the blood, lymph, and tissues that is an important component of the body's immune system. Also called white blood cell.

Linkage   The tendency for certain genes to be inherited together because of their physical proximity on the chromosome.

Lipoproteins   A class of serum proteins that transport lipids and cholesterol in the blood stream.

Lymphocyte   A type of leukocyte found in lymphatic tissue in the blood, lymph nodes, and organs. Lymphocytes are continuously made in the bone marrow and mature into antibody-forming cells.

Lymphokine   A class of soluble proteins produced by white blood cells that play a role in the immune response.

Macrophage   White blood cell produced in blood vessels and loose connective tissues that can ingest dead tissues and cells and is involved in producing interleukin.

Macrophage colony stimulating factor (M-CSF)   A natural hormone that stimulates the production of white blood cells, particularly monocytes (precursors of macrophages).

Meiosis   Process of cell reproduction whereby the daughter cells have half the chromosome number of the parent cells. Sex cells (haploid gametes) are formed by meiosis.

Messenger RNA (mRNA)   Nucleic acid that carries instructions to a ribosome for the synthesis of a particular protein (translation process).

Metabolism   All biochemical activities carried out by an organism to maintain life.

Metabolite   Organic compound produced by an enzymatic reaction or required for metabolism.

Microorganism   Prokaryotic organism without a true membrane-bound nucleus.

Mitosis   Process of cell reproduction whereby the daughter cells are identical in chromosome number to the parent cells.

Molecular genetics   Study of how genes function to control cellular activities.

Monoclonal antibody (Mab)   Highly specific, purified antibody. It is secreted by a hybridoma clone derived from a single B cell.

Monocytes   One of three types of white blood cells. Monocytes are precursors to macrophages.

Multigenic   Of hereditary characteristics, specified by several genes.

Mutagen   A substance that induces mutations.

Mutation   A change in the nucleotide sequence of a chromosome that is inherited.

Myeloma   A type of tumor cell that is used in monoclonal antibody technology to form hybridomas.

Nuclease   An enzyme that, by cleaving chemical bonds, breaks down nucleic acids into their constituent nucleotides.

Nucleic acids   Large molecules, generally found in the cell's nucleus and/or cytoplasm, that are made up of nucleotide bases. The two kinds of nucleic acid are DNA and RNA.

Nucleotide   DNA and RNA building block. Each nucleotide is composed of sugar, phosphate, and one of four nitrogen bases. The sequence of the bases within the nucleic acid determines what proteins are made.

Nucleus   The structure within eukaryotic cells that contains chromosomal DNA.

Oligonucleotide   A polymer consisting of a small number (about two to ten) of nucleotides. May be used as a probe in hybridization or as primer for the polymerase chain reaction.

Oncogene   Gene thought to be capable of producing cancer.

Oncology   Study of tumors.

Operon   Sequence of genes responsible for synthesizing the enzymes needed for biosynthesis of a molecule. An operon is controlled by an operator gene and a repressor gene.

Organic   A compound containing carbon.

Pathogen   Organism or virus that causes disease.

Peptide   Short sequence of amino acids.

Phenotype   The observable characteristics, at the physical, morphological, or biochemical level of an individual, as determined by the genotype and environment.

Plasmid   Extrachromosomal circular, double-stranded DNA molecule.

Pluripotent   Ability of a cell to develop into differentiated cell types.

Polymer   Macromolecule made up of a chain of repeated units.

Polymerase chain reaction (PCR)   Technique amplifying regions of DNA by *in vitro* replication of a DNA template.

Polymorphism   Variation in a population (least common allele occurring in 1 percent or greater of the population).

Prokaryote   Organism, such as bacterium, lacking a membrane-bound nucleus.

Protease   Enzyme that degrades proteins by hydrolyzing the peptide bonds.

Protein   A linear macromolecule composed of amino acids linked by peptide bonds. A protein can consist of one or more polypeptides.

Receptor   A protein, on a cell surface or within a cell, that binds to a ligand molecule and leads to a cellular response.

Recombinant DNA (rDNA)   The DNA formed by combining segments of DNA from different types of organisms.

Restriction enzyme   An enzyme that breaks DNA in highly specific locations, creating gaps into which new genes can be inserted.

Retrovirus   A virus that contains the enzyme reverse transcriptase. This enzyme converts the viral RNA into DNA, which can combine with the DNA of the host cell and produce more viral particles.

Ribonucleic acid (RNA)   Macromolecule consisting of ribonucleoside residues connected by phosphate. RNA is found in all cells, in both nuclei and cytoplasm.

Ribosome   A cellular component, containing protein and RNA, that catalyzes the synthesis of protein.

Sepsis   Presence in the blood or other tissues of pathogenic microorganisms or their toxins. Septicemia is a common type of sepsis.

Sequencing   Decoding a strand of DNA or gene to the specific order of its nucleotides: adenine, cytosine, guanine, and thymine.

Single nucleotide polymorphism (SNP)   Single-base difference in DNA sequence that can be observed between individuals in a population. SNPs are present in the human genome with an average frequency of 1 per 1,000 base pairs.

Somatic cell   Cell other than sex or germ cells.

Somatic cell gene therapy   Insertion of genes into cells for therapeutic purposes. It does not affect the genetic makeup of a patient's offspring.

Splicing   The removal of introns and joining of exons to form a continuous coding sequence in RNA.

Stem cell   A precursor cell that divides and produces differentiated cells.

Structural gene   A gene that codes for a protein, such as an enzyme.

Supressor gene   A gene that can reverse the effect of a mutation in other genes.

Telomere   Distal end of the chromosome arm, able to replicate and prevent shortening of the chromosomal end with each replication.

Template   A molecule that serves as the pattern for synthesizing another molecule.

Tissue plasminogen activator (tPA)   A protein produced in small amounts in the body that aids in dissolving blood clots.

Transcription   Synthesis of messenger (or any other) RNA on a DNA template.

Transfer RNA (tRNA)   RNA molecules that carry amino acids to sites on ribosomes where proteins are synthesized.

Transgenic organism   An organism formed by the insertion of foreign genetic material organism into the germ line cells of organisms.

Translation   Process by which the information on a messenger RNA molecule is used to direct the synthesis of a protein.

Tumor necrosis factor (TNF)   Rare protein of the immune system that appears to destroy some types of tumor cells without affecting healthy cells.

Vector   The agent (e.g., plasmid or virus) used to carry new DNA into a cell.

Virus   A submicroscopic organism that contains genetic information but cannot reproduce itself. To replicate, it must invade another cell and use parts of that cell's reproductive machinery.

Wild type   The form of an organism that occurs most frequently in nature.

Xenotransplantation   The process of transplanting organs, cells, or tissues from animals to humans. Donor animals may be genetically modified so that organs or other materials will not be rejected by the human immune system.

X-ray crystallography   Method of generating X-ray diffraction patterns (i.e., three-dimensional arrangement of atoms in a molecule) that is generated by the diffraction of X-rays through a crystal molecule.

Zygote   Diploid cell resulting from the union of male and female gametes (sperm and ovum).

INDEX

DuPont, 24, 26, 60, 72, 250
Duramed, 193
Dyson, Freeman, 3, 29

Ebeling, Thomas, 152
Educational content, 281–282
E-health, structure of, 257–259, 291. *See also* Internet
Eisai, 18, 277, 278
Eisenberg, David, 39, 124
Elan, 72, 75
Elitra, 78
EMEA (European Medicines Evaluation Agency), 197, 221, 236
Employer activism, 208
Enablers, 21
Enbrel, 15, 56, 59, 98, 112, 134, 160, 174, 243
Engerix-B, 98
Environmental biotech, 5
Eon, 166
Epivir, 56, 159
ePocrates, 271
Epogen/Procrit:
  arbitration over (Amgen/J&J), 74
  blockbuster status of, 15, 55, 56, 96
  chemical name, 97, 98
  DTC spending, 208, 275, 276
  global strategy and, 150
  in-licensing, 56, 74, 160
  marketing, 101, 123, 132, 134, 150
  patent battles, 192
  sales/growth data, 55, 96, 97, 98, 99, 123, 134
  search engine visibility, 279
  successor brands, 59, 180
Epogin, 98
Equity:
  alliance (system for building), 89
  biobrand (overview diagram), 132
  brand, and name change, 129
  network, 57, 81–90
Erbitux, 112
ES Cell, 19
Europe:
  alternative medicine, 39–40, 126
  biosector restructuring, 59
  consumer biotech knowledge survey, 37
  DTC ban, 280
  generics, 196
  genetically modified foods, 27
  health spending *vs.* performance, 216
  innovation flight, 220–221
  Internet, 108, 259–262, 268, 280, 285
  orphan drug status, 189
  osteoporosis, 171
  OTC, 199
  pediatric extensions, 190–191

pricing controls, 207, 215, 217, 219–225, 240, 244
public company data, 16
Evidence-based:
  marketing (*vs.* experience based), 94, 101, 107–108, 126, 290
  positioning, 142
  pricing, 232
Evista, 165
Evotec, 58, 73
Exelixis, 68
Exelon, 245

Facilitation, 286
FDA, 96, 145, 150, 153, 210, 272, 282
FDA Modernization Act (FDAMA) (1997), 190
Feldene, 186
Financial health (alliance metric), 85
FitzGerald, Niall, 127
Flonase, 276
Florida, 220
Flovent, 237
FluMist spray, 145, 210
Foods (nutraceuticals):
  agbio, 12, 26–27, 62–63, 99
  cross-industry deals, 62–63
  diet products, 101–102
  functional, 4, 105–106
  golden rice, 4, 27, 99
  medical, 4, 25–26, 105
Forest, 158, 159, 190
Fortéo, 165
Forward integration, 75
Fosamax, 72, 170–172, 213
Franchises, 153, 154, 164–165, 180–185
Friedli, 33
Fujisawa, 126
Fullerenes, 25
Functional genomics, 47, 110

Garnier, Jean-Pierre, 152
GenCom, 18
GeneFormatics, 70
Gene geography, 119
GeneLogic, 75
Genencor, 14
Genentech:
  alliances, 60–62, 68, 77, 80, 81, 145
    in-licensing, 154–155
    Lilly (Humulin), 8, 9, 11, 89, 137, 164
  financial/sales data, 14, 98, 168
  Herceptin, 98, 109, 113, 123, 135, 155, 278–279
  innovation timeline, 8, 9
  Internet, 278–279